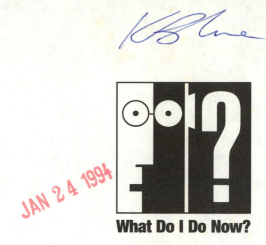

What Do I Do Now?

THE MACINTOSH BIBLE

WHAT DO I DO NOW?

DO NOW? BOOK

BY CHARLES RUBIN

PEACHPIT PRESS

THE MACINTOSH BIBLE "WHAT DO I DO NOW?" BOOK
Charles Rubin

PEACHPIT PRESS, INC.
2414 Sixth St.
Berkeley, CA 94710
(800) 283-9444
(510) 548-4393
(510) 548-5991 (fax)

Cover design by John Miller, Big Fish

Interior design by Olav Martin Kvern

Production and illustration by Kim Rush, Jan C. Wright, and Olav Martin Kvern

ISBN 1-56609-095-4

0 9 8 7 6 5 4 3 2 1

Printed and bound in the United States of America

Contents

Part 2: General Mac Problems

Acknowledgments

Lots of people helped with this book, either through direct support or simply by doing a terrific job of discovering things about the Mac and making those discoveries available to others.

From the Sedona area, I'd like to thank David Work and Dolly Yapp of Communications Plus; Dick Searle of Argosy Services; and Diane Parsinnen, Michael Sohaski, Dick Stites, Ramona Stites, Dick Dunham, and the other members of the Oak Creek Apples user group.

In the software and hardware community, my thanks to Ron Lichty, Caroline Rose, and the entire developer technical support staff of Apple Computer; Lucinda Rowley at Microsoft; Dennis Marshall at Claris; and all the sysops who maintain the Macintosh forums on CompuServe.

Lastly, of course, this book would not exist without the talents of Olav Martin Kvern, whose design makes the information easier to get to than ever; Jessie Wood, who unscrambled my editorial mistakes; and Roslyn Bullas, who always listens to my rants with equanimity.

My heartfelt thanks to you, one and all.

Introduction

The Macintosh can be a wolf in sheep's clothing. Beneath those cute icons and that smooth plastic exterior lie miles of circuitry and millions of lines of program code, pulsating and dancing frenetically, just waiting to misbehave. Thanks to Apple, the Mac isn't quite as susceptible to mind-boggling problems as a DOS or Windows machine, but anything this versatile is bound to mess up or confuse you at some point. There may be something wrong with the Mac's hardware or software, or you may simply not understand what's happening at the time, but the result is the same: you're stuck in the land of panic and frustration until you figure things out.

In this book, I've tried to offer the fastest, simplest ways out of a few hundred common Mac problems. Much of the book is devoted to very specific problems you may have with Mac hardware or software, but there's also a comprehensive guide to figuring out problems on your own. So if you get stuck and you can't find your specific problem, you should at least have some idea about how to diagnose and solve it anyway.

How to use this book

This book attacks Macintosh trouble from three directions: basic knowledge, conceptual problems, and operating problems.

The first part, basic knowledge, covers the fundamentals of Mac hardware and system software, explains the types of things that can go wrong, shows how to avoid some common problems, and offers general advice about how to troubleshoot and solve problems on your own. If you read Part 1 (chapters 1-7) from start to finish, you will know more about the Macintosh than half the people now using them, and you will be that much better prepared to rescue yourself from problem purgatory.

Parts 2, 3, and 4 cover conceptual problems and operating problems that occur as you use the Mac. By conceptual problems, I mean problems that arise from misunderstandings about what's going on. In the majority of problem situations, the computer and software are functioning perfectly—it's the user's level of understanding that needs repairs. Part 1 builds a foundation of understanding, a barrier between you and problems that arise out of ignorance; the conceptual problems and solutions in the other three parts deal with specific problems. Parts 2, 3, and 4 cover the most common operating problems—actual hardware and software malfunctions—as well.

Part 2 (chapters 8-17) is devoted to general problems with Macintosh system software. It's organized in functional areas having to do with different types of Mac operations. Most of the problems you'll have with a Mac are software-related, even if they don't appear to be, so check this section first for specific problems you have with your Mac. For example, a display problem with your monitor may be due to an improper software setting. Problems like this are covered in Chapter 13.

Part 3 (chapters 18-21) covers hardware problems that are unique to specific Macintosh computers, monitors, and printers. These problems are far less likely, but if you've tried software solutions to no avail, then this is where you should look next.

Part 4 (chapters 22-28) deals with problems you may run into while using seven of the best-selling Macintosh application programs. Most Mac owners use at least one of these programs. Space prohibits me from covering more than a dozen or two problems for each program, but I've tried to highlight the ones that seem to give most people trouble.

The best strategy is to read all of Part 1 so you'll be familiar with basic Mac operations, maintenance, and troubleshooting techniques. You may think you know most of this stuff already, but a little extra digging here can save you hours of head-scratching later when you're actually trying to solve a problem. If your Mac is attached to a network, you should also read the introductory section to Chapter 15. After that, use the table of contents, the Appendix, and the index to zero in on specific solutions.

What the book covers

This book covers technical basics and common alert messages and hardware problems for any Mac model, from a 512K to a Quadra or PowerBook. It covers all versions of the system software, from 4.2 through 7.1, although it assumes you're using System 6 or System 7. Problems that are unique to System 6 are identified with a special icon, and problems unique to a specific software version (6.0.7, for example), are identified in the problem headings.

In case you're wondering whether this book will have you pulling chips out of your Mac's insides, rest assured that it won't. Most of the problems you're likely to have with your Mac are software-related and will respond to software solutions. If faulty hardware is the culprit, this book will help you identify the problem so you can either fix it yourself (using a repair guide like *The Dead Mac Scrolls* from Peachpit Press) or take your Mac in for service.

In Parts 2, 3, and 4, the book follows a consistent format for presenting problems and solutions. First there's a heading, a graphic, or both identifying the problem. In most cases the alert text may vary slightly, depending on which system software version or Mac you're using, so don't be too literal. If an alert or problem heading is similar to one you've got, read the problem description to determine if this is the explanation you're looking for.

After the problem heading and description, the solution section tells you exactly what steps you should follow to recover from the problem. Follow the steps in order until your problem is solved—you may not need to use them all.

The secret decoder section

Every book has certain stylistic conventions to denote different kinds of information. In this book, I've used italic type the first time I use an important term or concept, like hardware or software. The names of Macintosh commands, buttons, checkboxes, and checkbox options are also shown in italics. When you're supposed to press certain keys on the Mac, those keys are shown in a keycap font. For example, if you're supposed to press the Command and Z keys, the text shows those keys as ⌘ Z.

Yeah, but what about...

Even at 380 pages, this book can't possibly resolve every problem you can
have with a Mac. Over the years, readers of previous editions of this book
have written with a variety of specific problems, and I've incorporated some
of them in this edition. But for every problem I've used there are many that
I've rejected because based on my experience (not to mention hours of
research in dozens of printed and online sources and consultations with
other Mac gurus) they are not common problems.

   At this very moment, the sudden startup of a room air conditioner may
have caused a random power spike during a file-saving operation under
MultiFinder on a Mac SE with 2.5 megs of RAM, which in turn caused a word
processor file to be written on top of the spreadsheet file that was open at the
same time. Or trying a free rotation with a rendering program has caused
somebody's Finder-enhancing extension to clash with the ROM on their
graphics accelerator card, producing random green spots shaped like a profile
of Alfred Hitchcock on their third-party monitor. If something like this has
happened to you, congratulations. Welcome to the zany world of computers.

 I'm assuming you're
using System 7, but I've
set aside sections that
explain System 6 opera-
tions when they're different. The
System 6-related paragraphs or
sections are set off with an icon
like the one shown here.

But for every truly unique and
unfathomable problem, there are
dozens and dozens of common
problems that happen all the time
to thousands of Mac users, many
of which can be easily resolved or
entirely avoided with a little common sense. If you're one of those
thousands with one of those dozens,
this book will show you what to do.

Chapter 1

Basic Mac Hardware and Software

All computers work through the interaction of *hardware*—the physical components—and *software*, the recorded instructions that tell the hardware what to do. Like a cassette player and a cassette tape, the hardware and software in your Mac are a team—each needs the other in order to accomplish anything. In this chapter, we'll look at the Mac's hardware and software components.

Hardware basics

Every Mac consists of at least a CPU (defined next), one or more disk drives, a monitor or display screen, a keyboard, and a mouse. Most Mac systems also include one or more hardware *peripherals*, such as a printer or an external hard disk drive.

The CPU

CPU stands for *central processing unit*. Technically, it refers to a specific portion of a computer's microprocessor chip. However, Apple uses the term CPU more broadly to mean *the box that holds all the computer's brains*, so we will too.

The brains of the CPU are on the *logic board*, a printed circuit board that contains a couple of dozen semiconductor chips, some other electronic components, and circuits connecting them all. It isn't necessary to know about every device on this board, but we'll refer to certain devices, chips, and groups of chips later, so we'll go over them here.

■ The *microprocessor* is the nerve center of the Mac—it executes the instructions that come from the software you run. Different Mac models have different microprocessors, which determine how fast a Mac performs its work and how much memory it can use. Some Macs have additional microprocessors (called *coprocessors*) that speed up certain functions like mathematical calculations and data transfers.

■ RAM *(random-access memory)* temporarily holds programs and data. When someone refers to the Mac's memory, they're talking about its RAM. Different Mac models can contain different amounts of RAM, from less than a megabyte (one million bytes) to over a hundred megabytes. When you open a program, the Mac loads some of that program's instructions into its RAM. When you quit the program, those instructions are removed from RAM, and the space they occupied becomes available for other programs or data. RAM can only retain data while the computer is turned on, so any programs or other data stored in RAM are lost when you turn the computer off.

■ The *PRAM (parameter RAM—pronounced P-RAM)* is a separate area of RAM used for storing system software settings that must be retained by your Mac even when it's turned off. This special RAM is powered by a small battery so it can store data when the Mac itself is not on. Some of the things stored in the PRAM are the current date and time and the location of the current startup disk.

■ The *ROM (read-only memory)* contains permanent information that can't be changed by the Mac. Instructions in ROM are physically etched into chips, so they're always available for the Mac to use whenever you turn it on. As Mac models have evolved, the ROM instructions have changed to accommodate the features of newer Macs. For example, ROMs in the earliest Mac models didn't have instructions for working with color, or for accessing 800K or 1.44MB floppy disk drives.

Most Mac models also contain one or more *expansion slots* into which you can plug various *expansion* or *interface cards*. (The earliest Macs didn't have any expansion slots, but enterprising manufacturers figured out how to expand them anyway.) Common types of expansion cards include accelerators (which make your Mac run faster); video cards (which let you use larger monitors with your Mac); and communications cards (which allow your Mac to communicate over telephone lines or over special types of computer networks).

Along with the logic board, your Mac CPU contains one or two *floppy disk drives*, in which you insert floppy disks to start up the Mac, feed it data or run a program. These days, most Mac CPUs also contain *internal hard disk drives*. Hard disks work like floppy disks (except they hold a lot more information), but the disk can't be removed. Hard disks spin faster and give you much faster access to your data. Finally, some of the newer Macs contain CD-ROM (Compact Disk-Read Only Memory) disk drives (for optical disks that can be read but not changed).

New Mac users often confuse memory (RAM) with storage (disk space). Memory is temporary (it's only maintained while the computer is on), while storage is more permanent (items on a disk remain there whether the computer is on or not). Hard disks typically store 20, 40, or more megabytes (MB) of information, while most Macs have from 1 to 8 MB of RAM. (A byte is enough to store about one character of text or one number.)

Finally, the CPU contains a power supply, various *ports* for connecting printers and other devices (described next), and (depending on the Mac model) a display screen and usually one or more expansion slots.

Peripherals

External hardware devices that plug into your Mac's CPU are all called *peripherals*, and they fall into four classes: input devices, output devices, storage devices, and communications devices.

Input devices let you control the Mac or bring information into it. For example, you use your Mac's keyboard and mouse to type information or choose commands. Instead of the keyboard and mouse that came with your Mac, you can buy other keyboards or alternative pointing devices such as trackballs or digitizing tablets. Other input devices include scanners and video cameras.

Output devices let you get information out of the Mac and put it in a specific form. The most common output devices are monitors and printers.

Storage devices not built into your Mac include external floppy disk drives; external hard disk drives; removable cartridge hard disks; CD-ROM drives (which play prerecorded optical disks); tape backup systems; and read-write optical drives (which can both play and record data on optical disks).

The most common *communications devices* are modems, which let your Mac send and receive data over a telephone line. Specialized modems called *fax modems* let you communicate with facsimile machines as well as with other computers.

Connecting peripherals to your Mac

You could simply plug in the Mac's CPU by itself and turn it on, but you couldn't command it without a keyboard, you wouldn't see the effects of your commands without a monitor, and you couldn't print anything without a printer. You have to set up all these peripheral devices and plug them together before your Mac will do anything useful.

Most of the peripherals that make up a basic Macintosh system plug into the CPU, sometimes through an expansion card in a slot on the logic board, but more commonly through a port. Every Mac has several ports on the back of the CPU case; above each port is an icon that identifies its purpose. You won't find all these ports on every Mac, but you may see several of these icons:

 The *external floppy disk drive port* is for connecting an external floppy disk drive.

  The *mouse* or *ADB port* is for hooking up the mouse or keyboard. The type of port you have depends on your Mac. Some Macs have two ADB *(Apple desktop bus)* ports. Mac Plus and older models have only one mouse port on the back of the CPU; the keyboard port is on the front of the machine and uses a completely different connector.

 The *video port* lets you connect a video monitor directly to the Mac. (Some Macs either have built-in monitors or they require you to connect a monitor via a video display card plugged into an internal slot.)

The *printer port* is where you connect the Mac to a local printer (that is, a printer used by just one Mac) or to an AppleTalk network. If you're connected to an AppleTalk network, your Mac can communicate with other Macs, printers, or other devices on that network.

The *modem port* is where you connect modems or direct-connect data cables so your Mac can transmit data to other computers.

 The *sound output port* is where you connect external speakers or headphones to the Macintosh, so that sounds play through them instead of through the Mac's built-in speaker.

 The *sound input port* is where you connect a microphone so you can record sounds and play them on your Mac-

 The printer and modem ports can be used inter-changeably to hook up local printers or modems. You can connect a modem to the printer port and a printer to the modem port, if you like, as long as you let your Mac's software know you've done that by using the Chooser DA (see Chapter 2, page 25). However, each of these ports works best if you use it for its stated purpose. And if you're attaching to an AppleTalk network, you must *always* connect it to the printer port.

intosh. Only newer Macs have a sound input port, but you can use a special adapter to record sounds through another port on older Macs.

 The *SCSI (small computer systems interface) port* is usually where you connect the Mac to an external hard disk drive. In addition to hard disks and other storage devices, most scanners are also SCSI devices that must be connected to this port. Some printers and even some monitors are SCSI devices, too. You can connect up to seven SCSI de-vices through this port by hooking the first device to the Mac's SCSI port, the second device to the first device, the third device to the sec-ond device, and so on, in what is called a *SCSI chain*.

Software basics

Although the ROM permanently stores some of the instructions the Mac needs, most of the Mac's software is stored on floppy disks or on a hard disk. There are three types of software on the Mac: system software, applications, and data files.

Each device in a SCSI chain must have a unique address, numbered from 0 to 6, so that your Mac knows which device it's talking to at any given time. Your Macintosh itself has SCSI address 7; therefore, if you plug in an external SCSI hard disk, it must have an address other than 7. If your Mac has an internal hard disk, that disk's SCSI address is always set to 0.

System software is the collection of files and programs the Mac needs to recognize and use its various hardware components, to understand and run the applications you use and the data files you create, and to perform other fundamental tasks.

Applications are programs that let you use your Mac to perform specific functions, like creating written documents (word processing programs), drawing graphics (graphics programs), calculating numbers (spreadsheet programs), and communicating with other computers (communications programs). Some applications combine two or more of these basic functions, or perform even more specialized functions, such as accounting or image processing.

Data files, or *documents*, are storage files created by applications or by the system software. When you write a letter with a word processing program and then save the letter to disk, you create a data file containing that letter.

What system software does

The system software is a go-between: it reads information about the state of the Mac's hardware and passes it on to application programs, as shown at left.

When you want to print a document, the system software tells the application which printer is selected. When you want to open or save a file, the system software tells the application which disks are available.

Applications

System Software

- which disks are available
- which printer is available
- which monitors are connected
- how many colors are available
- how much RAM is available
- sound volume
- time and date
- which network devices are available

Hardware

All applications rely on the system software for information about the current state of the Mac's hardware.

When applications are system software

Although applications and system software fall into two different categories, some applications are considered system software because they let you view or manipulate system software settings. Most of these applications are included in the Mac system software that comes from Apple, but you can also buy programs from other companies that let you adjust system software settings.

There are five types of system software applications.

- The *Finder*, *At Ease*, and (*MultiFinder* under System 6) are applications that allow you to view the contents of your disks, to open applications, or to manage files, folders and disks, One of these programs loads automatically when you start your Mac. Which of these you see depends on which Mac model and version of system software you're using.

- *Desk accessories (DAs)* such as the Chooser, Alarm Clock, and (if you're using System 6) the Control Panel, are all available under the Apple ( ) menu.

- *Extensions*, or *inits*, are programs that are loaded automatically when you start up your Mac. These include printer drivers (or *Chooser extensions*) that let your Mac work with different types of printers, and *system extensions* that enable other functions such as file sharing, special Finder capabilities, and macro capabilities.

- *Utilities*, such as the Font/DA Mover and Apple HD SC Setup, can be stored anywhere and are opened by double-clicking them, just like regular applications.

- *Control panel programs* (if you're using System 7) include Date & Time, File Sharing Monitor, General Controls, Labels, Monitors, Sharing Setup, Sound, Users & Groups, and Views. Most control panels can be located anywhere and are opened by double-clicking, although some of them are loaded automatically as extensions.

Before System 7 came along, DAs were distinguished from other applications by the way you installed and used them—you had to use the Font/DA Mover to install them, and you could only open them by choosing them from the menu. Under System 7, however, DAs work like other applications.

In Chapter 2, we'll see how to use some of these system software applications to view or change various settings in the Mac's system software.

System software essentials

Many of the operating problems you'll run into with a Mac are related to the system software, so let's look more closely at the various system software components and what they do. You need at least three system software components to make the Mac operate: a System file, a Finder or Finder alternative, and a System Folder. A Mac won't start unless it's connected to a disk drive that contains a System file, a Finder file, and a System Folder. We'll look at these three components more closely in the following sections.

The System file

The *System file* is basically a storage facility. It contains instructions that tell the Mac how to manage its screen, memory, microprocessor(s), disk drive(s), keyboard, mouse, and other devices. It also contains fonts, sounds, and (under System 6) desk accessories.

The System file is loaded into your Mac's RAM at startup, along with any extensions or inits you have installed. All this information loads into a portion of RAM called the *system heap*. Under System 6 the system heap is a fixed size (although you can change it with a utility program). Under System 7 the system heap expands or contracts automatically depending on how much space the System and related files need.

Since the total amount of RAM installed in your Mac must be shared by the system heap and any application programs you have running, using lots of fonts, sounds, or extensions will mean that there's less RAM available for any programs you want to run. See *Minimize the System file* on page 66 in Chapter 4 for more information.

The Finder

The *Finder* displays the Mac's desktop. You use it to view or open, copy, or erase files, folders, and disks. The Finder is set to open automatically each time you start your Mac. However, you can set your Mac to start up with another program.

If you're using a Macintosh Performa, your Finder desktop may contain the *Launcher*, a special window that contains buttons you click to open programs or documents.

You may also be using *At Ease*, which is an alternative to the Finder that makes it easier to work with documents and programs on the Macintosh Performa.

The System Folder

The *System Folder* is where the System, the Finder and other system software files are stored. When you install Mac system software using the Installer program, the Installer automatically creates a System Folder and puts the necessary files into it.

Other than the System and Finder, the files in the System Folder aren't absolutely necessary for starting the Mac, but you do need them to make various adjustments to the system software, as we'll see in Chapter 3.

The contents and organization of the System Folder vary, depending on whether you're using System 7 (or later) or a previous version of the Mac's system software. Since System 7 is now the standard, we'll look at it first. If you're still using System 6 or an earlier version, you should also read *The System Folder before System 7*, on page 15.

The System Folder under System 7

Under System 7, the System Folder looks something like this:

We'll start at the top of this window, looking at the folders first.

The *Apple Menu Items* folder contains DAs and other items you want to appear on the menu. Under System 7, anything you place in this folder appears on the menu when you display it. (See page 58 in Chapter 3 for more information about the Apple Menu Items folder.)

The *Control Panels* folder contains control panel programs. Each of

these programs controls an aspect of the system software, such as the networking setup or the way files are displayed in Finder windows. Some control panel programs are loaded when you start up your Mac. Under System 6, control panels are called *control panel devices*, or *cdevs*, and you can only use them through the Control Panel DA. (See page 44 in Chapter 3 for more information about System 7's control panel programs.)

The *Extensions* folder contains *Chooser extensions* and *system extensions*. As mentioned earlier, Chooser extensions allow the Mac to communicate properly with printers, modems, scanners, network file servers, and other devices. When you open the Chooser DA's window, for example, you see icons representing Chooser extensions called LaserWriter, ImageWriter, and StyleWriter, which allow the Mac to communicate properly with these printers. This folder also contains the PrintMonitor application, which allows you to print documents in the background while you work on something else. (See *Printing* in Chapter 2 for more about background printing, and see Chapter 3 for more details on Chooser extensions.)

System extensions are files that change the System file's standard settings. For example, one Apple-supplied system extension file allows the Mac to share files with other Macs on a network. The Mac loads these system extensions automatically each time it starts up, and they run unobtrusively in the background while you're doing other things with your Mac.

While Apple supplies a handful of system extensions, most are sold by other companies. For example, one third-party extension called Capture lets you select a portion of your Mac's screen and save it as a graphic file on disk by pressing a couple of keys. Another, called QuicKeys, modifies the System file so you can create macros (automated routines) that execute whole sequences of commands with a couple of keystrokes.

The *Fonts* folder was added in system software version 7.1. It stores all the fonts you want to make available to your application programs. Before version 7.1, fonts were installed in the System file itself.

The *Preferences* folder contains files that store user-adjustable settings for the Finder, file sharing options, and other system functions. You can also use it to store your own preference settings for various applications.

The *PrintMonitor Documents* folder is a temporary storage location for documents you've printed with the Chooser's *Background Printing* option turned on. This folder is automatically created the first time you print with the *Background Printing* option on. (For more information about printing in the background, see page 26 in Chapter 2.)

The *Startup Items* folder doesn't contain any system software files. Under System 7, programs that you place inside this folder are opened automatically each time you start your Mac. If you want a certain program to start whenever you turn on your Mac, place it inside the Startup Items folder. (See page 59 in Chapter 3 for more information about this folder.)

System enablers didn't exist before Macs that came out with system software version 7.1 or later. If your System Folder doesn't contain one and your Mac works fine, then your Mac doesn't need one.

Along with the System file, the Finder, and these additional folders, the System Folder holds the *Clipboard* and *Scrapbook files*. These files store items that you copy to the Clipboard or to the Scrapbook DA. If you use the Note Pad DA to store text, you'll have another storage file called *Note Pad File* in your System Folder.

Additionally, your System Folder may contain *system enablers*, which are special system extension files that configure the system software for the particular model of Mac you're using. These must be stored directly in the System Folder.

The System Folder before System 7

In pre-System 7 versions of the system software, the programs and files are not grouped in separate folders; they're all placed directly inside the System Folder, as shown at right. Although they aren't segregated, the items in the System Folder still fall into a few categories, as labeled in the illustration. Let's see how each of these categories works.

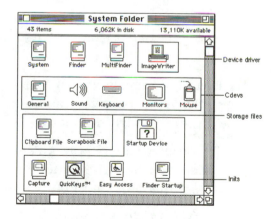

Device drivers or *Chooser resources* work exactly like Chooser extensions in System 7.

Cdevs, or *control panel devices*, are similar to control panel programs in System 7, except that they don't work like individual applications. Cdevs in your System Folder are loaded automatically when you start your Mac; they appear inside the Control Panel DA's window, from which you can select them after you've chosen the Control Panel DA. Each cdev displays a set of options that let you perform various system functions. (See page 41 in Chapter 3 for more details about cdevs.)

Inits are just like system extensions in System 7. The Mac looks for them and loads them automatically each time it starts.

If you're using a version of System 6, your System Folder will also contain a copy of the PrintMonitor program and storage files for the Clipboard, Scrapbook, and Note Pad.

One additional file you'll find in the System Folder is *MultiFinder*. MultiFinder is an extension of the Finder that allows you to open and run more than one program at a time as long as your Mac has enough RAM. (In System 7, MultiFinder's features are included in the Finder.) To use MultiFinder, you must have the Finder file in your System Folder. Also, you'll find that it takes at least 2 megabytes of RAM to run more than one program at a time.

PowerBook hardware and software

So far, we've looked at Macintosh hardware and software in general. Because of their portable design, PowerBooks have some unique characteristics. For example:

- Every PowerBook can run on battery power, so there are special system software programs you can use to monitor the battery charge and to control the brightness of the screen.

- To conserve battery power, PowerBooks can be put into *sleep mode*, which maintains the contents of RAM but shuts off power to the hard disk, display, and most of the rest of the system.

- Every PowerBook has a built-in trackball pointing device instead of a mouse.

- PowerBooks don't have internal slots that accept standard expansion cards. You can buy an internal modem for a PowerBook that connects to a special slot inside it, but other expansion options connect to one of the PowerBook's ports or to a Duo docking station (described next).

■ PowerBook Duo models have special peripherals called *docking stations* that make it easy to access expansion slots, monitors, and external hard or floppy disk drives.

PowerBooks have some unique troubleshooting and maintenance issues. We'll cover these in special sections later in this book, as well as in Chapter 19.

Third-party software

Apple's system software handles all the basic housekeeping chores for the Mac, but other developers have come up with programs that enhance the system software's operation or perform other important tasks. Some of these programs are so useful that they're considered essential. We can group these products into three categories: resource managers, Finder utilities, and diagnostic, backup, and repair tools. Let's see what these do and why you might want to use them.

Resource managers

Resource managers help you make more efficient use of system software or hardware resources on your Mac. Some make it easier to work with fonts, desk accessories, and sounds; others help you get the most out of your PowerBook. We'll take a brief look at these here; Chapter 6 contains more information.

Under the basic Macintosh software, every font you have in the Fonts folder (system software version 7.1 or later) or inside the System file (System 7.0) or System Folder (System 6 or earlier) is loaded into the system heap when you start your Mac. If you have dozens or hundreds of fonts, your system heap will take up a huge portion of your available RAM.

With a resource manager like Suitcase II or MasterJuggler, you can choose which fonts are loaded into memory at any given time. You can still have dozens or hundreds of fonts available in your System Folder, but you can regulate which of them is "open," or using up RAM, at any given time.

Most people who use lots of fonts consider Suitcase II or MasterJuggler essential pieces of system software. Apple should really make the standard system software work this way.

If you can't reduce the demands on your system heap with Suitcase II or MasterJuggler, you can enlarge the system heap itself under System 6 with a utility like HeapFixer or Heap Tool.

Another popular resource manager is Adobe Type Manager (ATM), which makes it possible to display Adobe PostScript fonts in any size on your screen without the need to have several specific sizes of screen fonts installed. PostScript fonts are used by most designers, desktop publishers, and graphic artists, and virtually everyone who uses these fonts also uses ATM.

Finally, PowerBook utilities like Connectix PowerBook Utilities and PB Tools give you more control over your PowerBook's sleep times, report the battery level more precisely, and perform other power-saving and security chores.

Finder utilities

Finder utilities change the Finder's basic operation in some way. Some programs make the menu work differently—for example, adding hierarchical menus to it or keeping track of recently opened folders there. Other utilities add new menus to the menu bar so you can locate folders or documents more easily. Like other system software enhancements, these programs use up RAM on your Mac, so your decision to use one should take that into account.

Some Finder utilities can conflict with one another or with other system software components. Others can slow down your Mac's operation. Make sure the utility's added features are really worth having, and don't use more than one utility at a time.

Diagnostic, backup, and repair tools

Apple supplies a program called Disk First Aid with its system software, but there are many troubleshooting, backup, and repair programs available that go well beyond it. These programs can examine and repair disks, recover deleted or corrupted files, optimize your hard disk so it operates at top speed, make a backup of your hard disk, and handle other important tasks.

Every Mac user should have at least one good disk diagnostic and repair program and one backup program, and should use them regularly. See Chapter 4 for more about preventive maintenance, and see Chapter 6 for descriptions of specific programs.

Chapter 2
Basic Mac Operations

In this chapter, we'll look at the Mac's basic operations from a system software perspective. As we go through these operations, you'll learn what happens when you start up a Mac, open disks, work with applications, and print files. We'll also discuss managing multiple applications with the Finder (System 7) or MultiFinder (System 6).

The startup sequence

Let's assume you've just set up your Mac for the first time. You have a StyleWriter connected to the printer port and an internal hard disk drive that contains a System Folder. When you turn on the Mac's power switch, here's what happens:

1. The instructions in your Mac's ROM tell it to check all its chips, send a startup sound through the speaker, turn on the screen or video circuitry, and search for a disk with a System folder on it.

2. The Mac checks for a floppy disk in its internal disk drive, but in this case it doesn't find one. It then checks for an external floppy disk drive, again without finding one. Finally, the Mac checks for a hard disk and finds what it's after. It loads the System file located in the System Folder on the internal hard disk and displays a "happy Mac" icon on the screen.

It's possible to replace the *Welcome to Macintosh* box with another screen, called a *startup screen,* so you may see something else when you start up.

3. As the System loads, the happy Mac is replaced by the *Welcome to Macintosh* box.

4. Under System 7, the Mac then loads any system enabler files from inside the System Folder.

5. One at a time, the Mac loads any system extensions (or inits under System 6) located in the System Folder or the Extensions folder. Generally, extensions are loaded in alphabetical order by name, although some have nonalphabetical characters in their names or special file types to ensure that they'll be loaded first. As the extensions load, most display an identifying icon in the lower left corner of the screen; however, some extensions don't announce themselves with an icon.

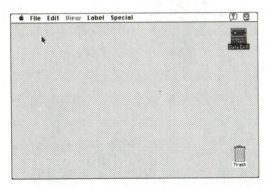

6. After loading the extensions in the Extensions folder, the Mac loads any startup items in the Control Panels folder, also in alphabetical order.

7. Still following the instructions in the System file, the Mac locates and loads the Finder or At Ease, and—depending on which program is loaded—the familiar desktop interface appears on the screen, as shown above.

The Finder's desktop displays icons representing any hard disks or other storage devices that are connected to the Mac, turned on, and have disks in them.

8. If you're using System 7, the Mac then opens any programs or documents in the Startup Items folder. If you're using System 6 and have set other programs or documents to open with the *Set Startup* command, those items are opened now.

9. The Mac waits for further instructions from you.

Selecting and opening objects on the desktop

Whether you're working with disks, files, programs, or even with data inside programs, one basic principle for interacting with the Mac always applies:

 Failing to select an item and selecting the wrong item are common mistakes for new Mac users. If you issue a command and nothing happens—or if it happens to the wrong item (say the wrong program or document opens)—make sure you've selected the right thing first.

Select first, then execute.

The whole Macintosh interface is based on pointing to something with a mouse or trackball, clicking the mouse or trackball button to select the item, and then working with it. (In System 7, you can also select an item on the desktop by typing the first few characters of its name.)

Before you can work with a disk, a file, or a program, before you can execute a command, before you can choose a printer or a network file server—before you can do anything—you must first select the item you want to work with.

When an icon, disk, command, or file name is selected, it's displayed in reverse video—that is, whatever is normally white turns black and whatever is normally black turns white, like a film negative. If an item isn't darkened, it isn't selected. Once you've selected an item on the desktop, you can open it or drag it from one location to another.

To open an object on the desktop, you point to the item, click it once to select it, and then choose the *Open* command from the File menu. You can also use a shortcut called *double-clicking* to open items in the Finder: instead of clicking an item once and then choosing the *Open* command, you double-click—click twice quickly—to open the item.

Viewing items on a disk

When you open a disk icon, you see a window that shows the disk's contents. The illustration on the next page shows a disk window displayed in a *list view*, arranged by item name.

Macintosh HD			
7 items	46.9 MB in disk		31.7 MB available
Name		Size	Kind
▷ ☐ Applications		—	folder
⌂ ClarisWorks		603K	application p
▷ ☐ Finances		—	folder
▷ ☐ Misc. Work		—	folder
☐ Standard Glossary		3K	Microsoft W
▷ ☐ System Folder		—	folder

 You can arrange item lists by size, kind, or other categories of information (or you can display items as separate icons that aren't in a list) by choosing different commands from the View menu in the Finder. The space used and available shown in the window header are available in list views only if you're using System 7.

The At Ease interface is different from the Finder. Instead of clicking disk icons to open them, you see a stack of folders, and you view different parts of a disk by clicking different folder tabs.

Disks are often divided into multiple levels, or hierarchies, of organization. The window at left shows that this disk contains individual files (both data files and applications) and folders, which represent a second level of organization. Folders can be placed inside other folders, so a disk's organization can be several levels deep. To see what's inside a folder, double-click it to open its window or—if you're using System 7—click the triangle next to its name. The Kind column tells which items are folders, which are applications, and which are documents.

All this information about the disk is maintained by the system software; the Finder is simply relaying it to you.

Working with applications

You can open an application in the same way you open a disk or folder, by double-clicking it. If enough RAM is available, the program loads and its opening screen appears. If there isn't enough RAM to accommodate the program, the Mac displays a message telling you so.

Opening files from inside an application

Once an application is open, you can create new files or open existing ones by choosing *New* or *Open* from the program's File menu. If you choose the *New* command, a new, empty file appears.

If you choose the *Open* command, the Mac displays a *directory dialog box* that looks like the one shown at right.

Depending on the program, the box may list all the files in a particular folder or only files that the current application can open. Each Mac application creates its own file type, and can open only a limited number of other applications' files. To open a file, you can either double-click the file's name or click its name once and then click the *Open* button.

The directory dialog box lets you view the files in different folders on a disk or switch from one disk to another. The pop-up menu above the list of files tells you what folder you're looking at, and the name above the buttons at the right tells you which disk you're viewing. In this example, the list shows the files inside the Auction Stuff folder on the disk named Macintosh HD.

 In integrated programs that combine several applications, the *New* command usually displays a dialog box that lets you choose the type of document you want to create.

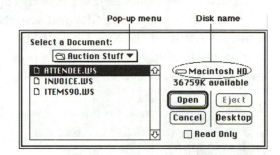

Pop-up menu · · · · · · Disk name

Select a Document:
🗁 Auction Stuff ▼
▢ ATTENDEE.WS
▢ INVOICE.WS
▢ ITEMS90.WS

Macintosh HD
36759K available
[Open] [Eject]
[Cancel] [Desktop]
☐ Read Only

 If you don't see the document you want in a directory dialog box list, check the folder name at the top of the list to make sure you're looking in the right folder.

The default location

The Mac always defaults to a particular disk location, so you often need to use a directory dialog box to navigate to different folders when you want to open documents. For example, if you open your program from a folder called Applications and immediately choose the *Open* command inside that program, you'll see the contents of the Applications folder in the directory dialog box. To view a different area of the disk, click the pop-up menu to select another folder, or click the *Desktop* button at the right to access a list of all the disks that are currently available to your Mac. Then you can select a new disk and view its contents by double-clicking its name.

Opening a document from the desktop

In most cases, you can use a shortcut to open a particular document and the program that created it at the same time. Since each program's document type is unique and is stored with its document, the Mac's system software can usually tell what program created a document. When you double-click a document's icon on the desktop, the Mac finds the program that created the document, opens it, and then opens the document itself.

Occasionally document types aren't specified, so the Mac can't always tell which program created a file, and sometimes the program that created a file is not available. If the Mac doesn't know which program to load when you double-click a file or can't find the program it needs to open it, you'll see a message to that effect.

 It's a good idea to save your work every few minutes, so you'll have it safely stored on your disk in case something goes wrong. A few applications (like FileMaker Pro) automatically save changes to files as you make them. You can also buy a system extension that automatically saves every open document at intervals that you choose.

Saving documents

Once you've created or opened a document, you can save it quickly by choosing *Save* from the program's File menu. If you're saving a document that you originally opened from the disk, it is automatically saved to the same folder and disk from which it was opened. If you're saving a new file, the directory dialog box appears so you can name the file and choose a folder and disk location for it. If you want to save an existing file to a different location or under a different name, use the *Save As* command on the program's File menu to display the directory dialog box, and then specify the new name or location.

Printing

Now, suppose you've finished writing a memo in Microsoft Word and you want to print it on your StyleWriter printer. Let's assume you're using the Mac for the first time, so even though the printer is connected, the system software isn't aware of it. To tell the Mac you're using a StyleWriter, you use the Chooser DA:

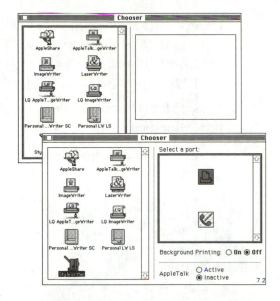

1. Choose the Chooser DA from the menu. You see a window similar to the one shown at right.

2. Click the StyleWriter icon to select it. The icon is highlighted and the large box at the right displays the icons of the two Mac serial ports, as shown at right.

3. If it's not already selected, click the printer port icon to tell the Mac that the StyleWriter is connected to that port.

4. Click the *On* button to turn background printing on. This way, the print job will be "spooled" to the PrintMonitor Documents folder when you print it, and you can do other things with your Mac while the job is printing on your StyleWriter.

 Early versions of the StyleWriter Chooser extension didn't support background printing. If the *Background Printing* option doesn't appear in the Chooser when you select the StyleWriter, get a newer version of the StyleWriter extension.

5. Click the close box at the upper-left corner of the Chooser window to close the Chooser DA. Now the Mac knows it has a StyleWriter printer connected to its printer port, and can relay that information to your applications when you choose their *Page Setup* and *Print* commands.

You can select only one device to print to at a time. If you ever want to print to a different device, you'll have to notify the Mac's system software by selecting that device in the Chooser.

Now that you've told the Mac which printer you want to use, you're ready to print your memo.

1. Choose *Page Setup* from Word's File menu, and adjust or confirm any settings it displays. Because you've already selected the StyleWriter with the Chooser, Word knows you'll be printing on a StyleWriter and the page setup options apply to that particular printer.

2. Choose *Print* from the File menu. Word displays the StyleWriter dialog box, which contains its printing options.

3. Select the options you want and print the file.

 If your Mac seems sluggish while you're printing a document with background printing on, it's probably because the Mac is performing some printing chores behind the scenes and can't immediately respond to your commands.

About background printing

With background printing turned on, the Mac automatically loads the PrintMonitor program whenever you issue a *Print* command from any application. The PrintMonitor program saves the document to the PrintMonitor Documents folder inside the System Folder and then returns control of the Mac to you.

As it works behind the scenes, PrintMonitor feeds the document to your printer, page by page. You can instruct the Mac to print several documents one after the other, and they're saved in the PrintMonitor Documents folder until their turn comes up. Meanwhile, you retain control of your Mac so you can continue with other work while the printing is handled in the background.

If you're running System 7, the PrintMonitor program's name is added to the Application menu shortly after you issue a print command. Once all the printing is done, PrintMonitor quits automatically. If you're running MultiFinder under System 6 (see the next section), PrintMonitor's name appears at the bottom of the menu. The program prints documents by itself without your intervention, but you can also adjust its operation.

When you choose PrintMonitor from the Application menu (System 7) or menu (System 6 MultiFinder), you display its window and menus. The window shows which documents are printing or waiting to be printed, and you can change the order in which documents are printed, or pause or cancel printing of a particular document or documents.

Because it prints in the background, PrintMonitor usually does its job invisibly. When a problem (such as a paper jam) does crop up, PrintMonitor notifies you. (See Chapters 3 and 14 for more information about PrintMonitor.)

Managing multiple applications

Both versions 6 and 7 of the Mac's system software allow you to have several applications open at once; however, this feature works somewhat differently in the two versions. Under System 6, you must use a special program called MultiFinder to manage multiple applications. The System 6 Finder can manage only one application at a time. Under System 7, there is no Multi-Finder, because the Finder itself is capable of managing as many applications as you wish, as long as you have enough RAM to accommodate them.

There are also differences in the way Systems 6 and 7 handle DAs, control panels (cdevs), and standard applications. In the next section, we'll look at the way things work under System 7. If you're using System 6, you can skip ahead to *Managing multiple programs under System 6.*

 To find out how much RAM you have available at any time, choose *About This Macintosh* (under System 7) or *About The Finder* (under System 6) from the menu.

Managing multiple programs under System 7

Under System 7, DAs, control panels and standard applications all work the same way. To install these programs you simply drag them onto a disk, and to open them you just double-click their names or icons.

You can open as many programs, DAs, or control panels at once as you want, provided you have enough memory. Each program requires a specific amount of memory, and asks the system software to set that amount aside when you try to open the program. If you don't have enough memory, the system software alerts you and the application won't be opened. (See Chapter 3 for information about adjusting the amount of memory used by applications.)

When you first install System 7, you'll find a selection of DAs on the menu. This is simply a matter of convenience; normally DA names appear on the menu because the DAs themselves have been placed inside the Apple Menu Items folder in the System Folder. Once it's listed on the menu, you can choose a DA's name there to open it. Alternatively, you can open the Apple Menu Items folder and double-click individual DA icons. All control panels are stored inside the Control Panels folder. You can double-click them there to open them.

As you open different DAs or standard applications under System 7, their names appear on the Application menu, which is indicated by an icon at the far right of the menu bar. By pulling down this menu and choosing a program's name, you can activate any program listed there. As soon as you quit a program, its name is removed from the Application menu. You can always tell which program is currently active because its menus appear in the menu bar and its icon appears as the Application menu icon.

Control panel program names don't appear on the Application menu—to activate an open control panel, you must choose the Finder from the Application menu and click in the control panel's window.

Managing multiple programs under System 6

Under System 6 and earlier versions of the system software, standard applications work differently from DAs and control panel devices (called *cdevs* in System 6).

DAs are a special kind of application that must be installed directly inside the System file using either Apple's Font/DA Mover or a resource manager like Suitcase II or MasterJuggler. Because they require special installation, DAs are stored in a distinct type of file called a *suitcase*.

Once they are installed in the System file, the DAs' names appear on the menu, and you must choose them there to open them. You can open more than one DA at a time under System 6, as long as there's enough memory available.

 You need at least 2 megabytes of memory to run multiple programs under System 6. Although it's possible to run MultiFinder on a Mac with only 1 megabyte of memory, that amount won't allow you to launch and manage multiple programs.

You must install cdevs in the System Folder, and you can only access them by choosing *Control Panel* from the menu. (See page 41 in Chapter 3 for more information.)

As mentioned earlier, System 6 lets you decide whether to run only one application at a time or as many as you have room for in RAM. Using the Finder alone limits you to running only one program at a time—if you're running a word processor and you want to open a spreadsheet program, you must quit the word processing program first. By switching to MultiFinder, you can run several application programs at once, just as you can under System 7.

To run MultiFinder, you must have both the Finder and MultiFinder programs in your Mac's System Folder. When you're running MultiFinder, the Finder itself always runs along with any other programs you start up, so if necessary you can always switch to the Finder desktop to work with disks or files without having to quit other programs.

As you open programs under MultiFinder, their names are added to the bottom of the menu, and you activate different programs by choosing their names there. The program that's currently active is the one whose menus and icon appear in the menu bar.

Chapter 3
Adjusting System Software

System software typically does its job without your help, but you can adjust it to better suit your working situation, or to compensate for problems such as low memory or improper monitor settings. In this chapter, we'll look at all the ways in which you can make these adjustments. You'll need to know these basic techniques to solve many of the problems covered in later chapters of this book.

This chapter is not a substitute for your *Macintosh User's Guide*. This isn't a complete guide to using system software. Instead, we'll focus on the aspects of adjusting system software that relate to the troubleshooting techniques covered later in this book.

Although some of this material may be familiar, you should at least skim this chapter. If you do get stuck in the middle of a problem-solving session and can't remember how to make a particular system software adjustment, you can always refer back to these pages.

There are six basic ways to control the Mac's system software:

- Finder commands

- Desk accessories such as the Chooser (or the Control Panel in System 6)

- Control panel programs

- System extensions (or inits)

- The System file itself

- System Folder folders

We'll look at these methods in the following sections. System 7 added several new facilities for adjusting system software, and if you're using System 6, the sections on control panels and System Folder folders don't apply to you. Look for the System 6 icon next to sections that apply specifically to System 6.

Finder commands

Among the Finder's commands, seven allow you to view or adjust various characteristics of the system software.

- *About This Macintosh* shows you how your Mac's RAM is being used, and how much is available.

- *Get Info* lets you lock a desktop item, change its icon, or change the amount of memory a program uses.

- *Sharing* lets you make folders from your disk available to other users on a network.

- *Make Alias* lets you create aliases.

- *Restart* restarts your Mac.

- *Set Startup* (System 6) lets you switch from the Finder to MultiFinder or set other programs to open when the Mac starts up.

- *Shut Down* turns the Mac off or quits the system software so you can shut it off yourself.

In this section we'll look at each of these commands in turn.

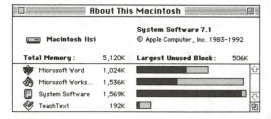

About This Macintosh...

When you want to see how much of your Mac's RAM is available for use, or how much is being used by the system software and any programs and documents you have open, choose *About This Macintosh* from the menu. You see a window like the one shown at left.

As you can see, the window lists each program you have open in alphabetical order, rather than in the order in which they were opened. The bars at the right represent the total amount of memory set aside for each program (the exact amount is shown to the left of each bar), and the darker bar shows how much of that memory block is actually in use. Memory can be used by the program itself or by any documents you have open. With system software, the memory used includes the System, Finder, and any open extensions and control panels.

 A block of memory set aside for a program or system software can't be used for anything else, even though the program or software may not be using the entire block at a given time. To make more memory available for another program, you have to quit a program that's currently running to free up an entire memory block.

Above the bars, the Largest Unused Block number shows the largest block of unused memory. This isn't necessarily the total of your unused memory— it's just the largest continuous area of memory. Programs normally need a continuous block of memory when you open them, so this number tells you roughly how large a program you can open at any given time. It's normal for this number to fluctuate by a few K while you have the window open.

Get Info

When you select an item on the desktop and choose the *Get Info* command (or press ⌘ I), the Mac displays a window containing information about that item.

The information you see in this window depends on the type of item you've selected. However, most information windows contain the same information:

- An icon that identifies the item on the desktop.

- The name, kind, size, and location of the item.

```
════ Microsoft Word Info ════
        Microsoft Word
        Microsoft Word 5.0
 Kind : application program
 Size : 852K on disk (870,675 bytes used)

Where : Macintosh HD : Applications :

Created : Mon, Dec 2, 1991, 9:01 AM
Modified : Tue, Apr 7, 1992, 2:13 PM
Version : 5.0, © 1987–1991 Microsoft
          Corporation
Comments :
┌─────────────────────────────┐
│                             │
│                             │
└─────────────────────────────┘
          ┌ Memory Requirements ┐
           Suggested size :  1024    K
           Minimum size :  [512]   K
□ Locked   Preferred size :  [1024]  K
```

- The date and time the item was originally created and last modified.

- The version number of the item (if it's an application).

- A *Locked* checkbox you can click to lock the item so it can't be renamed or deleted.

Information windows let you set different options for different types of items (documents, programs, aliases, folders, disks, and the Trash). Before we get into these item-specific settings, we'll look at one function you can perform in any information window.

 You can't change the icons for system software components such as the System Folder, Scrapbook, and Apple Menu Items folder.

Changing an item's icon

In every information window, you can select the item's icon and change it by pasting in a different icon from the Clipboard. For example, you might design your own special icon, using a paint or draw program, and then use it to replace your hard disk's icon. To do this:

1. Select the new icon in the drawing program or the Scrapbook (wherever you have it stored) and press ⌘ C (or choose *Copy* from the Edit menu) to copy it to the Clipboard.

2. On the desktop, select the item whose icon you want to change and press ⌘ I (or choose *Get Info* from the File menu). That item's information window is displayed.

3. Click the item's icon in the information window. A selection box appears around it.

4. Press ⌘ V (or choose *Paste* from the Edit menu). The copied icon replaces the current icon in the information window.

5. Close the information window. The item is now represented by its new icon on the desktop.

Locking an item

Except for disk and folder windows, all information windows also have a *Locked* checkbox in the lower-left corner. When you check the *Locked* box, the item is locked on the disk so that you can't delete it, rename it, or alter it in any way. You can open a locked item, but when you do, an alert appears telling you that the item can't be changed. If you try to delete a locked item, an alert tells you that it can't be thrown away.

Typically, you'll lock documents to prevent others from changing their contents. Although you can lock applications or system software files, it's not a good idea to do so because most of these don't work properly when they're locked.

Changing an application's memory size

When you run System 7 (or MultiFinder under System 6), you can have more than one application running at a time. For this scheme to work, your Mac needs to know how much memory it should assign for use by each program. Every new application that you launch asks the Mac for a certain amount of memory. If that much memory isn't available, your Mac displays a message saying so.

Applications tend to be conservative when asking the system software for memory. A program will ask for enough memory to let you work with a small or moderately sized document, but you may run short if you try to work with a large document. If an application ends up needing more memory than it originally asked for, the application will quit—often unexpectedly.

When you select an application and choose the *Get Info* command, the information window that appears contains a box displaying the suggested, minimum, and preferred amount of memory set aside for the application.

The suggested size is the amount of memory the program automatically asks for. If the program's memory size has never been reset,

You can't reset memory sizes for control panels or desk accessories. Under System 7.0, the *Preferred size* box is called *Current size*, and there's no minimum memory box.

In System 6, the *Preferred size* or *Current size* box is called *Application Memory size*.

You can't change the current memory size of a program while it's running. If you get a message that says your program is running out of memory, you must quit the program before you can reset its memory size. Also, although it's possible to reset a program's memory size to less than the suggested size, it's a bad idea. Doing so may make it impossible to run the program at all, or it may cause the program to crash.

the preferred size will match the suggested size, as it does in the information window for the Microsoft Word application shown on page 33. Under System 7.1 or later, the *Minimum size* box lets you set a smaller, alternate amount of memory under which to run the program if the preferred amount isn't available.

To reset a program's memory size:

1. Quit the program if it's running, then select the program's icon on the desktop and choose *Get Info* from the File menu.

2. Double-click the number inside the *Preferred size* box and type the amount of memory you want to use. It's best to increase the size by at least 20 percent.

3. Double-click the number in the *Minimum size* box and type a number smaller than the preferred size, if you like.

4. Close the window. The next time you run it, the program will ask the system for the new current size you've set.

Creating a stationery document

Document information windows have a *Stationery pad* checkbox in the lower-right corner. By checking this box, you can turn any document into a *stationery pad*, a special type of document that always opens as an untitled document when you double-click it, even though it contains information and has a unique name on the desktop.

By making a document into a stationery pad, you can store standard formatting or text that you want to appear on all new documents when you first open them. For example, you could add your name and return address to the top of a Word document and save it with the name Letterhead; then you could use the *Get Info* command to change the Letterhead document into a stationery pad. After that, your name and address would appear at the top of an untitled document whenever you double-clicked the Letterhead document on the desktop.

To turn a stationery pad back into a standard document (which opens with its own name), just remove the check from the *Stationery pad* checkbox in the document's information window.

Finding an alias's original

An *alias* is a remote-control switch; it lets you open a file, disk, or folder that's stored in another location. Alias names always appear in italics. When you select an alias and choose the *Get Info* command, the info window contains a *Find Original* button. When you click this button, the Mac searches your disk for the original program, document, disk, or folder that the alias represents. (See *Make Alias* on page 38 for more information on aliases.)

Turning off the Trash warning

The Trash info window has a *Warn before emptying* checkbox at the bottom. By checking or unchecking this box, you can choose whether or not the Mac will display a warning about the contents of the Trash when you choose the *Empty Trash* command from the Finder's Special menu. By default this checkbox is checked and the Mac alerts you before it empties the Trash. You can uncheck the *Warn before emptying* checkbox to disable the warning, and the contents of the Trash will be discarded immediately when you choose the *Empty Trash* command.

Notes on the *Get Info* command for System 6

Aliases, icons that can be selected and replaced, the *Warn before emptying* checkbox in the Trash information window, and the *Stationery pad* checkbox in document information windows are features exclusive to System 7; System 6 users don't have these options. However, you can bypass the Trash warning in System 6 by holding down the Option key when dragging items to the Trash.

Sharing

System 7 offers built-in file-sharing capabilities for Mac users who are connected to each other on a network. The *Sharing* command lets you share selected disks or folders with other users on a network, control exactly who can access those shared items, and view the current sharing information for any item you can select on the desktop. In Chapter 15, we'll go over these activities in detail.

If you're running your Mac under System 6, the *Sharing* command isn't available, and you can't share your files with other Macs on the network. However, you can still access other shared files on the network from your Mac if it's set up to use AppleShare. (See Chapter 15 for more information.)

 For an alias to work properly, the alias and its original item must both be on disks that are currently available to your Mac. If the original for an alias is damaged or deleted from your disk, you'll get an alert message when you try to open the alias.

Make Alias

An *alias* is a stand-in for a folder, document, or program on your disk that acts just like the original item when you select it or open it, but takes up only a fraction of the space of the original. By using aliases, you can open programs, DAs, control panels, folders, and other items from many different places on your disk. For example, the *Control Panels* item on the ⌘ menu is an alias for the real Control Panels folder, which is located inside the System Folder; when you choose the *Control Panels* alias from the ⌘ menu, the real Control Panels folder opens.

To make an alias:

1. Select the item for which you want to make an alias.

2. Choose *Make Alias* from the File menu. A copy of the original item appears next to it with the name *<item name> alias* in italics. Below, for example, the alias for Microsoft Works has been named *Microsoft Works alias*.

3. Once you've created an alias, you can move it anywhere you want on your disk and it will open the original item when you open it. For example, you could drag the Microsoft Works alias onto the desktop. Then, whenever you double-clicked the alias, the Microsoft Works program itself would start up.

You can make as many aliases for an item as you like and place them in different locations on your disk. If you need to access a certain folder frequently, you can put an alias for it on the desktop, and also place one inside every other folder on your disk.

To remove an alias, just select it and drag it to the Trash. Deleting an alias has no effect on the original file. You can also rename an alias without affecting the name of the original.

Restart

The *Restart* command is the software version of shutting your Mac off with the power switch and then turning it on again, but it's a lot easier on your Mac's power supply and disk drives. Restarting is usually the first thing

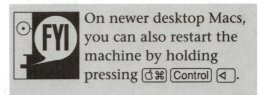

On newer desktop Macs, you can also restart the machine by holding pressing ⌘ Control ◁ .

you do when your Mac crashes and its screen locks up. Most of the time, a re-start solves the software problem that caused your Mac to crash and puts you back in business.

You must also use the *Restart* command when you want to activate new system extension files or inits you've added to your disk, because these only become active during the Mac's startup sequence.

Set Startup

On Mac SE and newer Mac models, you can set different startup items in System 6 with the *Set Startup* command on the Special menu in the Finder. This command

Mac Plus and older models aren't compatible with the *Set Startup* com-mand, so it's not avail-able on these machines.

lets you modify your System file so it looks for an application other than the Finder and loads it along with the Finder at startup. If you always work with Microsoft Word, for example, you can make it the startup application; then Word will load automatically when you start your Mac, saving you the extra steps of waiting for the Finder to load and then launching your program.

You also use the *Set Startup* command to switch between the Finder and MultiFinder. Under the Finder, you can only set one startup application, because the Finder only allows the Mac to run one application at a time; under MultiFinder, however, you can set several startup applications or DAs, because MultiFinder lets you open several applications at once. Whether

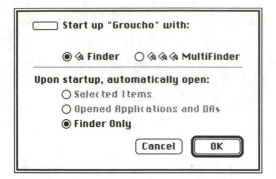

you're setting one startup application or several, the procedure is pretty much the same:

1. On the desktop, select the icon(s) for the application(s) that you want to open automatically at startup.

2. Choose *Set Startup* from the Special menu. The Mac displays a dialog box like the one shown above.

The disk name is at the top of the dialog box and your options are controlled with the radio buttons below.

3. Click the options you want to select, and then click the *OK* button to reset the startup application. Your Mac will automatically load the applications you've chosen the next time you start or restart it.

Shut Down

The *Shut Down* command purges everything from your Mac's memory and—depending on the Mac—either turns it off or clears the screen except for a dialog box that says it's okay for you to turn it off. The dialog box contains a *Restart* button that you can click if you change your mind and want to start up again instead.

You should always use the *Shut Down* command before turning off your Mac, because it quits any programs you have running and closes down the system software in an orderly way. If you have files open that haven't been saved or that have changed since you last saved them, the *Shut Down* command gives you a chance to save them. If you don't use the *Shut Down* command, not only will your Mac take longer to start the next time you use it, but some of your system software files could be damaged in the process.

Desk accessories

Control Panel

 If you're using System 6, control panels aren't double-clickable programs as they are in System 7. Instead, functions such as controlling the sound or the number of colors displayed on a monitor are handled with the Control Panel DA, which looks something like the one shown at right.

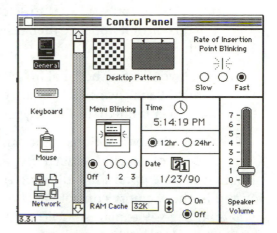

The far left section of this window contains icons representing various cdevs (control panel devices), each of which controls some aspect of your Mac's performance. Each cdev icon in the Control Panel DA corresponds

 Some init files (like QuickKeys) also show up as icons in the Control Panel.

to a file in your Mac's System Folder. Your Control Panel may look different from the one shown here, because your System Folder may contain a different collection of cdevs. Apple supplies a number of cdevs with its system software, but many others (like the Network cdev shown here) are available from third-party software vendors.

When you select an icon from the cdev list, the settings controlled by that cdev are displayed in the rest of the window. In the preceding illustration, the General icon is selected, so its settings are displayed.

Cdev icons generally appear in the Control Panel in alphabetical order from top to bottom, but no matter which cdevs you have in your System Folder, the General icon is always at the top of the list. In addition, it is always selected automatically when you open the Control Panel DA, because it contains most of the system settings you'll typically want to change.

To use the Control Panel DA:

1. Choose the Control Panel DA from the menu. The Mac displays the Control Panel window, shown above.

2. Click the buttons or icons at the right to change the General settings, or click a different cdev icon at the left to view another group of settings. If the icon you want to select isn't in view, you can scroll the list of icons until it appears, then select it and change the settings you want.

3. When you've finished making changes, click the close box to put the Control Panel away. Most changes you make in the Control Panel DA take effect immediately after you close its window.

The General cdev's options are much like those in System 7's General Controls control panel, described on page 45; however, the General cdev also includes the option for adjusting the size of the RAM cache, which is located in the Memory control panel under System 7. *Adjusting memory options* on page 49 explains how the RAM cache works. The only thing that's different about the RAM cache in System 6 is that you can turn it on and off.

System 6 also includes cdevs that correspond to System 7's Monitors, Sound, and Startup Disk control panels (except that the Startup Disk control panel is called the Startup Device cdev in System 6). For more information about these features, see page 45 *(Monitors)*, page 47 *(Sound)*, and page 49 *(Changing the Startup Disk)*.

Chooser

As you'll recall from Chapter 2, the Chooser DA is what you use to tell the system software which peripheral or network devices you want to use. When you start your Mac, the System file determines which Chooser extensions are present in the System Folder, and those icons appear in the Chooser window when you display it.

Most new Chooser extensions display an icon in the Chooser as soon as you copy them into your System Folder. In some cases, however, you have to restart the Mac to make the icon appear.

If you haven't copied a device's Chooser extension file into the System Folder, your System file won't detect that device, and its icon won't show up in the Chooser.

To use the Chooser, choose it from the menu. The Mac displays the Chooser window, which looks like the one on the next page.

The icons on the left side of the window indicate which Chooser extensions you currently have installed in your System Folder. (Under System 7, these extensions are grouped in the Extensions folder inside the System Folder.)

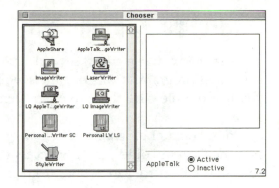

There are two distinct procedures for choosing devices to work with, depending on whether you're choosing a network file server for file sharing or another peripheral device. The procedure for choosing a network file server is covered on page 220 in Chapter 15. When you're choosing a printer, a modem, or any peripheral other than a file server, you can handle the whole procedure with the Chooser window itself. With the Chooser window open:

1. Select the icon that represents the type of device you want to use. If there's only one device of that type, its exact name appears in the list at the right, and that name is selected. If more than one device of that type is connected to your network, or if your network has zones, the list contains several names.

2. If your network has zones, select the name of the zone where the device you want is located. (If your network doesn't have zones, skip to step 3.)

3. Select the name of the device you want to use. If you don't click the actual device name, your Mac won't know which device you want; or it may assume that you want the device at the top of the list because that one may be automatically selected.

4. Click the close box to quit the Chooser. Any selections you make with the Chooser take effect immediately.

Remember, your Mac's system software only knows which devices to use when you select them with the Chooser. When you hook up a printer or other network device for the first time, you must select it with the Chooser or your Mac won't realize it's there. (By the way, you should *never* connect or disconnect devices while your Mac is turned on.)

Control panel programs

In System 7, you can adjust several aspects of the system software using control panel programs. Control panels work like other applications and DAs—you just double-click them to open them, and a window filled with options appears.

Control panel programs are usually located in the Control Panels folder inside the System Folder. You can access them there or, as a shortcut, you can choose the Control Panels alias from the menu to open the Control Panels folder.

 Apple uses *control panel* to refer to both the program and its open window, so we will too. It's confusing, but you have been warned.

Over a dozen control panel programs come with System 7. Some offer convenience features like a world time map, or allow you to check or adjust minor items such as the sensitivity of the mouse. In this section, we'll focus on the control panels and options that you'll use to solve the problems described later in this book. For a complete description of all the standard Mac control panels and what they do, consult a general guide to System 7 such as *The Macintosh Bible Guide to System 7.1*.

The control panels we'll be discussing fall into five functional areas:

■ Adjusting the Mac's look and feel

■ Changing the startup disk

■ Adjusting memory options

■ Adjusting file-sharing options

■ Adjusting PowerBook and Mac Portable options

Adjusting the Mac's look and feel

The control panels you use to adjust the look and feel of the Mac are General Controls, Monitors, Sound, and Views.

General Controls

The General Controls control panel looks like the illustration shown at right.

For our purposes, the important options on this control panel are *Time* and *Date*. If your Mac's clock or calendar is wrong, this is where you reset it. To reset the time or date, click directly on the digit(s) for the hour, minute, second, day, month, or year you want to change. A pair of arrows appears to the right of the date or time. You can click the up or down arrow to choose a new number; or just type the numbers you want from the keyboard. When you're finished, click the clock or calendar icon above the time or date to reset the Mac's internal clock or calendar.

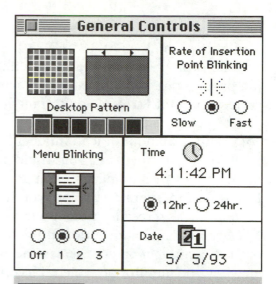

 Any items that were date- or time-stamped before you reset the clock will bear their old dates and times until you open and modify them; then the Mac will update these items.

Monitors

The Monitors control panel automatically records which monitor (or monitors) you have connected to your Mac. In the example shown at right, only one monitor is connected, and its icon appears in the center of the control panel with the number *1* on it.

If you have more than one monitor connected to your Mac, you'll see a numbered icon for each monitor in the center of this control panel. One icon will have a menu bar on it, and your Mac's menu bar will be located

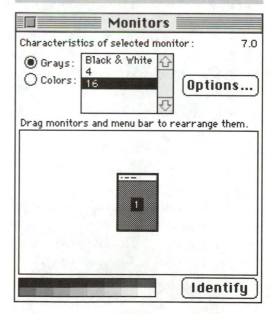

on the monitor that icon represents. You can move the menu bar by dragging it from one icon to another.

When you have two or more monitors connected, the mouse pointer jumps from one monitor to another when you drag it to the edge of the current monitor's screen. You can move the icons around in the control panel to change the way the pointer moves from one monitor to another. For example, if monitor icon number 2 is to the right of monitor icon number 1 in the control panel, you would drag the pointer off the right edge of monitor 1's screen to make it jump to monitor 2's screen. If monitor 2's icon is to the left of monitor 1's icon, you would drag the pointer off the left side of monitor 1's screen to make it jump to monitor 2.

Clicking the *Identify* button at the bottom right of the control panel displays a number on your screen to show which monitor you're currently viewing (the monitor on which the control panel is displayed), so you can always tell which monitor is number 1, which is number 2, and so on.

The buttons at the top of the Monitors control panel let you select whether to display grays or colors on the current monitor (assuming it's capable of showing colors). If the monitor is displaying colors and you want it to display only grays, click the *Grays* button in this control panel. If it's showing only shades of gray and you want it to show colors, click the *Colors* button.

The *Options* button is for Macs that have built-in video display capabilities. This button lets you choose how much RAM you want set aside for video operations. The more memory you set aside, the more shades of gray or colors you can display. However, setting a lot of memory aside for video can slow down your Mac, and it can take away memory you might otherwise use to run programs. Once you've chosen how much memory to set aside, options for selecting different numbers of colors or grays appear in the scrolling list to the left of the *Options* button.

When you drag the menu bar, rearrange the icons in the Monitors control panel, or change the amount of RAM you want set aside for video, these changes don't take effect until you restart your Mac.

If a monitor connects to the Mac through an add-in video card, the card itself has its own RAM, and you automatically see options for selecting the number of colors or grays you want in the scrolling list— you won't have to click the *Options* button. In this case, the number of colors or grays on your screen

changes as soon as you make your
selection and close the control panel.

Sound

If you have an earlier Mac model like
the Plus, you may not see the complete Sound control panel, which
looks like the illustration shown at
right.

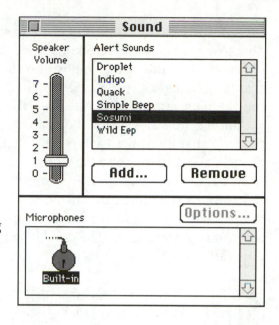

The slide bar at the left lets you
change the volume of sounds coming
through the Mac's speaker. Just drag
the slide to the setting you want (0
turns the sound off). In the scrolling
list, you can select a different sound
to replace the usual beep.

The Microphones box at the bottom of the control panel only appears if
your Mac model has a built-in microphone or sound input port. This box lets
you select different microphones for recording sounds, assuming you have
more than one microphone connected.

Any changes you make to the Sound control panel take effect
immediately.

Views

The Views control panel, which lets you change the way information appears
in windows, looks like the one in the illustration shown below.

At the top of the control panel are
options you can use to change the
font and size of the text that identifies items in list view windows. For
our purposes, however, the important options are in the Icon Views
and List Views areas at the center
and bottom of the control panel.

The Icon Views buttons let you
choose either a straight grid or a stag-
gered grid for displaying icons in

icon view windows. Examples of these styles appear to the left of the buttons. The *Always snap to grid* checkbox forces the Mac to align icons along the current grid. If you're trying to position the icons in a window and they keep snapping to a grid, you need to uncheck this checkbox. (You can always use the *Clean up* command on the Special menu to realign items to a grid.)

Among the List Views options are buttons that let you choose the size of the icon that identifies each type of item in a window. At the right, there are checkboxes that tell the Mac which categories (or columns) of information to show in list view windows. For example, if you're looking for Kind information about a document in a list view window and it isn't showing, you need to open this control panel and click the *Show kind* checkbox to display that column of information. The default settings for these options appear in the illustration on the previous page.

 Checking the *Calculate folder sizes* box makes your Mac display windows more slowly, because calculating folder sizes takes time.

When you check the *Calculate folder sizes* checkbox, the Mac automatically calculates and displays the total size of items inside every folder and shows this information in the Size column for each folder in a list view. (Normally, folder sizes are not shown.) The sizes are calculated one at a time, from the top of the window to the bottom, and appear individually as they're calculated, in place of the dashes that normally appear.

Macintosh HD		
7 items	41.9 MB in disk	36.7 MB available
Name	Size	Kind

Finally, the *Show disk info in header* checkbox causes your Mac to show the total amount of used and free space on a disk in all window headers. The information appears just below a window's title bar, as shown in the illustration above.

Normally, information about the number of items in the window and the total space used and available on the disk appears only in icon view windows; checking this box makes it available in list view windows as well.

Any changes you make in the Views control panel take effect as soon as you close the control panel.

Changing the startup disk

As explained in Chapter 1, when you turn on your Mac, it automatically looks for a System Folder, first on a floppy disk and then on its internal hard disk. The first disk it finds that contains a System Folder becomes the startup disk. If you're using a Mac SE or newer model, the Startup Disk control panel lets you specify an alternate startup disk if you have one connected to your Mac. The Startup Disk control panel looks like the one in the illustration shown at left.

Any hard disk that you have running and connected to your Mac appears in this control panel. To specify a startup disk other than the one your Mac normally uses, just select its icon here and then close the control panel. The next time you turn on the Mac, it will start from the disk you've chosen, provided that disk contains a System Folder.

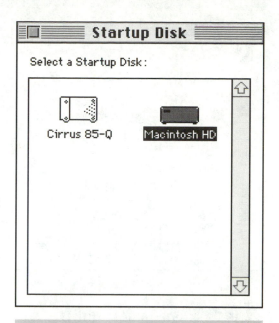

 If you have another disk connected and running that doesn't show up in the Startup Disk control panel, try restarting the Mac. You may have turned the disk on after the Mac was already running, so the disk wasn't recognized on the SCSI bus.

Adjusting memory options

The Memory control panel lets you adjust the way your Mac uses its RAM to handle file storage and system-related functions. Depending on which Mac model you're using, your Memory control panel may be missing some of the options on the full control panel, which looks like the one on the next page.

The Disk Cache section at the top lets you adjust the size of the disk cache, a special section of memory that's used to hold frequently used instructions so they can be quickly swapped into and out of RAM without being read from disk every time.

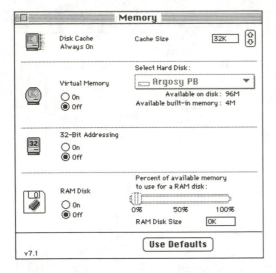

Under System 7, the disk cache must be at least 16K (and on some models the minimum is higher). You can use the arrows at the right of the Cache Size box to change the size of the cache. If you use applications that frequently swap instructions from disk, enlarging the cache makes those programs run a little faster.

On Macs using a 68030 or 68040 processor, Mac LCs, or Mac IIs using a 68020 processor and an optional paged memory management (PMMU) chip, you can set aside part of your hard disk as *virtual memory,* which is disk space that your Mac uses like extra RAM. The Virtual Memory area in the Memory control panel is where you turn this feature on and specify how much disk space you want assigned to it. If your Mac can't take advantage of virtual memory, this area won't appear in your Memory control panel.

 Since a RAM disk is part of your Mac's RAM, anything you copy there is wiped out when you turn off your Mac. Be sure to copy items from the RAM disk back to a real storage disk before shutting down or restarting.

Like virtual memory, 32-bit addressing is only available on certain Macs that use 68020, 68030, or 68040 processors. This feature lets your Mac use far more physical RAM than it could under System 6—up to 128 megabytes on some models. If your Mac can't use 32-bit addressing, this area won't appear in the Memory control panel.

Finally, the RAM Disk area also appears only on certain Macs. It lets you set aside a portion of your available RAM as an electronic disk. Once you've turned this feature on and dragged the slider to indicate how large you want the RAM disk to be, you can copy programs or documents to the RAM disk and then access them much more quickly than you could from a floppy disk or hard disk.

Adjusting file sharing options

Three control panel programs are used to turn on file sharing and adjust its various options: Sharing Setup, Users & Groups, and File Sharing Monitor. The Sharing Setup control panel lets you set up your Mac for file sharing and turn file sharing on. This control panel is the first tool you use to begin sharing files from your Macintosh with others on your network.

If you want to share your Mac's files with specific people on your network and assign specific access privileges to those people, you use the Users & Groups control panel to register those people by name. The File Sharing Monitor control panel tells you which other users on a network are currently connected to your Mac.

For PowerBook users, an extra control panel called the Auto Remounter lets you set your Mac up so any shared network volumes are automatically remounted when you restart your PowerBook or wake it up from sleep mode.

We'll see how to use all these control panels in Chapter 15.

Adjusting PowerBook and Mac Portable options

Some special features of the Mac Portable and PowerBook models are controlled by additional control panel or desk accessory programs. We'll look at these programs here.

Battery

The Battery control panel is installed on PowerBook models, and displays the

amount of battery charge left with a bar as shown here.

As the battery drains, the black bars become white from right to left. When the battery charge is down to 15 percent or less, you see messages warning that the battery needs charging. You can then plug in the power adapter cord to continue working as the battery recharges. When the battery is recharging, a lightning bolt appears across the battery icon in the control panel.

When you click the flag icon, you see a button you can click to put the PowerBook into sleep mode. Sleep mode turns off the hard disk, some processor functions, and screen backlighting to conserve power. (Of course, you can also choose the Sleep command from the Special menu to put the PowerBook to sleep.)

Brightness

The Brightness desk accessory was supplied with the original Macintosh Portable, and was the means by which you adjusted the screen's brightness. This DA displays a simple slider mechanism, and doesn't need any further elaboration here.

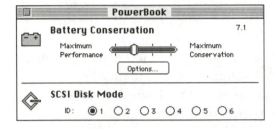

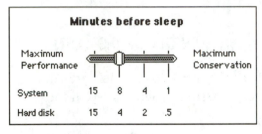

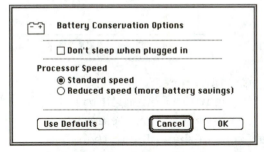

PowerBook

The PowerBook control panel comes on most PowerBook models. It allows you to make tradeoffs between performance and battery conservation. The control panel looks like the one in the illustration shown at the top left.

The four settings on the slider determine how long the PowerBook waits before going to sleep if there's no input from the keyboard or mouse. The scale doesn't show them, but the four sleep settings control both the hard disk and the rest of the system, defining specific numbers of minutes before sleep. What the settings mean is shown in the illustration at the middle left.

By clicking the different ID buttons in the SCSI Disk Mode area, you change the SCSI ID of the PowerBook itself. You can use a special SCSI cable to connect the PowerBook to another Mac and then use the PowerBook as an external hard disk for that Mac. The buttons here let you set the PowerBook's SCSI ID number when you use it as an external disk.

Finally, clicking the *Options* button in the Battery Conservation area reveals a dialog box like the one shown above.

Click the checkbox to shut off sleep mode when you're running under AC power. Click the *Reduced speed button* to cut down the processor's speed and in return gain a little more battery life.

PowerBook Display

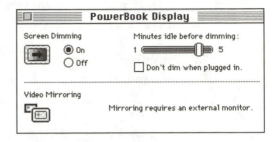

The PowerBook Display control panel lets you control the interval at which the screen is dimmed and how your PowerBook displays video on an external monitor. The control panel looks like the one in the illustration at right.

You can turn screen dimming on or off, drag the slider to set the interval of inactivity required before the screen dims, and click the checkbox to turn off screen dimming when you're running under AC power.

Video mirroring allows you to display on an external monitor the same thing that is showing on your PowerBook's screen. When you've connected a monitor to the PowerBook's video port, the Video Mirroring section in this control panel contains *On* and *Off* buttons. Click the *On* button to turn video mirroring on, then restart the Mac.

 Screen dimming turns off the PowerBook's backlighting—a major battery user. Don't confuse this with sleep mode, which also shuts down the hard disk.

The System file

You can modify the System file itself to change which fonts and sounds are available to your system software, and thus to your application programs. Changing the System file not only changes the look and sound of your Mac, it also affects the amount of memory your System file uses.

The procedures for changing the System file depend on which version of system software you're using. Before we go into these, however, let's look at a special type of file used to store fonts and (under System 6) desk accessories.

About suitcases

Geneva   Before System 7 came out, all fonts and desk accessories were stored in files called *suitcases*. Under System 7, DAs are separate programs. Fonts can be stored as individual files, or you can store groups of font files in suitcases. Suitcase files are so called because their icons look like the one shown above.

Combining groups of fonts into suitcases is still a handy option. You can use version 4.1 or later of the Font/DA Mover under System 7 to create or change suitcases.

Under System 6, the only way you can install fonts or DAs is to open a suitcase file using the Font/DA Mover utility and then copy some or all of the fonts or DAs from it into the System file.

Under System 7, you don't need the Font/DA Mover; you can open suitcase files by double-clicking them, and you can install fonts or sounds by dragging their individual files into the System file.

Changing fonts, sounds, and DAs under System 6

Under System 6, fonts, sounds, and desk accessories are all stored directly in the System file. You use the Font/DA Mover to add fonts or desk accessories to or remove them from the System file, and you must use a special utility to add or remove sounds.

To add or remove fonts or DAs, open the Font/DA Mover utility that came with your system software. You'll see a dialog box like the one in the illustration above.

The list at the left shows the current contents of the System file on your startup disk (the disk name is shown below the list). The list shows fonts or desk accessories, depending on which of the two buttons is selected at the top of the box.

To remove a font or desk accessory, select it in the list and click the *Remove* button.

To install a font or desk accessory, click the *Open* button underneath the right-hand list, navigate to the font or DA suitcase file (or the other System file) that contains the file you want to install, and open it. The fonts or DAs in that file appear in the list above. Then select the font or DA in the list and click the Copy button to add it to your System file.

To install or remove sounds under System 6, you need a shareware utility like Sound Master (available through user groups or online information services); or you can use a resource manager like Suitcase II or MasterJuggler.

 You can also use the Font/DA Mover to create new suitcase files in which to store collections of fonts or DAs. Just click the *Open* button underneath the right-hand list, click the *New* button in the directory dialog box that appears, and type a name for the new suitcase file.

Changing fonts and sounds under System 7.0 or 7.0.1

If you're working under System 7.0 or 7.0.1, you can open the System file or any suitcase file by double-clicking it. The item's window opens, and then you can drag files into or out of it. However, although you can open the System file window at any time, you can't add or remove fonts or sounds while any other application except the Finder is running.

To install individual font or sound files, just drag them into the System file window, onto the System file icon, or onto the System Folder icon.

To add fonts from a suitcase, you can either open the suitcase and drag individual fonts from it into the System file window, or you can drag the whole suitcase onto the System file or System Folder icon. If you drag a suitcase onto the System file or System Folder icon, however, the Mac will unpack the suitcase, installing all the files inside it into the System file, and will then delete the suitcase itself. So, if you want to install some fonts without deleting the suitcase in which they were stored, you need to open the suitcase and drag-install the fonts into the System file manually.

To remove fonts or sounds, open the System file window and then drag the items you want to remove out of it.

 To maintain all the contents of a suitcase and copy some fonts into the System file (instead of moving them), hold down the Option key while dragging font files from the suitcase window to the System file window.

Changing fonts and sounds under system software version 7.1 or later

If you're using system software version 7.1 or later, there's a separate Fonts folder inside the System Folder that stores all the fonts you want installed on your Mac. Any fonts or font suitcases inside the Fonts folder are automatically added to the System file when you start up your Mac. However, when you open the System file window, you won't see these installed fonts, because they're stored in the Fonts folder.

You add or remove fonts by dragging them into or out of the Fonts folder. And, unlike System 7.0 or 7.0.1, you can store font suitcases in the Fonts folder without unpacking them. (If you drag a suitcase onto the System Folder icon, the whole suitcase is placed inside the Fonts folder intact.)

To add or remove sounds, you open the System file window and drag them into or out of it.

System extensions or inits

System extensions (called inits under System 6) are automatically loaded at startup. Each system extension modifies the operation of the system software in a specific way. Your Mac comes with Apple-supplied extensions that enable file sharing and networking, for example. You can also get other extensions to enable functions like QuickTime, macro capabilities, adding features to directory dialog boxes, compressing files automatically when they're saved, or accessing a CD-ROM drive, to name just a few.

Each time you install one of these system extensions and restart your Mac, you are modifying the system software. All this modification has two potential side effects:

1. Some extensions may conflict with others or may be incompatible with your version of system software, causing system crashes or less serious problems.

2. Using lots of extensions increases the amount of RAM used by your system software, leaving less memory in which to run applications.

In order to minimize or deal with these problems, it pays to know how to install, remove, activate, and deactivate extensions or inits.

Installing or removing extensions or inits

Under System 7 and later, extensions are all stored in the Extensions folder inside the System Folder. To install an extension, drag it inside the Extensions folder. Alternatively, you can drag the extension onto the System Folder icon—the Mac automatically knows the item belongs in the Extensions folder and asks you to confirm this.

Technically, removing an extension requires only that you drag it outside the Extensions folder. To make absolutely sure the extension doesn't load at startup, however, drag it completely outside the System Folder.

Deactivating extensions or inits

You can always deactivate an extension or init by removing it from the System Folder and restarting your Mac, but System 7 offers a simpler alternative: hold down the Shift key as you restart your Mac, and none of the extensions in your System Folder will be loaded.

 Under System 6, all inits go directly inside the System Folder. To install them, just drag them inside the System Folder or onto the System Folder icon. To remove inits, drag them outside the System Folder.

 If an extension or init was installed at startup, dragging it outside the System Folder ensures it won't be installed when you restart, but the modification performed by that extension or init is still in effect until you do restart your Mac. So if you're having a problem and you want to remove an extension or init to resolve it, remember to restart the Mac after removing the item.

 If you frequently have problems with incompatible inits or extensions, you'll want to activate some and not others. You can always drag certain inits or extensions outside the System Folder, but it's much easier to use an extension manager program. See Chapter 6 for more information.

The System Folder folders

Under System 7, you can use four of the folders inside the System Folder to adjust the system software: the Apple Menu Items folder, the Extensions folder, the Fonts folder (under System 7.1 and later), and the Startup Items folder. Items that belong in these folders are placed in them automatically when you install System 7 with the Installer program or when you drag new items onto the System Folder icon on the desktop.

 Some system extensions or Chooser extensions may work properly even if they're not inside the Extensions folder, but it's best to keep all these files in their proper place.

The Apple Menu Items folder

The Apple Menu Items folder contains the programs, DAs, control panels, folders, and documents that appear on the menu. If you want an item to appear on the menu, just drag it (or an alias for it) into this folder. Placing individual DAs, control panels, folders, documents, programs, or aliases on the menu gives you easy access to them at any time. To remove an item from the menu, simply drag it out of the Apple Menu Items folder.

The Extensions folder

The Extensions folder is where you store all your Chooser and system extension files. If you drag any Chooser extension or system extension file onto the System Folder icon, your Mac automatically places it inside the Extensions folder.

The Fonts folder

The Fonts folder under System 7.1 and later stores all the fonts and font suitcase files you want installed in your System file. If you drag any font or font suitcase onto the System Folder icon, the Mac automatically places it inside the Fonts folder, and any fonts in the Fonts folder become available to the System file at startup.

The Startup Items folder

The Startup Items folder is where you place any program, document, or alias that you want to open automatically when you start your Mac. Once an item is inside this folder, the Mac attempts to open it along with the Finder at startup.

The Mac opens the items in the Startup Items folder one at a time in alphabetical order. It will fail to open an item in only two situations: when there isn't enough memory available, and when the Mac doesn't know which program was used to create a document because the document's Kind designation doesn't say.

System Folder operations under System 6

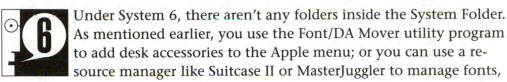

Under System 6, there aren't any folders inside the System Folder. As mentioned earlier, you use the Font/DA Mover utility program to add desk accessories to the Apple menu; or you can use a resource manager like Suitcase II or MasterJuggler to manage fonts, sounds, and desk accessories. To install inits, you simply drag them into the System Folder and restart your Mac.

Chapter 4

Keeping Your Mac out of Trouble

Most common Mac problems arise from mistakes you've made rather than from some diabolical streak in your hardware or software. Even when your hardware or software is at fault, something about the way you use the Mac is often at the root of—or has at least aggravated—the problem.

In this chapter, we'll look at some daily and periodic things you can do to minimize the occurrence of problems with your Mac.

Twenty-one ways to avoid problems

In this section we'll recommend some general operating procedures that will help you prevent hardware and software failures. Although some of these may seem obvious, it's amazing how many people overlook them. These procedures apply to all Macintosh models. For some other, PowerBook-specific suggestions, see *Ten ways to save your PowerBook battery* on page 69.

1. Make sure everything is plugged in securely before you start your Mac.
Everyone checks the plugs when setting up or moving the Mac or its peripherals, but people often sit helpless in front of a dead Mac because the janitor knocked the power cord out of the wall with a vacuum cleaner the night before. You don't need to hand-tighten every connection each day, but you should definitely try this simple solution first if your Mac doesn't start up, or if you can't locate your network printer or file server with the Chooser.

2. Never plug anything into or unplug anything from the Mac while the Mac or the other component is turned on.

This basic rule is the best way to prevent serious electrical problems with your equipment.

3. Don't cover up any of the cooling vents on a Mac, hard disk, monitor, printer, or other component.

It's tempting to treat the Mac as furniture, perhaps using it as a bookend or stacking papers on top of it. Remember though, the Mac, its monitor, and other components generate a lot of internal heat, and unless that heat is dissipated through unobstructed cooling vents, it will shorten the life of the semiconductor chips and other electric components inside the machine. Giving your Mac and other components enough breathing space is an easy way to avoid expensive repairs.

4. Don't place external components too close together.

Your Mac and some peripherals create radio frequency interference (RFI), which can cause problems with monitors and disk drives in particular. If you're using more than one monitor on your Mac, make sure they're at least a few inches apart, because the RFI between one monitor and the other can distort the screen images.

5. Don't place liquids near your Mac.

Lots of Macs have been put out of action at least temporarily because someone set a can of soda or a coffee cup within spilling distance. Spilled liquids can cause anything from a sticky keyboard to an electrical short in the CPU that can ruin your Mac's logic board. Make a habit of keeping liquids off the table that holds your Mac.

 If you're using an external floppy disk drive, the best place for it is on the right side of the Mac as you face it. In most Macs, the power supply is on the left side, and the power supply emits the most RFI. Placing the external floppy drive on the left can cause files on your floppy disks to become corrupted.

6. Allow plenty of room for your Mac's cables.

Lots of Macs are bristling with cables in the back, and this can make it hard to fit a Mac comfortably on a workstation that's set against a wall. People usually try to fix this problem by shoving the Mac as far back as they can in order to free up space in front for the keyboard. If you push a Mac to the wall, though, you usually end up squashing the cables, and that can cause problems.

Every cable coming out of your Mac is filled with smaller wires, and every wire can only be bent so far. Past a certain point (or *bend radius,* as the techies would say), wires begin to break. In a SCSI cable linking an external hard disk with your Mac for example, a few broken wires inside the cable can cause intermittent disk problems that are maddeningly difficult to diagnose. The simplest way to avoid cable problems is to allow cables to bend naturally. Don't squash a cable against the wall, wrap excess cable into a tight bundle, stretch a cable to make it span too big a gap, or otherwise force it to assume shapes that it wouldn't normally take on.

7. Don't quit programs or the Finder by turning off the power switch.

Always use the *Shut Down* command before you turn off the power. Choosing *Shut Down* may seem like an extra step when you're just going to turn off the computer anyway, but this command does more than empty the Mac's memory and black out the screen.

During the shut-down sequence, the Mac quits all the programs it's currently running, gives you a chance to save any documents you may have forgotten to save since the last change, and stores information about the current state of the Finder desktop so the Mac knows what to display the next time you start up from the same disk. If you simply turn off your Mac, it will take longer to start the next time (because it will have to determine how the Finder should look, instead of knowing that in advance). What's more, you could damage some system software files by hitting the switch without using *Shut Down.*

If your Mac is locked up so you can't use the *Shut Down* command, you'll probably have to use the power switch to turn the machine off so you can restart it; however, newer Mac models have a keyboard shortcut ((⌘) (Control) (◁)) that will restart the machine if it's locked up.

There's also a system extension by Paul Mercer, called Programmer's Switch, that lets you restart any Mac II or SE model by pressing (⌘) (Control) (◁) . This program is available on electronic bulletin boards and from user groups.

8. Don't move, hit, or shake the Mac, a hard disk, or a laser printer while it is turned on.

This one is really obvious, but it's easy to get careless and toss a book down on the desk so it hits an external hard disk. If you do this, you're risking a hard disk crash and the loss of your data.

Moving a running Mac is like moving a television set while it's on, except you're not only jiggling a tube that's generating thousands of volts, you're also in danger of disconnecting SCSI devices or external floppy drives. Moving a laser printer is even worse—you could end up spilling toner all over the inside, and everything you print afterwards will have polka dots.

9. Don't restart, shut down, or turn off your Mac while it's printing or accessing any storage device.

This trespass is sort of like driving away from a gas station with the fuel hose still pumping gas into your tank: you're cutting off the flow of data from its source, which can damage (or at least thoroughly confuse) the peripheral that's left in the lurch. Doing this with a hard disk could cause a head crash, which can destroy data on the disk.

10. Don't store more than one copy of the System file, Finder, or System Folder on the disk you use to start the Mac.

As explained in Chapter 2, the Mac looks for a System file and a System Folder on startup. If it finds more than one, it loads the first System file it locates, but it may then become confused about which System file is in charge, resulting in unexpected system crashes and other unpleasantries.

It's not difficult to see how this problem occurs: when you copy a new application to your hard disk from the original floppy, it's easiest to copy the whole disk, which sometimes contains its own System Folder. To keep extra System Folders off your hard disk, make sure you copy only program files from original application disks and periodically use the *Find* command on the File menu in the Finder (if you're running System 6, use the Find File DA or another file-finding utility) to search for duplicate System or Finder files or for System Folders.

If you do end up with more than one System Folder on your startup disk, you can tell which ones are extraneous by checking the icon that represents each of them. When it locates a System Folder and uses its files to start up, the Mac identifies that System Folder as the one that's in charge and places a small Mac on its icon, like the one shown at left.

System Folder

To determine which of your multiple System Folders you should keep, select the window that contains each one, choose *Icon* from the View menu in the Finder, and look for the System Folder icon that has a Mac on it.

11. When you connect more than one SCSI device to your Mac, make sure each device has a different SCSI address number before you start the system.

Some people like to have different System Folders available for different purposes. If you partition your hard disk into multiple volumes, it's okay to have a System Folder in each volume because the Mac treats each volume as a separate logical disk. You can then use the hard disk's partitioning software to decide which volume your Mac uses to start up.

You can have up to seven SCSI devices connected to your Mac's SCSI port, but each device must have a different address (from 0 to 6). If two devices have the same address, your Mac won't be able to use either of them properly. Usually you set the address either with software that comes with the device, or by using a wheel or button on the back of the device itself. Check the device's manual for instructions.

12. Never turn any SCSI device on or off while the Mac is running.
Turn SCSI devices on before you start the Mac and turn them off after you turn off the Mac. The Mac always scans its SCSI port during the startup sequence. If you have a SCSI device connected but not turned on, the Mac won't recognize it.

You may get into the habit of turning on your hard disk and your Mac at the same time. That's probably OK with a small-capacity hard disk (under 100 megabytes), because the drive warms up so fast that it's ready to go by the time the Mac has scanned the SCSI bus. If you have a large hard disk or a removable cartridge hard disk, you'll have to wait until the drive's Ready light comes on to turn on the Mac.

If you turn off a SCSI device while the Mac is still running, the Mac will probably continue to think the device is available. This is especially problematic with storage devices: if you try to save to a SCSI device that is no longer turned on, you'll cause a system crash.

When the System file's size reaches about a megabyte under System 6, it's pushing the limit of memory set aside for it and you'll begin to have problems printing or starting up. If you must use a System file this large, use HeapFixer or Heap Tool, two shareware utilities available from user groups or bulletin boards, to make your system heap larger. Under System 7, the system heap is automatically enlarged as the System file requires more space.

13. Minimize the System file.

The System file in a basic Macintosh running under System 6 contains over 300,000 bytes of complex instructions. Under System 7, a typical System file occupies over a megabyte. As you start up and use the Mac, parts the System file are read and modified by the Chooser, control panels, extensions, Finder, and various other DAs and applications. It's like having 15 editors working on a manuscript at the same time and expecting the results to be perfectly consistent.

The System file's size and the complexity of its interactions with other Mac software are responsible for many software errors; there's no sense in aggravating the situation by making the System file any larger than necessary. Each time you add a font, sound, or DA to your System file, it gets more cumbersome. Adding extra extensions to your System Folder or Extensions folder also increases the amount of memory the System file requires to run.

The next time you feel an urge to load up the System file with all sorts of fonts, sounds, and DAs you'll rarely use, or to enhance it by adding lots of dubious extensions to your System Folder, remember that you're only making it harder for the Mac to manage something that's already tricky.

 If you decide to use a resource manager, be sure to remove any duplicate copies of desk accessories or fonts that you'll be installing with the resource manager program.

14. Use a resource manager.

If you want to use lots of fonts (and DAs under System 6), use a resource manager like Suitcase II or Master-Juggler to manage them. With a resource manager, you can store DAs or fonts outside the System file, and open them only as you need them. Rather than having a hundred fonts installed and using up memory all the time, for example, you can use a resource manager to locate and open fonts as you need them.

15. Minimize the System Folder.

Don't use the System Folder to store any files except those essential to the operation of the System file. The Installer program you use to install System files puts important files into the appropriate folders in the System Folder. Other programs you install may also place system-related files (like preferences files) in the System Folder.

But don't store any files in the System Folder that don't have to be there, such as data files or applications. The more cluttered the System Folder becomes, the longer it takes the System file to locate and load the resources it needs.

Remember, anything you can do to make the Mac's system-related tasks easier and faster will cut down on system errors.

16. Leave some empty space on each disk.

The fuller a disk becomes, the more likely that files on it will become fragmented (see *Periodic maintenance* on page 70), and the longer it will take to read or write files. In extreme cases, when the disk is completely full, your Mac may not have enough room to manage files or the disk directory and you'll get error messages. Try to leave 5 percent or so of empty space on each disk.

17. Leave some available RAM space.

Try not to open so many programs that you use up all the available RAM in your Mac. The closer you come to using up all your Mac's RAM, the more likely it is that you'll have "out of memory" problems or crashes. When you must open so many programs or documents that your Mac's RAM is nearly all used, try not to keep everything open any longer than you have to.

18. Use compatible versions of all programs and system software.

You can't stop the march of technology. Eventually every piece of software on your Mac will become obsolete with respect to the current state of the art. This doesn't matter if you never change any of your software and don't need to share files with other Mac users. (Somewhere out there, isolated Mac users are still happily using 512K Macs with system software and applications created in 1986.) If you're like most users, though, you'll gradually acquire new programs or upgrade old ones as the years go by.

When you consider adding or upgrading a program or system extension, check with the manufacturer to make sure the new arrival is compatible with your current version of system software. Otherwise, you'll need to upgrade your system software.

19. Use a virus detection or repair program.

Viruses can cause such headaches that it's well worth the expense and effort to use a virus fighting program to prevent them. This is particularly true if you share files or programs with other users or download files from electronic bulletin boards or information services.

20. Don't do more than one thing at a time. Wait for an operation to finish before you begin the next operation.

Everybody becomes a speed freak once they master the basics of computing. As soon as you've mastered the steps for printing a document or performing some other procedure, somehow your Mac—once such a marvel of technology—becomes slower than a sloth on snowshoes. Then, instead of calmly waiting those agonizing milliseconds while the Mac obeys each command, you pile commands on top of one another in the hope that the Mac will remember and execute them all in the proper order.

Most of the time your Mac can keep up, but sometimes it can't and then you'll have a problem. C'mon, give the Mac a break. How would *you* like it if your boss gave you a full week's orders in two seconds and expected you to remember and follow them all flawlessly?

21. Keep it simple.

Every month, dozens of new hardware and software products appear for the Mac, and all of them seemingly do something you need to have done, or make your Mac better in some way. But invariably, the people who make the most changes to their basic Mac system are the ones who have the most problems, especially software-related problems.

I try to keep my Macs as "plain vanilla" as possible. Although I'm aware of all sorts of Finder helpers, compression programs, and nifty system extensions that could make my Mac a little better in countless ways, I try to live by the old adage: "If it ain't broke, don't fix it." Of course, software and hardware vendors don't like this attitude much, but then they're not the ones who lose files or hours of work because of problems caused by adding too many goodies to a Mac. For me, this philosophy has kept my Macs basically problem-free for many years.

Ten ways to save your PowerBook battery

Anyone using a PowerBook knows that the biggest challenge is to keep the machine running as long as possible under battery power. PowerBooks are supposed to run for three hours on a battery charge, after which they'll maintain the current contents of RAM in sleep mode for up to two days, but these limits depend a lot on how you use the PowerBook. Here are some tips to maximize battery life.

1. Discharge the battery completely at least every three months.

It's easy to keep the power cord plugged in as you use the PowerBook, so the battery is typically recharging constantly and never gets to the point where it's completely

 Some collections of PowerBook utilities have battery conditioning utilities that totally discharge the battery and then recharge it automatically.

discharged. If you use mostly AC power for a long period of time, however, the battery never runs totally empty and it will eventually become unable to take a full charge. So, at least once every three months, disconnect the power cord and run on battery power until the bitter end, ignoring the battery charge warnings, until the PowerBook puts itself to sleep. Then plug in the power cord and recharge the battery for at least eight hours, or remove the battery and put in the optional charger for at least five hours.

2. Set screen dimming to the shortest possible interval with the PowerBook Display control panel.

Screen backlighting takes up more juice than any other PowerBook feature, so set screen dimming to occur as frequently as you can stand without really interfering with your work.

3. Turn down the screen's brightness to the lowest level you can tolerate.

Again, the lower the brightness level, the less power you'll use.

4. Set the PowerBook control panel to maximum battery conservation, and use the *Options* button to set the reduced processor speed.

5. Put the PowerBook to sleep whenever possible, even if only for a minute or two.

If you copy your system software and working programs and documents into RAM, you can then drag the hard disk's icon to the Trash to keep it from running at all. After the screen, the hard disk is the second biggest battery hog on a PowerBook.

6. **If your PowerBook has 6 MB of RAM or more, set up a RAM disk as a startup disk with the Memory control panel and copy your System Folder, application programs, and documents into it at startup.**

7. **Don't use virtual memory.**
Using virtual memory makes your hard disk work harder, and the hard disk is a major drain on battery power. Check the Memory control panel to make sure this feature is off.

8. **Use the Chooser to turn AppleTalk off if you're not connected to a network.**
It takes battery power to maintain a connection through the serial port, and the PowerBook tries to do this whenever AppleTalk is on.

9. **Use the Sound control panel to set the sound level at zero.**
Making sounds through the speaker also consumes power. Setting the sound level at zero doesn't turn off the startup sound.

10. **Quit any communications program when you're not using it.**
Communications programs use modem power whenever they're running (even in background), so don't leave such a program open if you're not using it.

Periodic maintenance

The activities outlined in this section are on the order of a regular oil change or tune-up for your car, and they apply to every Macintosh. They won't necessarily keep your Mac from breaking, but they'll keep it running more smoothly, help eliminate some potential problems before they occur, and make it easier to recover from problems that do crop up.

Make backup copies of everything.

There's one thing you can be certain of: sometime, somehow, you'll have a problem with your Mac that will cause you to lose some data. If you make regular backup copies and save an extra copy of your work to a second disk several times a day, you'll protect yourself against potential disaster. The more often you back up your data, the less work you'll lose when trouble strikes.

The best way to protect yourself is with a backup utility program, because it copies everything on your hard disk. If you simply drag-copy files to another disk, you'll invariably miss items like the Scrapbook or other important files, and you won't be able to copy invisible files at all. A backup program will ensure that you get everything.

In addition to a master backup made with a utility program, you should also make at least one set of backup floppy disks for every program you have, including all the system utilities and setup programs that came with your Mac, your hard disk, and any other components. You'll need working copies of these utilities to perform many of the repair techniques described in this book.

Sometimes one of the system software installation disks or your hard disk setup program becomes damaged and the only remedy is to use another copy that works properly. You won't be able to do that if you haven't made at least one backup copy.

Keep all your original, master disks in a safe place and lock them to prevent them from being accidentally erased or overwritten. If you end up having to use a backup set of floppy disks, keep them locked as you use them. This way, if the problem is causing disk damage, the disks will be protected.

Rebuild the desktop file

The desktop file is an invisible file found on every disk. It contains information about the files and programs on the disk and how you view them in the Finder. As a disk is inserted (or as the System file recognizes it at startup time), its desktop file is read into the Mac's memory. As you work with the disk (adding and deleting files), the desktop file grows because it stores information about files even after they've been deleted. This can create two problems:

■ First, all that reading and writing of information makes a file increasingly prone to minor disk errors, which can cause data to be written incorrectly. This may show up when you try to open a file and can't, when a disk's icon doesn't look right, or when the Mac tells you a disk is damaged or unreadable.

■ Second, after several weeks or months, you end up with a desktop file that contains all sorts of information your Mac no longer needs because it concerns files that have been deleted. An extra-large desktop file takes longer to read, so you have to wait longer and longer for your Mac to display disk icons and windows in the Finder.

You can keep your disks in optimum shape by periodically rebuilding the desktop file on each disk. How frequently you need to do this depends on how many changes you make to the files you store on your hard disk, and on how often you change them. If you add or change a few files a day, you only need to rebuild the desktop file every month or so. (For complete instructions, see *Rebuild the desktop file* on page 109 in Chapter 7.)

Replace the System file

As explained earlier, the System file is a large and complex piece of software that is modified continually as you use the Mac. Sometimes a disk writing error causes problems in the System file that don't show up immediately. If you begin having minor, intermittent problems with disk access, printing, or startup, it's a good idea to replace the System file on your disk. Even if you don't begin to notice problems, replacing your System file every three months or so will help prevent them. (For complete instructions, see *Replace the system software* on page 112 in Chapter 7.)

Avoid disk clutter

What's good for the System Folder, System file, and desktop file is also good for your disks in general. The more files and folders you have on a disk, the larger its desktop file, and the longer it takes to display the disk's contents. Most computer users waste from 10 to 30 percent of their disk space by storing old memos, letters, and other data files they no longer need, or large applications they never use. Again, the principle applies: a lean Mac is a happy Mac. If you haven't used a file in several months, you can probably copy it onto a floppy disk and get it from there when—or if—you ever need it again.

Defragment your hard disk

File fragmentation is another factor that can affect your Mac's performance. When you begin storing files on a new hard disk, the files are stored side by side in concentric rings. However, when you enlarge an existing file, your Mac has to fragment the file, or break it up, and store it in two or more places because the original space created for that file is now too small for it, and other files are stored immediately next to it.

A fragmented file takes longer to load and store, because the disk has to read or write in two, three, or more places. Fragmentation is inevitable on hard disks, and it doesn't usually become a performance problem until 30 percent or more of the files on a disk are fragmented.

Check for fragmentation every couple of months with a disk utility program like DiskExpress, Mac Tools, or Norton Utilities for Macintosh. If the utility shows that 30 percent or more of the space on your disk is fragmented, you can defragment it using the same program. (This can be a bit risky, so be sure to back up your entire disk before you run a defragmentation program.)

A safer alternative is to make a complete backup copy of your disk, reformat the disk to erase everything on it, and then restore the backup copy. When you restore the files, they are written to the disk in unfragmented blocks.

Chapter 5
What Can Go Wrong

The Mac is a general-purpose computer that can do thousands of different things. But in a machine that's so versatile, there are also many different possibilities for problems. In this chapter, we'll go over the basic types of things that can go wrong with your Mac and how the Mac lets you know when there's a problem.

Three problem areas

There are three types of problems on a Macintosh (or any computer):

- Hardware problems
- Software problems
- User error

Let's look at each category in turn.

Hardware problems

Computers are basically pretty reliable, and hardware problems are the least likely ones. A rule of thumb is that if you're going to have a hardware problem related to a manufacturing or component defect, it will happen when the computer is new. This is why many computer dealers "burn in" each computer, letting it run for 24 hours or more to see if any such problems occur before delivering it to the customer.

If you're the electroni- cally adventurous type, get a copy of *The Dead Mac Scrolls* by Larry Pina from Peachpit Press. It shows how to repair hundreds of specific Mac hardware problems.

If you've used the computer for even a few hours and no hardware problems have occurred, then you probably won't encounter such a problem until the computer is get- ting old (after several years), or until the computer is physically damaged in some way. Of course, if you don't follow the suggestions in Chapter 4, you significantly increase the likelihood of hardware problems. And even if you take all the precautions, sometimes you just get lucky and end up with a machine that has some unbelievably annoying defect.

Each time you start it up, the Mac does a series of self-diagnostic checks. Problems with memory chips, video, the processor, or other major compo- nents are reported with a sad Mac icon and the failure of the machine to start. (See *The sad Mac icon* on page 80.) If no failures are reported at startup, a hardware problem usually announces itself with some physical sign—a distorted or black screen, funny noises or smells coming from inside the CPU or from a peripheral, or the plain failure of something to work.

This book won't have you opening up cases or soldering logic boards. If a hardware-related problem can be fixed quickly and simply, we'll show you how. Otherwise, you'll have to take the Mac to a technician.

Software problems

Software problems are the second most likely source of trouble. These fall into several subcategories:

- Memory problems

- File corruption problems

- Incompatibilities

- Viruses

Most software problems are memory-related. When applications or the system software don't have enough memory (or enough of the right area of memory), things go wrong. The program may quit, or announce that it doesn't have enough memory, or it may simply slow down or begin per- forming erratically.

Another source of trouble is file corruption. System software, program, and document files are read from and written to your disk constantly. A tiny electrical surge during reading or writing can cause a small error that garbles the file. Often the problem isn't bad enough to keep you from running the Mac or opening a program, but it shows up in smaller ways—part of a file will be trashed, or a file can't be found, or the file won't open properly. A simple remedy for problems like this is to reinstall the system software or application, or to open a backup copy of the file. (See Chapter 7 for more on these techniques.)

Incompatibilities are a third type of problem. Sometimes portions of the system software (extensions or inits are common culprits) just don't get along with each other, or with your application programs. As system software evolves, older applications or extensions become incompatible. Again, these problems often don't announce themselves in dramatic ways. Rather, little things start going wrong. The best prevention for these types of problems is to check for and maintain version compatibility between your application programs, extensions, and system software, as suggested on page 67 in Chapter 4.

Viruses are the fourth major software-related problem. Most people are pretty virus-conscious these days and most people use virus-fighting programs, so these beasts aren't as common as they once were. However, viruses can be pesky, because they cause minor or seemingly intermittent problems, such as:

- Unexpected crashes or restarts when you move items on the desktop

- Intermittent system errors when you open or print documents from within applications

- Sluggish performance when opening windows on the desktop

- False "disk unreadable" messages when you insert floppy disks that are really okay

The best way to eliminate this source of trouble is to use a virus-fighting program. See Chapter 6 for more information.

User error

Unpleasant as it may be to admit, user error is by far the most common source of problems on the Macintosh. In the majority of situations, everything is working as it should, but we simply don't understand it. Perhaps the computer beeps because we're trying to do something that's not allowed, or we expect to see information on the screen that isn't there, or we get an alert message that we don't understand.

Since user errors are such a big part of the problem, we'll cover dozens of common ones later in this book.

How the Mac reports problems

The Mac has several different ways of getting your attention or alerting you to a problem or potential problem. Let's look at these in order of severity.

The system beep

The system beep (or boing, or clank, or whatever sound has been substituted for the beep) is the Mac's main way of getting your attention. Either the Mac's system software or an application or DA you're running can trigger a beep when you do something that isn't permitted in a given situation, like clicking outside a dialog box on the screen.

The system beep is just a reminder that something won't work—a gentle nudge that tells you you've made an operator error, rather than a sign that something's wrong with your Mac. Since most people commit these small transgressions quite regularly, the system beep can become annoying. If it bothers you, you can eliminate it by lowering your Mac's speaker volume to 0 in the Sound control panel.

Alerts

An alert is a type of dialog box that appears on the screen when something has gone wrong or when the Mac needs to call your attention to something.

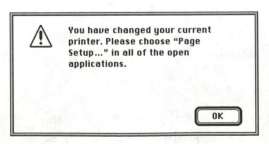

Some alerts—like the *Printing In Progress* message that pops up during a print job—just let you know what's going on. Others warn you of a problem, and these are always announced by one or more system beeps and a flashing menu bar or Application menu icon.

Alert boxes contain brief messages that try to describe the problem and—sometimes—tell you what to do about it.

You may even be given a chance to do something immediately by clicking a button in the alert box. In other cases, your only option will be to click an *OK* or *Continue* button that puts the alert box away. In general, System 7's alerts are much more specific and helpful than those in System 6.

There are three types of alerts: stop, note, and caution. Sometimes alert boxes contain only text and one or more buttons, but usually each type of alert has an icon, as in the illustration above.

In addition to icons and messages, some alert boxes contain a message ID number that refers to a technical explanation of the problem. See *System error codes* on page 82.

System errors

System errors are special alerts distinguished by the dreaded bomb icon.

This is a sure sign that you're out of luck for the moment. These messages can be extremely frustrating because while your Mac is still functional enough to display an alert box, the alert's only purpose is to tell you that your program is dead and your data is history.

In some System Error situations you can use your Mac's interrupt switch and type some code numbers to regain enough control to save any open files. See *Restart the Mac and try again* in Chapter 7.

System error alert boxes always contain an ID number in the lower-right corner. These error codes help programmers determine what has gone wrong, but they probably won't help you fix the problem or avoid it in the future. If you simply can't contain your curiosity about the codes, however, see *System error codes* on page 82.

Once in a while you'll see a system error message that includes a *Resume* or *Continue* button. Clicking the button rarely does any good. If your Mac is hurting badly enough to display a system error, your best—and often only—option is to restart the machine and hope the problem doesn't recur.

Freezes

In a freeze, you lose control over the Mac but it doesn't display the System Error message. Typically, the pointer freezes on the screen and the Mac no longer responds to any keyboard or mouse input. In most cases, the only solution is to restart the Mac. (See *Restart the Mac and try again* in Chapter 7 for more information about restarting in freeze situations.)

Crashes

A crash is a warning only in the sense that a blowout is a warning of a tire problem. As with a freeze, your Mac is so screwed up it can't even display a system error message. Instead of simply locking up, however, the screen may dance and jitter, or display a random pattern of wavy lines. Sometimes these symptoms are also accompanied by a buzzing or crackling noise. Believe it or not, these dramas are often software-induced (any bizarre sounds you hear are a sort of electronic funeral march played through the Mac speaker, not the sound of your logic board going up in smoke). Again, the best remedy is to shut off your Mac, wait a few seconds, then turn it on again.

The sad Mac icon

The sad Mac icon only appears during the startup sequence, and alerts you to a hardware problem that prevents your Mac from working properly. The sad Mac looks like this:

 Every sad Mac has one or two rows of numbers beneath it—depending on the model—which identifies the problem. On Mac II models, the sad Mac is usually accompanied by a different-sounding startup chime than you hear when everything is okay. To a trained ear, the specific chords of the chime indicate the problem. When you have a sad Mac problem, you're out of luck until you fix the specific hardware problem that causes it.

On Mac Plus and earlier models, the sad Mac has one row of six-digit numbers. The first two numbers indicate the class of problem, and the last four indicate specific problems within a class. On Mac SE and newer models, there are two rows of numbers. The last four digits of the upper number indicate the problem class, and the second row identifies the specific problem. On the Mac Portable, the third pair of numbers in the upper row indicates the problem class.

For most of us, the sad Mac icon means a trip to the local Mac repair technician. There are dozens of different problem-specific codes and remedies. However, there are only a handful of class codes, and since one class is software-related, we'll look at the class codes here.

Mac Plus and older (first two digits of six-digit code)

Code	Problem
01	ROM test failed
02, 03, 04, or 05	RAM test failed
0F	Software error (probably a bad System file, Finder, disk directory, or disk boot blocks)

Mac SE and newer (last four digits of upper number)

Code	Problem
0001	ROM test failed
0002-0005	RAM test failed
0006-0009, 000A-000E	Other logic board chip or bus failure
000F	Software error (probably a bad System file, Finder, disk directory, or disk boot blocks)

Mac Portable (third pair of digits of upper number)

Code	Problem
01	ROM test failed
02, 05, 16	RAM test failed
06	ADB chip failed
08, 0E	Data bus failed
0B, 0C	SCSI or disk controller failed
10, 11, 14, 15	Logic board chip failure

With these codes in hand, you can at least zero in on the problem area. If you get an "0F" or "000F" code, try starting the Mac from another disk and replacing the system software on your normal startup disk. If this fails, the disk directory is probably damaged, and you'll need to use a disk diagnostic and repair utility (see Chapter 6).

For further information about and solutions to specific sad Mac problems, see *The Dead Mac Scrolls* by Larry Pina, from Peachpit Press. Also the *Troubleshooting Guide* that comes with 911 Utilities, part of the Superset Utilities from Datawatch software, has a comprehensive list of sad Mac codes (see Chapter 6).

System error codes

This section lists the system error code numbers you're likely to see in alert boxes, and explains what they mean. As you can see, all these numbers are negative ones (probably because errors are a very negative experience on the Mac). Many of the explanations won't mean much unless you're a Mac programmer, however. Error numbers above 100 are quite rare, so these are summarized in groups.

Code	Problem
-1	bus error
-2	memory address error
-3	illegal instruction
-4	zero divide error
-5	check trap error
-6	overflow trap error
-7	privilege violation error
-8	trace mode error
-9,-10	line trap errors
-11	miscellaneous hardware exception error
-12	unimplemented core routine error
-13	uninstalled interrupt error

System error codes (continued)

Code	Problem
-14	I/O Core Error
-15	Segment Loader Error
-16	floating point error
-17	package 0 not present [List Manager]
-18	package 1 not present [reserved by Apple]
-19	package 2 not present [Disk Initialization]
-20	package 3 not present [Standard File]
-21	package 4 not present [Floating Point Arithmetic]
-22	package 5 not present [Transcendental Functions]
-23	package 6 not present [International Utilities]
-24	package 7 not present [Binary/Decimal Conversion]
-25	out of memory
-26	can't launch file
-27	file system map has been trashed
-28	stack has collided with application heap
-33	directory full
-34	disk full
-35	no such volume
-36	Input/Output error
-37	bad file or volume name
-38	file not open
-39	end of file
-40	tried to position to before start of file
-41	memory full or file won't fit
-42	too many files open
-43	file not found
-44	diskette is write protected

System error codes (continued)

Code	Problem
-45	file is locked
-46	volume is locked (software lock)
-47	file is busy
-48	duplicate filename
-49	file already open
-50	error in user parameter list
-51	refnum error
-52	get file position error
-53	volume was ejected
-54	permissions error (on file open)
-55	volume already mounted
-56	no such drive
-57	not a Macintosh disk diskette
-58	volume in question belongs to an external file system
-59	file system internal error: during rename the old entry was deleted but could not be restored…
-60	bad master directory block
-61	write permissions error
-64	drive not installed or Font Manager error
-65	font not declared
-66	font substitution occurred
-67 through -84	disk read/write errors
-85	can't find menu bar definition
-86	recursively defined menus
-87,-88	couldn't load menu resources
-90	FPU instruction executed, but machine has no FPU
-91 through -98	AppleTalk errors
-99	can't load patch resource

System error codes (continued)

Code	Problem
-100	no scrap exists
-101	memory parity error
-102	System is too old for this ROM, or no object of that type in scrap
-103	booting in 32-bit on a 24-bit system
-104	need to write new boot blocks
-105	need at least 1.5 MB of RAM to boot 7.0
-108 through -117	memory manager errors
-120 through -123	HFS errors
-124 through -127	MFS errors
-126 through -128	Menu Manager errors
-130 through -132	HFS file ID errors
-145 through -157	Color QuickDraw and Color Manager errors
-185 through -199	Resource Manager errors
-200 through -232	Sound Manager errors
-250 through -261	MIDI Manager errors
-290 through -293	Start Manager errors
-300 through -351	Start Manager errors
-299	Notification Manager error
-360 through -400	Device Manager errors
-450 through -463	Edition Manager errors
-470 through -489	SCSI Manager errors
-500	QuickDraw region too big
-600 through -606	Process Manager errors
-620 through -625	Memory Dispatch errors
-800 through -816	Database Access errors
-850 through -863	Help Manager errors
-900 through -932	PPC Toolbox errors

System error codes (continued)

Code	Problem
-1024 through -1029	AppleTalk NBP errors
-1066 through -1075	AppleTalk ASP errors
-1096 through -1105	AppleTalk ATP errors
-1273 through-1280	Data Stream Protocol errors
-1300 through -1308	HFS errors
-3101 through -3109	AppleTalk ATP errors
-4096 through -4101	Print Manager errors
-5000 through -5044	AppleTalk Filing Protocol (AFP) errors
-5500 through -5502	SysEnvirons errors
-5550 through -5553	Gestalt errors
-8132 through -8160	LaserWriter Driver errors
-11000 through -11005	Picture utilities errors
-13000 through -13005	Power Manager errors
-23000 through 23048	MacTCP errors

Chapter 6

Diagnostic and Repair Tools

There are several hardware and software tools you can use to diagnose, repair, or recover from problems. In this chapter, we'll look at popular products and services in each of several key categories:

- Backup programs
- Extension managers
- Resource managers
- Hard disk setup utilities
- Diagnostic and repair utilities
- Software diagnostic utilities
- Virus utilities
- Network utilities
- Miscellany
- Component-level repair shops

These lists are not comprehensive, and the mention of a product here shouldn't be considered an endorsement of that particular product (although I couldn't help opining about some of them). For more detailed information about these hardware and software products, check *MacWorld* or *MacUser* magazine, or consult your local computer retailer.

Backup programs

A backup program is the single most important tool in your fight against Mac problems, because it ensures that you'll have a second or third copy of your files and programs if something happens to the ones you work with each day. Apple used to supply a backup program with its other system software utilities, but now you need to get one from another developer.

Key attributes you should consider when choosing a backup program include whether or not it works with your backup medium (some programs don't work with tape drives, for example); how convenient it is to use; whether it lets you make partial backups; and how fast it is.

DiskFit Pro, $125, Dantz Development Corp., 510-849-0293. This program, a favorite for years, has the advantage of producing backup files that can be opened from the Finder. It doesn't support tape drives, however.

Fastback Plus, $189, Fifth Generation Systems, 504-291-7221. This program has built a reputation by performing backups more quickly than most other programs.

MacTools, see page 93. This utility collection from Central Point Software includes Central Point Backup, which supports all types of media.

Norton Utilities for Macintosh, see page 93. This utility collection from Symantec includes a backup program.

Redux, $79.95, Inline Design, 203-435-4995. This program has been around a long time and gives you lots of flexibility in choosing which files to back up, but it doesn't support tape drive systems.

Retrospect, $249, Dantz Development Corp., 510-849-0293. This product has lots of extra features, such as the ability to set up regular, timed backups, and the ability to back up to all types of media. A network version, Retrospect Remote, allows backups across a network.

Extension managers

Extension managers let you turn system extensions or inits on or off without having to drag them into or out of the System Folder. Because they save a lot of file dragging, these products make it much easier to identify and deal with extension conflicts.

Conflict Catcher and Other Innovative Utilities, $79.95, Casady & Greene, 408-484-9228. Other extension managers let you decide which extensions are loaded or not loaded at startup. Conflict Catcher does that as well, but its unique feature is its ability to detect extension conflicts as the extensions are loaded. It thereby prevents system crashes that result from extension conflicts before they have a chance to occur, and then runs a series of tests to locate the problem extension.

 The software diagnostic program Alert! also includes an extension manager. See page 95.

Extension Manager, free from online services and user groups. This product from Apple Computer lets you turn extensions on or off. It's simple and lacks the features of other programs, but then it doesn't cost anything, either.

INITPicker, $79.95, Inline Design, 203-435-4995. This product was one of the first extension managers. It lets you turn extensions on or off, or create and save different sets of extensions that you can load at different times.

Resource managers

Resource managers help you make better or more efficient use of system-level resources such as fonts, sounds and desk accessories, thereby helping you save disk or memory space.

Adobe Type Manager, $99, Adobe Systems, 415-961-4400. If you use PostScript fonts, this program makes it possible to display them in any size on your screen without having to have several different sizes of screen fonts installed. It also allows you to scale and print PostScript fonts on a QuickDraw printer such as the StyleWriter.

Connectix PowerBook Utilities, $99, Connectix Corp., 800-950-5880. This collection of utilities helps you get more out of your PowerBook. Features include better battery management through more sleep options and a more precise charge-level indicator; password protection; selectable power-usage settings for home, office, and other environments; keyboard shortcuts for hard disk power, backlighting, and dialog box and menu control; and file synchronization to ensure that you have the same versions of files on your PowerBook as on your desktop Mac; and more.

HeapFixer, CE Software, 515-224-1995. This utility is included with most of CE Software's products (which include DiskTop, Quick-Mail, and QuicKeys). It lets you adjust the size of the system heap in System 6. This is one way to resolve out-of-memory problems when you're using a lot of system extensions or have a lot of fonts installed in the System file under System 6.

Heap Tool, shareware, available from user groups and bulletin boards. Like HeapFixer, this utility lets you adjust the size of your system heap under System 6. It's somewhat easier to use than HeapFixer.

MasterJuggler, $49, ALSoft, 713-353-4090. MasterJuggler is an extension that manages fonts, sounds, and desk accessories. It lets you easily find and open only the fonts and sounds (and DAs under System 6) that you want open at any given time, rather than installing them in the System file and using up memory for them all the time. With MasterJuggler, you can open up to 120 font or DA suitcase files at a time. The program also adds functionality to your menu, adds sounds to various Macintosh events, and resolves font number ID conflicts.

PBTools, $99.95, Inline Design, 800-453-7671. This collection of utilities helps you use your PowerBook more efficiently. Features include displaying the battery level precisely in volts; allowing more sleep options than the PowerBook control panel does; performing a "deep discharge" to drain the PowerBook battery so you don't have to run it down manually; thickening the screen cursor so you can see it more easily; and hot keys to aid screen navigation.

Suitcase II, $79, Fifth Generation Systems, 504-291-7221. The original font and DA manager, Suitcase II is still the market leader in this category. Like MasterJuggler, it lets you open and close font, sound, and DA files on the fly and resolves font ID conflicts.

Hard disk setup utilities

If you own a hard disk, you already own a hard disk setup utility, because one comes with every hard disk you buy. Lately, though, there's been a rise in third-party utilities for setting up disks. Here's why.

In many cases, the hard disk setup utility you own was designed for your hard disk and not for others. (For example, Apple's HD SC Setup utility only works with Apple hard disks.) So if you buy more hard disks, you may end up with several different setup programs, and you need to remember which one works with which disk.

Another problem has been System 7. When you install System 7 on a System 6 disk, you need to update your hard disk driver. If you have an older hard disk, your setup program may not be compatible with System 7, so you'll need to find a setup program that is.

So the point of buying third-party hard disk setup programs is that they work with any hard disk, and they're System 7 compatible. All setup programs perform basic functions such as testing, reformatting, installing drivers on your disk, and partitioning the disk into multiple volumes. Some of the more elegant ones offer other features, such as support for removable devices such as CD-ROM or removable cartridge hard disks, or a "drive light" that flashes in your menu bar to show when a disk is being accessed.

DiskMaker, $89, Golden Triangle Computers, Inc., 800-326-1858. This utility is simple to use and has all the basic features.

Drive 7, $79.95, Casa Blanca Works, 415-461-2227. This was the first System 7-compatible disk formatter from a company that doesn't sell hard disks. Along with all the basic features, Drive 7 supports removable cartridge hard disks, CD-ROM drives, and SuperMac DataFrame disks (a discontinued product line that was once one of the most popular names in Mac hard disks).

Hard Disk Toolkit Personal Edition, $79, FWB Software, 415-474-8055. FWB makes hard disks, and this product is a stand-alone version of the program it includes when you buy one of its hard disks. This program is a stripped-down version of FWB's $200 Hard Disk Toolkit, but without the performance testing features and extensive reference manual.

Silverlining, $149, LaCie Ltd., 800-999-3919. Like FWB, La Cie is a hard disk vendor, and Silverlining is included on any La Cie hard disk you buy. This product has received excellent reviews, but is more expensive than most others.

Diagnostic and repair utilities

This category includes programs that diagnose and repair disk or other hardware configuration problems and recover damaged or deleted files. One of the basic repair and diagnostic programs should be a standard part of any Mac user's toolkit. A good package should at the minimum diagnose and repair disk problems, repair damaged files, and recover deleted files. Some of the best packages combine these basics with disk optimization, virus protection, and other features.

Apple TechStep, $995, Apple Computer, Inc., 800-950-2442. This handheld device connects to the Mac and lets you perform a variety of tests on nonfunctioning Mac CPUs and SCSI hard disks. It has plug-in ROM cards that customize it for tests on specific Macintosh model groups.

ALSoft Power Utilities, $129, ALSoft, 713-353-4090. This collection of utilities includes DiskExpress II (described next), MasterJuggler (see Resource managers, page 90), a disk partitioning utility, a screen saver, a disk diagnostic program, and a menu enhancement utility. However, the collection doesn't perform key operations such as repairing damaged disks or files, or undeleting files.

DiskExpress II, $89.95 ALSoft, 713-353-4090. This program is strictly a disk optimizer. It checks your hard disk for file fragmentation, and can reorganize the files on your disk to eliminate it. File fragmentation occurs naturally as your hard disk fills with files, and it can slow down your access to files (see page 73 in Chapter 4).

Disk First Aid, free, Apple Computer, Inc. This program performs basic repairs on damaged disk directories. It's included with the system software. It's a very simple program that doesn't recover or undelete files.

MacTest Pro, $89 or $99, Apple Computer, Inc., 800-950-2442. This program lets you choose different tests to diagnose various parts of Macintosh hardware, including the processor, NuBus cards, hard disks, and other components. There are three different packages, depending on which group of Mac models you want to test.

MacTools, $149, Central Point Software, 503-690-8090. This bundle of utilities includes a disk diagnostic and repair program, a file recovery program, a disk optimizer, a backup utility, and a virus detection program.

Norton Utilities for Macintosh, $149, Symantec Corporation, 408-253-9600. Like Mac Tools, this bundle of utilities includes disk diagnostics and repair, file recovery, disk optimization, and backup. It doesn't include a virus program, but it does offer other useful utilities such as Directory Assistance, which makes it easier to find and open files, and KeyFinder, which makes it easy to tell which key creates which character in any font.

Public Utilities, $149, Fifth Generation Systems, 504-291-7221. Another utility bundle, Public Utilities is unique in that it continually scans your disk for problems when your Mac is idle, and automatically alerts you to problems and recommends defragmentation when it becomes necessary. Like the other disk diagnostic and repair packages, Public Utilities examines and repairs disk problems, and repairs and recovers files.

Safe & Sound, $49.95, Central Point Software, 503-690-8090. This product is a simpler version of the utilities in Mac Tools, except that it's all combined in one program. Functions include disk diagnosis and repair, examining and repairing files, and detecting and eliminating viruses. This program's best feature is its one-button operation: just click a button and it performs all the diagnostics, reports problems, and gives you a chance to fix them.

SCSIProbe, free from online services and user groups. This simple control panel program displays every connected device on your SCSI bus and lets you mount devices. Most disk setup programs also perform this function, but it's handy to have this ability in a control panel.

Snooper, $49.95, Central Point Software, 503-690-8090. Snooper is a comprehensive hardware diagnostic tool that does much more than test hard or floppy disks. It tests your Mac's RAM, ROM, CPU, serial and SCSI ports, and other logic board components, disk drives, and video and audio input and output systems. It reports problems, and then suggests remedies when a component fails its test. You can also run performance tests and compare your Mac system with the performance of other Macs.

Superset Utilities, $149.95, Datawatch Corp., 919-490-1277. This collection of utilities also covers all the bases in disk and file diagnostics and repair. It includes 911 Utilities, a complete disk and file diagnostic and recovery program that comes with a terrific troubleshooting manual; Virex, one of the industry's leading virus detection, prevention, and repair programs; an undelete program; a disk and file security program; and a remote control utility that lets you control another Mac from yours across a telephone line or network. The only missing element is disk optimization.

Software diagnostic utilities

These utilities examine all the files on your hard disk and then produce reports. The reports list all your application programs, extensions, control panels, DAs, fonts, and system software programs, along with program version numbers, the amount of space each item takes up, the amount of application memory each program is set for, and other useful information. In addition, these programs report extension or control panel conflicts and advise you what to do about them.

All these programs work by scanning your disk and comparing the names of programs found with a database of the latest program version numbers and known compatibility problems, which are supplied by software vendors. Because program versions and compatibility problems change frequently, the commercial software diagnostic programs (Alert! and Help!) have subscription services that entitle you to free updates of the compatibility information.

Alert!, $49.95, Central Point Software, 503-690-8090. This program scans the software on your Mac and reports compatibility or configuration problems. It produces a report showing all the software, version numbers, and problems, if any. Along with diagnostics and suggested solutions, Alert! lets you implement some of those solutions right from inside the program: you can turn extensions on or off, change the order in which extensions load, change applications' memory size, or turn off 32-bit addressing. Alert! comes with network communications modules that allow you to diagnose and repair other Macs on the same network or accessible via telephone lines.

Compatibility Checker, free, Apple Computer, Inc. This program comes with System 7 installation disks. It lists installed and current version numbers of all your programs, tells whether or not you should upgrade, and in most cases lists each vendor's phone number so you can call about an update. The Compatibility Checker's information is only as current as the last system software release, however, so although it's free, this program isn't likely to be as current as the commercial products.

Help!, $149, Teknosys, 813-620-3494. Help! is similar to Alert!, except that it reports problems and suggests solutions, but doesn't offer its own facilities for repairing problems. It also doesn't allow you to diagnose or repair remote Macs. But if you get less, you also pay less.

Virus utilities

These programs deal with viruses on your disks. Some scan floppy disks and hard disks automatically as they're mounted to the desktop, detecting the virus before it can spread. Some only scan disks manually, when you tell them to. Some can repair viruses once they're detected. The best packages do all three of these things, but you may be able to get along with less performance, depending on your computing style, how often you share disks or files with other users, and how vulnerable your Mac is to viruses.

Disinfectant, free from user groups and bulletin boards. This program scans disks manually and repairs most common viruses.

Many virus programs are free or shareware, so the question arises: why pay for something you can get for free? The answer is that the commercial programs offer all three functions (prevention, diagnosis and repair), while you must combine two or three shareware programs to accomplish the same thing. Also, registering with a commercial virus utility vendor usually means you get regular notices about new viruses and upgrades to the program that deal with them. With most shareware or freeware programs, you'll need to keep your eye open for new versions. (The exception is VirusDetective—see below.)

Gatekeeper, free from user groups and bulletin boards. Rather than scanning for viruses themselves, this system extension scans your system's activities for telltale signs of viruses attempting to spread, and prevents such operations from being carried out. Sometimes it detects activities that are normal, but you can learn to distinguish the real problems from the false alarms. This program does not repair virus damage or detect the presence of viruses themselves.

MacTools, see page 93. The Central Point Anti-Virus utility included in this package includes an extension that automatically scans disks for viruses as they're mounted or inserted, and removes viruses it finds.

Superset Utilities, see page 94. This collection includes Virex (see below).

Symantec Antivirus for the Mac (SAM), $99, Symantec Corporation, 408-253-9600. Like Virex, this program includes a virus-detecting extension that scans disks as they're inserted or mounted to the desktop, as well as a manual detection and repair program. Symantec maintains a free virus information hotline and sends updates for new viruses to registered users.

Virex, $99.95, Datawatch Corp., 919-490-1277. This program is known for regular updates to combat new viruses, and has a subscription service that entitles you to updates for a year for $75. It performs automatic detection of viruses on disks as they're inserted, and then repairs any viruses it finds.

VirusDetective, shareware, available from user groups and bulletin boards. This program is a desk accessory that scans inserted floppy disks whenever it's running, and can scan any disk manually at any time. When you register as a user, you get two disks filled with virus information and the latest version of the program, plus free updates about new viruses or virus-fighting strategies.

VirusBlockade II Ltd., shareware, available from user groups and bulletin boards. This system extension is a companion to VirusDetective, and automatically controls when VirusDetective scans your disks.

Network utilities

Network utilities are essential for anyone managing or troubleshooting problems on a network. These utilities perform tasks such as displaying the characteristics of all connected devices and testing the network's performance, and can also make it easier to update software on several networked Macs.

LANSurveyor, $695, Neon Software, 510-283-9771. This program is a profiling tool that produces a graphical map of your network, and then allows you to do performance tests by comparing response times between various devices or groups of devices.

NetMinder, $595 (Ethernet version), $395 (LocalTalk version), Neon Software, 510-283-9771. NetMinder is a more sophisticated troubleshooting tool, allowing you to design custom tests for specific types of data transmitted between specific devices. It also produces various types of reports to analyze the data you collect.

Network SuperVisor, $495, CSG Technologies, 412-471-7170. This is another profiling tool. It collects network traffic information, allows you to create network maps, and has a database feature so you can store and analyze network information easily.

Network Vital Signs, $449, Dayna Communications, 801-269-7200. This program monitors network performance as well as the status of printers, servers, and routers. It can also notify the administrator of performance problems and help to isolate them.

NetWorks, $1195, Caravelle Networks Corp., 613-596-2802. This product monitors networks and network devices for problems and then alerts the network administrator, either by displaying a message on the administrator's Mac, sending an electronic mail message, or sending a message to a remote pocket pager. NetWorks checks for communications problems on AppleTalk and TCP/IP networks and devices, reports on LaserWriter status, and monitors free disk space on network servers.

RouterCheck, $895, Neon Software, 510-283-9771. This program provides detailed information about network routers, checks for zone consistency, and recommends corrective action.

StatusMac, $449, On Technology, 617-876-0900. StatusMac allows you to check the configuration of every Mac connected to a network. It produces reports that tell you which versions of application and system software are on each Mac, whether or not any program or system software files are damaged, and which model Mac is in each location. It also automates the process of updating software to each Mac on the network.

TechWorks Net Utilities, $129, Technology Works, 512-794-8533. This bargain-priced collection allows you to collect configuration information on each connected network device; perform simple traffic tests; and monitor, name, or configure LaserWriter printers. It also alerts you automatically to performance problems as they crop up.

Miscellany

Crash Barrier, $79.95, Casady & Greene, 408-484-9228. This system extension tries to detect and prevent system crashes. It works with some types of crashes, but not with many others.

Can Opener2, $125, Abbott Systems, 800-552-9157. This utility can open just about any file and display its contents, which you can then select and copy elsewhere. This is a handy tool when you don't have a file's parent application and you can't seem to open it using import commands in other programs.

Orphan Finder, $69.95, Tuesday Software, 800-945-7889. A more elegant alternative to Can Opener, this utility scans your disk looking for files whose parent applications are missing, and then allows you to assign other applications to "adopt" them so you can open them.

Component-level repair shops

Apple dealers are only authorized to do subsystem-level repairs. This means that if one chip on your logic board is bad, they replace the whole logic board and charge you accordingly. As a result, you might spend $500 to repair one component that costs $15. It's usually much less expensive to have the failed component replaced. Some component-level repair companies are listed below, but there are plenty of people in this business now, so check the computer section of your local yellow pages.

Drivesavers, Ontrack Data Recovery, and other data recovery services can usually repair crashed hard disks and save your data.

Larry Pina's *Dead Mac Scrolls* from Peachpit Press helps you zero in on specific component failures and lets you know, approximately, how much the component repairs will cost.

800 We Fix Macs, Santa Clara, CA	800-933-4962
CJS Systems, Berkeley, CA	510-849-3730
Drivesavers, San Francisco, CA	415-883-4232
MacSwap, Woodbridge, NJ	800-622-7927
Maya Computer, Dobbs Ferry, NY	800-541-2318
MicroDoc, Eugene, OR	503-344-5335
Ontrack Data Recovery, Eden Prairie, MN	800-752-7557
Shreve Systems, Shreveport, LA	800-227-3971
Soft Solutions, Eugene, OR	503-461-1136
Sun Remarketing, Smithfield, UT	800-821-3221

Chapter 7
Basic Troubleshooting and Repair Techniques

In this chapter, we'll look at the basic techniques you'll use in later chapters to recover from Mac problems when they do occur. If you're already familiar with these techniques, you can skip ahead and just refer back to this section when you need a reminder.

Basic troubleshooting

Troubleshooting is a process of eliminating possible causes of a problem until you hit on the real cause. There are five basic ways to solve a problem:

1. Make sure it's really a problem. Just because you see an unfamiliar dialog box doesn't mean there's a problem.

2. Retrace your steps, looking at the commands or operations you've performed since the problem occurred, and figure out whether something you've done might have caused the problem.

3. Know your system and then check and change any hardware or software settings that could be causing the problem (such as low memory or the wrong Chooser selection).

4. Try basic repairs to see if the problem goes away. Sometimes performing a basic repair such as rebuilding the desktop or zapping the PRAM will correct the problem.

5. Ask for help.

Although these steps are numbered, they're not necessarily to be taken in order. For example, examining system software settings (step 3) may be one of the ways you look for changes you've made (step 2).

Let's look at these one at a time.

Make sure there's a problem

Just because you see something unfamiliar on the screen, or the program doesn't behave the way you expect, it doesn't mean there's something wrong. And even when there's definitely something wrong, it may be a one-time problem that never shows itself again. The first step is to see if you have a genuine, repeatable problem.

 Look for any Read Me files that came with the program when you installed it. Manufacturers often use Read Me files to report potential problems and workarounds that were discovered after the manual was printed.

Did you goof?

As mentioned before, a lot of the computer "problems" people have are the result of user error or ignorance. For example, sometimes I'm typing a little too fast and hit a combination of keys together that produces subscript type in my word processor. In this case, the software hasn't gone crazy—I've made a mistake.

Most of the mistakes you can make with system software operations (such as working with disks or files in the Finder) are reported with alert boxes, but many applications assume that you know what you're doing. If you're working in an application and something doesn't happen the way you think it should, think back over the last few commands or mouse clicks you've made and then consider whether you've made a mistake (see *Retrace your steps* on page 103).

If you can't discover a mistake (and it's often difficult to see our own mistakes), try repeating the procedure again to see if you get the same result. If you do, check the program's manual to make sure you're taking exactly the right steps. It's amazing how changing one small step of a complex procedure can produce a different result and plunge us into confusion.

Once doesn't count

If you encounter a spontaneous system crash or freeze, or your program quits, or something else happens that seems to be independent of any commands you've issued, don't panic and assume that your computer is kaput. Some problems are one-time glitches, and you can recover from them by restarting the machine, quitting and restarting the program, or closing and reopening the document. When it comes to computer problems, the basic rule is, "Once doesn't count." If you try one of the basic repair techniques discussed later in this chapter and the problem goes away, write it off as a minor, one-time problem.

Of course, there are also major problems like hard disk crashes or file corruption that will only happen once, and others that will continue to recur unless you take more repair steps. That's where the remaining chapters of this book come in. Still, it's always worth trying a simple remedy like restarting the Mac to see if the problem clears up.

Retrace your steps

When repeating a procedure or trying a simple repair doesn't do the trick, it doesn't mean the problem can't be solved. In fact, the problem is probably just a little more complex. Even complex problems are usually caused by some action you've taken—it's simply a matter of thinking back farther.

For example, you may have changed a system software setting and set up a problem situation that didn't announce itself until an hour later, when you used a particular program or tried printing a document. In this case, you'd have to remember changing that setting to get to the root of the problem.

The minute you experience a problem, stop right there and jot down the last few things you've done. If you were doing something you've done many times before without incident, then think about what's different this time:

■ Did you change a system software setting?

■ Do you have a different set of programs running or documents open?

If you can remember a change you made, try undoing the change and repeating the process. If the problem goes away, then you know the change was the cause of it. If not, you'll have to dig deeper in search of the difference between this particular situation and the ones in which you've successfully carried out the operation in the past.

Even if you can't discover the problem on your own, it will be a big help to any technical support person you call if you can report the steps you took just before the problem occurred.

Know your system

The more you know about your system, the easier it will be to zero in on a problem. You should always know the state of your hardware and software and how to check the various user-adjustable settings for potential problems. Even if you end up having to call someone else for help, you'll need to be able to tell that person the current state of your Mac.

 A software diagnostic program like Alert!, Compatibility Checker, or Help! can quickly produce a list of all the software installed on your Mac. See Chapter 6.

Here's what you need to know about the state of your system and how to determine it. (Check Chapter 3 for more information on system software settings, or Chapter 15 for more on file sharing settings.)

- **Which model Mac are you using?** Check the front of the Mac.

- **How much RAM do you have installed?** Choose *About This Macintosh* (or *About The Finder* under System 6) from the menu in the Finder and check the Total Memory figure.

- **Which version of system software are you running?** Choose *About This Macintosh* (or *About The Finder* under System 6) from the menu in the Finder and look in the upper right corner of the dialog box. On Macs using software older than System 6, you'll have to select the System and Finder files (one at a time) in the Finder and choose *Get Info* from the File menu to check the version number of each file separately.

- **Which version(s) of application program(s) are you running?** Select each program's icon in the Finder (one at a time) and choose *Get Info* from the File menu.

■ **Which extensions or inits (and which versions) are you running?** Look inside the Extensions folder under System 7. Select each extension and use the *Get Info* command to find out the version number. Under System 6, look inside the System Folder itself for items with the Kind designation *extension* or *startup document*. Use *Get Info* on each of these to determine its version number.

■ **Which expansion cards do you have installed?** If you're using a modular Mac, shut it off, pop open the top, and look. In compact Macs (the Classic, SE, etc.) or PowerBooks, you should know if there are any expansion cards installed; or you can ask the machine's owner.

■ **Which brands and models of peripherals are you using?** You should be able to tell by looking at the items connected to your Mac.

■ **What's the address of each SCSI device connected to your Mac?** If you have the SCSI Probe control panel, open it. If not, check the back of each device—many SCSI devices have a wheel or button you push to set the address, and the address is showing. Otherwise, open the setup program that came with the device to determine its address.

■ **Which printer is selected in the Chooser?** Choose the *Print* command from the File menu in any program or the Finder and look at the upper left corner of the Print dialog box. The printer type (and name, if it's a network printer) appears there.

■ **How much RAM are your system software and any open applications using?** Choose the *About This Macintosh* command (or *About The Finder* under System 6) from the menu in the Finder.

■ **How much RAM are other applications set to request when they're opened?** Select a program's icon and choose the *Get Info* command.

■ **How many colors or shades of gray is your Mac set to display?** Open the Monitors control panel.

■ **How loud is your Mac's speaker set?** Open the Sound control panel.

■ **What date and time are set on your Mac's internal clock/calendar?** Open the General Controls control panel or the Control Panel DA.

■ **How large is your disk cache?** Open the Memory control panel (or the Control Panel DA in System 6).

- **Are you using virtual memory, 32-bit addressing, or a RAM cache?** Open the Memory control panel.

- **Do you have file sharing on?** Open the Sharing Setup control panel.

- **Are other users sharing files on your Mac?** Open the File Sharing Monitor control panel.

- **Which users or groups are registered on your Mac?** Open the Users & Groups control panel.

- **Who has access to items you're sharing from your Mac?** Select the item you want to know about and choose the *Sharing* command from the File menu.

- **How often is your PowerBook set to sleep?** Open the PowerBook control panel.

- **How much battery life do you have left in your PowerBook?** Open the Battery DA.

If your Mac is locked up or won't restart, you won't be able to determine some of these settings. Keep a written record of things that don't change frequently, such as total RAM or which expansion cards are installed. That way you'll have the information readily available if you need to call someone else for help.

Try basic repairs

If the problem isn't obvious from your understanding of your system settings and you can't discover a mistake you've made, it's time to try some basic repairs. In this section, we'll go through a handful of fundamental repair operations you can try when things go wrong. Many of these techniques are suggested elsewhere in this book as complete or partial solutions to specific problems.

Restart your application

If your problem is with a particular program, you can sometimes resolve minor glitches by quitting the program and restarting it. Of course, you'll want to save any documents before you quit.

Save the file with a different name

If you're having problems with a particular document, you can sometimes eliminate them by saving it with a different name and then working with the new copy. Use the *Save As* command to save the document with a different name to a different disk or folder, quit the program, restart the program, and then open the copy.

Try a backup copy of the file

If working with a renamed version of the document doesn't help, try opening a backup copy of the document. (You did make one, didn't you?) Before opening the backup copy, however, make a copy of it in the Finder so you'll still have an undamaged copy in case your program is somehow trashing every document it opens.

Restart the Mac and try again

Restarting the Mac flushes out the whole system, emptying the RAM and reloading the system software. Sometimes this is enough to repair minor problems such as RAM fragmentation or minor application software glitches. There are several different conditions under which you can try restarting, and what you do depends on what's going on with your Mac at the time.

1. If your Mac isn't frozen, save any open documents and quit any open programs. Then choose *Restart* from the Special menu in the Finder; or (in System 6 or earlier) choose *Shut Down* and then click the *Restart* button in the dialog box that appears.

2. If you're running more than one program in System 7 or under MultiFinder and the program you're in is locked up, try pressing ⌘S to save your document first. Then press ⌘ Shift Option Esc. You may be able to quit only the program that's frozen and then return to the Finder or another program you have running. If this works, you should save any other open documents and then restart the Mac. If this procedure doesn't work, go on to step 3.

3. If your Mac is displaying a System Error message or is frozen and won't respond to commands, try pressing the interrupt button on your Mac's programmer's switch, if it has one, or pressing the keyboard sequence for an interrupt (check your Mac's *User's Guide* for the key sequence).

You should see a blank alert box with a > symbol in it. Type *SM 0 A9F4* and then press ⌐Return⌐. Then type *G 0* and press ⌐Return⌐ again. (Be sure to press the zero key for *0*, not capital o.) If the gods are smiling on you, you'll be returned to the Finder, where you can save any open documents and then restart in the usual way (step 1).

4. If your Mac is displaying a System Error message, or if it is frozen and step 3 doesn't work, you'll have to force a restart in one of the following ways, depending on which Mac you have.

   ■ If you're using a Mac IIsi, LCII, or newer model, press ⌐⌘⌐ ⌐Control⌐ ⌐◁⌐. If you're using a startup floppy disk, it will be ejected when you restart and you'll have to reinsert it.

   ■ If you have a programmer's switch on the front of your Mac II model or on the side of your Mac SE, Classic, Plus, or 512K model, press the front or right-hand side of the switch to restart. (The programmer's switch has two sides, and you push the side that is closest to the front of the Mac SE, Classic, Plus, and 512K models, or on the right on Mac II models.)

   ■ If all else fails, turn off the Mac with its power switch, wait 10 seconds, and then turn the Mac on again. If you're using a startup floppy disk, it will be ejected when you restart and you'll have to reinsert it.

 Be sure to throw away an existing copy of a program before installing a new one. If the program is infected with a virus, this is the only way to be sure you've eliminated the problem.

Reinstall your application software

If you're having problems with a particular program but not with others, try throwing away the program and all its related files (but not the documents you created with it) and reinstalling the program from its original program disks. If a program is corrupted or infected with a virus, installing a fresh copy can clear up the problem. (Use the same installation procedures you used to install the software originally—see your software user's manual.)

Use another startup disk

If the system software on your hard disk (or the disk you normally use to start your Mac) becomes damaged, you'll have to start your Mac with another startup disk in order to repair the damaged disk. A Macintosh startup disk is any floppy disk or hard disk that contains a System Folder, which must include at least a System file and a Finder file. Make one or two startup disks like this and keep them handy. You'll need them to perform many of the repair operations covered later in this book.

If you're using System 7, it's a lot easier to make startup floppies using a version of System 6, because the System Folder in System 7 is too large to fit on a standard floppy disk. Even on high-density, 1.44 MB floppy disks, you have to eliminate lots of system software files to make a System 7 startup disk, so it's simpler just to use a System 6 startup floppy. A copy of the System 7 *Disk Tools* disk will also work for this purpose.

If you have a disk repair utility, it may have come with an emergency startup floppy that contains a System Folder and a copy of the disk repair program. Use this if your normal startup disk won't work, because you can then run the repair program to diagnose the problem.

Rebuild the desktop file

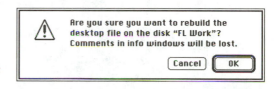

For reasons described in Chapter 4, rebuilding the desktop file can reduce the time it takes to start your Mac, or the time it takes to return to the Finder after you quit an application. Here's how to rebuild the desktop file on any disk:

1. Hold down ⌘ Option as you insert a floppy disk or as you start up from a hard disk. Either way, keep the keys pressed down until you see a message like the one in the alert box above. (The text of this alert box is a little different under System 6.)

2. Click the *OK* button or press Return; you see a box saying that the desktop file is being rebuilt. This operation can take anywhere from a few seconds to a few minutes, depending on how many files the disk contains.

When the desktop file has been rebuilt, the Finder desktop appears. The only problem with rebuilding a disk's desktop file is that doing so erases any comments you've entered in the Get Info windows for files on that disk. If you've used Get Info windows to store comments about certain files, you should review those comments and record any important ones before you rebuild your desktop file.

Turn your extensions off

Extension conflicts can cause a wide variety of problems, such as crashes when you start the Mac or load a program. A simple way to check is to turn all your extensions (or inits) off so they're not loaded when you restart your Mac. If the problem goes away when you restart, you know it was caused by an incompatible extension.

 Under System 6, make a new folder on your startup disk, drag your System and Finder files into it, and then restart. The folder containing the System and Finder becomes the new System Folder, and any inits in the old System Folder won't be loaded.

If you're using System 7, you can disable all your extensions at startup by holding down the Shift key as your Mac restarts. If your startup screen shows the *Welcome To Macintosh* message, you'll see *Extensions Off* underneath it.

If turning off your extensions solves the problem, then try turning them back on one at a time, restarting the Mac each time until the problem resurfaces. To do this under System 7, make a new folder outside your System Folder and put all the extensions

 If you have an extension manager program (see Chapter 6), you can also use it to turn off all your extensions or inits.

in it, and then drag them back into the Extensions folder one at a time, restarting the Mac after you drag each one. Under System 6, drag the extensions from the old System Folder to the new one you created, restarting after you move each extension. If you're using an extension manager, of course, you can simply turn the extensions back on one at a time.

Check the SCSI chain

Some problems you may have starting up or using disks can be traced to connections between various devices attached to your Mac's SCSI port. Before you diagnose your Mac's SCSI chain, turn off your Mac and any peripherals connected to it.

1. If you have more than one device connected to your Mac's SCSI port, make sure each device has a unique address. Every externally connected SCSI device must have an address from 1 to 6, and no two can have the same address. On some devices, you can see and change the address with a button or a wheel on the back panel. Other devices come with special software that lets you set the address.

2. Make sure the last device in the SCSI chain is terminated. Some SCSI devices require you to insert a special terminating connector between the device and the SCSI cable, and others are self-terminating. Check the device's manual for more information. Also, make sure no terminating connectors are plugged into any other devices in the SCSI chain—only the device at the end of the chain should have a terminator.

3. Be sure all the devices are plugged in securely. If any of them use 25-pin connectors, unplug these connectors (with everything shut off, of course) and check for bent or missing pins.

4. Check the cables coming out of the back of each device to be sure they're not bent at severe angles or stretched too far, as this can cause wires inside the cable to fray or break. If a cable looks like it might be damaged, try replacing it with another cable that you know works.

5. Make sure all the devices in the SCSI chain are turned on. Technically, you're supposed to be able to run properly with some devices on and others off, but in practice this setup has an adverse effect on some programs and device drivers. If you've had some devices turned off and a problem clears up once you turn everything on and restart the Mac, you'll know this was the cause.

 Unless you've selected a particular device with the Startup Disk control panel or Startup Device cdev, the Mac scans down the chain from device 6 to device 0 and starts up from the first device that has a valid System Folder. Internal hard disk drives always have the address 0.

6. If you have several devices connected to the SCSI port and a problem persists after you've checked their addresses and connections, looked for terminators, and turned all the devices on, there's one more thing you can try. Shut everything off and disconnect every device except the one that's not working properly (assuming this is possible—obviously, if you're starting up your Mac from an external hard disk and having trouble with a SCSI printer, you'll have to keep both of them connected). If the problem clears up when fewer devices are connected, the culprit is probably the SCSI circuitry in one of the devices you've unplugged.

Check the power source

If the Mac or peripheral doesn't come on at all, the first thing to check is the power source.

1. Make sure the power cord is plugged securely into the AC outlet and to the back of your Mac. Sometimes the cord wiggles out a little from the connector on the Mac.

2. If you're using a surge protector that has a reset switch, press the reset switch. If you're using a power strip, make sure the fuse or circuit breaker in it isn't blown.

3. Try plugging another device into the AC outlet to make sure the outlet has power.

Replace the system software

The purpose of replacing your system software is to eliminate problems caused by a damaged System file or by related files, or to make sure such problems don't occur. When you replace the system software, you replace the entire System Folder.

The safest and best way to replace a System Folder is to use the Installer. This procedure takes several steps; you can't simply throw away your old System Folder and install a new one. If you did, you would also toss out any custom fonts, DAs, sounds, extensions, and other files that you added to the System Folder later. Here's the best procedure:

1. Start your Mac with a startup floppy disk or another startup hard disk. (Use the Startup Disk control panel to change the startup hard disk if you have two or more of them.)

2. Open the System Folder on the hard disk whose system software you want to replace.

3. Drag the System file out of the System Folder and into another folder on the disk.

4. Rename the System Folder (we'll call it System Stuff here).

5. Restart your Mac using the *Install 1* disk that's part of your installation package. (The disk containing the Installer will have a different name—usually *System Tools*—if you're using System 6.) If the Installer program doesn't load automatically when you start up the Mac, click the Installer icon to load it.

6. Click the *OK* button on the Installer's welcome screen, and then click the *Easy Install* option on the main Installer screen to install a complete set of system software files.

7. Check the name of the disk drive in the upper part of the Installer dialog box to make sure it's the disk on which you want to replace the system software. If it isn't, click the *Switch Disk* button until the correct disk name appears.

8. Click the *Install* button or press [Return]. The Installer installs a new System Folder and informs you when the installation is complete.

9. Restart the Mac with the disk containing your new System Folder.

 If you're not sure which items in the System Stuff folder or System file are custom ones, drag the items one at a time to the new System Folder icon. If you see a message saying that an item with that name already exists, click the *Cancel* button—this isn't a custom file and shouldn't be copied to the new System Folder.

 System 6 users must manually install items from the old System file and the System Stuff folder. Under System 6, you can't double-click the System file to open it, so you must use the Font/DA Mover to copy any custom fonts or DAs from your old System file into your new one. To copy your other custom files from the System Stuff folder, simply drag them into the new System Folder. Once that's done, you can delete the System Stuff folder.

10. Open the System Stuff folder and copy any custom system extension files, DAs, or preferences files it contains into the new System Folder by dragging them onto the new System Folder icon. They'll automatically be installed in the proper folders within the System Folder.

11. Open the old System file that you dragged into a different folder and copy any custom fonts or sounds from it into the new System file by dragging them onto the new System Folder icon. They'll automatically be installed in the new System file.

12. Delete the old System file and the System Stuff folder when you're done.

Check for viruses

If your system is behaving erratically or you have problems opening, saving, or printing files, especially if you've recently installed or downloaded a file from someone else's disk, run a virus detection program to check for a possible infection. Viruses can make your Mac's file system erratic, interfere with printing, make it difficult to open or save files, slow down the Mac's operation, and do other destructive things. If you can't quickly isolate a problem, you can quickly confirm or eliminate a virus as the problem by running a check.

Whether you're using a shareware, free, or commercial virus detection program, try to use the most recent version so you'll stand the best chance of detecting the latest viruses.

Replace the hard disk driver

If you start your Mac from a hard disk, the file the Mac needs to recognize that disk (the hard disk driver) may become damaged over time, eventually creating problems during the startup sequence. One remedy is to reinstall the hard disk driver. Hard disk drivers come with the setup software that accompanies each hard disk; the manual for your hard disk should tell you how to install its driver.

 When you install System 7 or later on a hard disk that previously contained System 6, you should immediately replace the hard disk driver to update it for System 7.

The procedure for replacing a driver is usually the same one you used to install it in the first place—

you start your Mac from the hard disk's utility software disk and then install the driver from that disk onto your hard disk. (Usually there's a command or button that says *Install Driver* or *Update Driver*.) If you're using an Apple hard disk, the software for installing the driver comes on one of the system software disks and is called Apple HD SC Setup.

Use a disk repair utility

If your disk won't start up your Mac, or if you can't find or open a file because it's damaged, you can use a disk repair utility like the ones described in Chapter 6. These perform various operations to restore damaged hard disk files, so you can boot your Mac from the disk or recover data files from it. Disk First Aid is included on the Macintosh system software disks (instructions are included in Apple's system software user's guide), but it doesn't perform every type of repair you might need. You're probably better off buying one of the other programs covered in Chapter 6.

Zap the PRAM

As explained in Chapter 1, your Mac's parameter RAM, or PRAM, stores information about the location of the current startup disk, as well as the date, time, and other information. If this portion of the Mac's memory becomes corrupted, you may have problems starting your Mac or getting it to recognize a hard disk drive once you're up and running. If your Mac's PRAM becomes corrupted, you can remedy the problem by erasing (zapping) it. There are three ways to do this: one for any Mac running under System 7; another for SEs, IIs, or Portables running under System 6; and a third for Mac Plus or older machines.

If you're running under System 7, hold down ⌘ Option P R while restarting your Mac. After emitting a beep, the Mac will restart. Once the Mac begins restarting, you can let go of the keys. The PRAM will be erased and rebuilt. After that, reset the Mac's clock and calendar with the General Controls control panel, then reselect the startup disk with the Startup Disk control panel.

If you have a Mac SE, Portable or II and you're running under System 6:

1. Leave your Mac running.

2. Hold down ⌘ Shift Option while you choose the Control Panel DA from the menu. You see a dialog box explaining that you're about to zap the PRAM and asking if you really want to do so.

3. Click the *Yes* button to proceed.

4. Restart the Mac with your hard disk so the Mac can restore its PRAM with the correct information about the startup disk you want to use.

5. Reset the Mac's clock and calendar using the Control Panel DA.

6. Reselect the startup disk with the Startup Device cdev in the Control Panel DA.

If you have a Mac Plus or a 512KE, 512K, or 128K model running under System 6, the only way to erase the PRAM is to physically remove the battery that maintains it. The battery is located behind a door above the power switch on the back panel of the Mac. To erase the PRAM:

1. Turn off your Mac.

2. Remove the battery and wait about an hour. (A capacitor on the Mac logic board maintains power to the PRAM for a few minutes even if no battery is installed, so it won't be erased unless you leave the battery out for awhile.)

3. Replace the battery.

4. Restart the Mac. The correct information about your startup disk is read into the PRAM.

5. Reset the Mac's clock and calendar using the Control Panel DA.

Call for help

If you're unable to diagnose or repair the problem yourself, you'll have to call for help. You can get help from the software manufacturer's technical support line, from a friend who knows more about the program or the Mac than you do, or from a user group bulletin board or hotline.

 A program's serial number is usually printed on a label on the program disk; or you can usually display it by choosing the *About* command for the program from the menu.

In any case, keep the appropriate telephone numbers handy, along with their hours of operation and the serial number(s) of the program(s) you use. If you use a software manufacturer's support line, you may be asked for the serial number to verify that you're a registered owner of the program.

Some companies have electronic bulletin boards or fax numbers you can use to report problems and ask for help. If you're not in a particular hurry, using one of these is a more efficient use of your time than hanging around on hold waiting for someone to respond.

Before you call for help, have the following information ready:

1. Your Mac model and hardware and software configuration.

2. The version number and serial of the program and the amount of memory it has been allowed (use the *Get Info* command to see this).

3. A concise description of what happened and the operations you performed just before the problem occurred.

Chapter 8

Starting Up

This chapter covers problems you may encounter when starting up your Mac. In most cases there's a simple explanation and quick solution for these problems, but it can also be a serious hardware problem that's holding you up.

Nothing happens when you turn on the power switch.

Problem: Either the Mac isn't getting power for some reason, the logic board battery is dead (on newer Mac models), or the power supply needs to be replaced.

Solutions:

- Check the power source (see Chapter 7).

- Take the Mac in for service. If your Mac has a keyboard power switch (◁), the battery may be dead. Otherwise, your power supply is probably bad.

The startup disk is ejected.

 Problem: The disk is ejected because you've tried to start up the Mac with a disk that either doesn't contain a System Folder or contains damaged system software files.

Solution: Either insert another startup floppy disk or shut off the Mac, hook up a hard disk that contains a System Folder, turn the hard disk on, and then turn the Mac on again.

Problem: The Mac can't find a startup disk and is waiting for you to insert one. If you're starting up from a hard disk, the disk is either off or disconnected; it isn't ready to be read when the Mac looks for it; or its System Folder is missing, damaged, or incomplete.

Solutions:

■ Insert a startup floppy disk. To start from a hard disk, shut off the Mac, hook up a hard disk that contains a System Folder, turn the hard disk on and wait for it to spin up to speed, then turn the Mac on again.

■ Try a different startup disk. (Use the emergency startup floppy from a disk diagnostic and repair program, or use the *Disk Tools* or *Utilities 1* disk from a set of system software installation floppies.) If the Mac starts, there's a problem with your regular startup disk.

■ If the Mac won't start from any startup disk, shut it off and disconnect the mouse from the Mac, then restart. If the Mac starts up okay, the mouse button is stuck in the down position—try loosening the screws on the mouse case to free it (see page 127).

■ If you already have a startup hard disk connected and running, then the Mac is having trouble finding it or identifying it as a startup disk. Check the SCSI chain (see page 111).

■ If the SCSI chain checks out okay, run the hard disk's setup software and see if it recognizes the disk. If it does, update the driver on the hard disk and try restarting again. If the setup software doesn't recognize the hard disk, you probably have a problem with the hard disk. Contact the disk's manufacturer.

 If a hard disk isn't up to speed when the Mac scans its SCSI bus looking for a disk, the Mac won't see the disk and you'll see the question mark icon. With external hard disks, the basic rule is: Turn the disk on before you turn on the Macintosh, and turn the Macintosh off before you turn off the hard disk.

■ If you were able to update the hard disk's driver but the Mac still doesn't start up, reinstall the system software on the disk using the Installer program (see page 112).

■ If the problem persists after you reinstall the hard disk driver and system software, try using the hard disk to start up a different Mac. If it starts that Mac up, there's

something wrong with your Mac. Run a CPU diagnostic program like
Snooper, or take the Mac in for service. If the hard disk won't start up a
different Mac, take the hard disk in for service.

Sad Mac icon

 Problem: There's a hardware problem with your Mac—a bad memory
chip or worse. The code number underneath the sad Mac icon tells
you or a technician the general nature of the problem. See page 80
in Chapter 6.

 Problem: The Finder file is
either missing from your
startup disk or it's
damaged

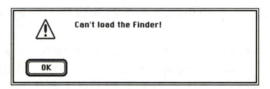

Solution: Start up your Mac from another startup disk and then reinstall the
system software files on the problem disk (see page 112).

The Mac freezes or displays an error message during the startup sequence.

Problem: Your Mac's hardware is okay but there's a problem with the software.
Sometimes the Mac locks up with the *Welcome To Macintosh* box on the
screen; other times it locks up when a particular system extension or init file
is loaded. Some of the alert messages you may see when your Mac locks up or
crashes include:

- Sorry, a system error has occurred

- Stack collision with heap

- System file may be damaged

- Illegal instruction

- Coprocessor not installed

- Address error

- Bus error

Whatever the specific text of the message, the most likely causes for a problem like this are:

- SCSI peripheral not turned on (Mac Plus only)

- Incompatible extension or init files

- Too much system software (System 6 only)

- Damaged or missing system software files

- Damaged boot blocks or an incompatible driver on your disk

- Corrupted PRAM

- Damaged or incompatible startup application

Solutions: There are several different solutions, depending on the specific problem. Before you try any of them, look through this entire section to see which solutions seem most applicable to your situation.

SCSI problems If you're using a Mac Plus and you have one or more peripherals connected to the SCSI port, make sure all your peripherals are turned on. The Mac Plus won't start properly if any connected SCSI devices aren't turned on. Try turning on all the peripherals, waiting for any external hard disks to warm up (10 seconds or so), and then restarting. If the Mac still won't start properly, check the SCSI chain (see page 111).

If you're not using a Mac Plus (or you are and the SCSI chain checks out okay), then whichever of the following solutions you try, you'll need to use a different startup disk. Insert a new startup floppy disk or connect and turn on another hard disk with a working System Folder on it. Then follow one of the three restart procedures described on page 107.

 If your Mac locks up with a startup floppy in the drive, try restarting with the mouse button held down to eject the floppy disk. If this doesn't work, you'll have to remove the floppy manually (see page 149 in Chapter 10).

Once you've got your Mac running again, you can continue searching for the problem on your normal startup disk. Here are the possible problems and solutions.

Incompatible extensions, control panels, or inits If your System Folder contains a lot of startup files (which includes extensions and certain control panels under System 7 and inits and certain cdevs under System 6), one of them may be incompatible with the others or with the operating system. This is particularly likely if you've just added a new one to your System Folder, or if you've just upgraded to a newer version of the system software. The best way to find out if a startup file incompatibility is the problem is to control which ones load at startup (see page 110).

Too much system software If you're running System 6 (or an earlier system version), only a certain amount of RAM is set aside for the system software, no matter how much RAM you have installed in your Mac. (System 7 allocates RAM space for system software as it's needed.) The RAM space that's been set aside is called the *system heap*, and if you're trying to run more system software than will fit into it, you can have problems starting up or experience sudden system crashes. There are two things to check:

■ **The size of your System file.** A System 6 Mac shouldn't have a System file larger than a megabyte or so. You can find out the System's size by checking its Size information in a list view window on the desktop, or by selecting the file and choosing the *Get Info* command. If your System file is too large, it's because you have too many fonts or DAs installed in it. (To remedy this problem, see *Minimize the System file* on page 66.)

■ **The number and size of any inits inside your System Folder.** Any inits you load at startup increase the amount of system heap space used. Many inits are only a few kilobytes in size, but some inits for antivirus programs or electronic mail programs can be over 150K apiece. As a rule, your system heap can't afford to spend more than a total of 150K on init files. If your inits are using more than this, you'll either have to eliminate some of them from your System Folder or increase the size of your system heap to accommodate them. To increase the size of the system heap, use HeapFixer or Heap Tool (see *Resource managers* on page 89 in Chapter 6).

Damaged or missing system software files If eliminating system extension or init files doesn't work and your Mac still won't start up properly, try replacing the system software on your disk (see page 112).

Damaged boot blocks or incompatible hard disk driver If replacing the system software doesn't work, then the startup instructions, or boot blocks, on your hard disk may have become damaged, or the disk's driver may be incompatible (particularly if you've just upgraded to System 7). If so:

■ Start up your Mac with a startup disk that contains your hard disk setup program.

■ Choose the option in the hard disk setup program that lets you reinstall or update the driver on your hard disk.

■ Remove the system software files from the problem disk and reinstall new system software with the Installer program (see page 112).

■ Restart the Mac with the original startup disk.

Corrupted PRAM The data stored in your Mac's PRAM may have become corrupted, so your Mac can no longer identify your startup disk as the correct one. In this case, zap the PRAM (see page 115). Even after you zap the PRAM, though, you should reset the startup disk with the Startup Disk control panel (under System 7) or the Startup Device cdev in the Control Panel DA (under System 6).

Damaged or incompatible startup application If you've set another startup application to load when your Mac starts up, the program may be damaged or incompatible with your version of the system software. Reinstalling the system software will cancel any startup applications you had set, and should fix this problem. If the problem recurs when you set the startup application again, however, delete the startup application and install a new version or (if you've just upgraded your system software) consult the manufacturer to see if there's a newer version that's compatible with your new system software.

The hard disk icon doesn't appear on the desktop.

Problem: In this case, your Mac seems to start up all right, but then the startup disk's icon doesn't appear on the desktop. Either your Mac's PRAM is corrupted, the desktop file needs to be rebuilt, or the disk directory is corrupted.

Solutions:

■ Zap your Mac's PRAM, and then restart the Mac (see page 115).

- Use the Startup Disk control panel or the Startup Device cdev (under System 6) to select the disk as the one you want the Mac to start up from, then restart and see if the icon appears.

- Rebuild the desktop file on the hard disk (see page 109).

- Replace the system software (see page 112).

- Update the hard disk's driver (see page 114).

- Check the SCSI chain (see page 111).

- Run a disk diagnostic and repair utility to see if the disk's directory or file map is damaged, and repair it if necessary.

- Try using the disk to start up a different Mac. If it starts that Mac up and its icon appears there, there's something wrong with your Mac. If the icon still doesn't appear, take the hard disk in for service.

Your Mac won't start up from a CD-ROM disk that contains a valid System Folder.

Problem: Some Macs don't support CD-ROM startups, and you're probably using one of them. These Macs are the 128K, 512K, 512Ke, Plus, SE, SE/30, Portable, II, IIx, IIcx, and original Classic.

Solution: If you're using a Mac that supports CD-ROM startups, check the SCSI chain (see page 111).

Your Mac keeps trying to start up from a hard disk that crashes on startup.

Problem: Your regular startup hard disk has a hardware or software problem, but you can't get your Mac to start up from another disk.

Solutions:

- To start up from a floppy disk, insert the disk immediately after you hear the bong or chime when your Mac restarts. (If possible, use an emergency startup floppy that also contains a disk repair program.) Once the Mac is running from the floppy disk, you can run a disk repair or formatting program to repair the hard disk.

- To start up from an external hard disk (rather than from an internal hard disk that crashes), make sure the external hard disk is running,

If you insert the floppy before restarting or when the Mac is off, the disk will be ejected at startup. then hold down ⌘ Shift Option Del as you restart the Mac. The Mac starts from the external disk, and you can then run a disk repair or formatting program to fix the startup disk.

The Mac starts okay, but it doesn't respond to the mouse or the keyboard.

Problem: Either the mouse or keyboard cable isn't properly connected, there's a temporary software problem that prevents the Mac from recognizing them, or the Mac itself has a hardware problem.

Solution:

- Shut down the Mac and turn it off. Remove the mouse and keyboard cables, and look inside the cable connectors for bent pins. If a pin is bent, try straightening it with a pocket knife, a small needle-nose pliers, or a small screwdriver. (If you can't straighten a bent pin, you'll have to buy a new cable.) If all the pins look straight, make sure none of them is loose. Then carefully plug all the cables back into the proper ports and make sure they're pushed in firmly. Restart the Mac.

- Check the mouse itself to make sure the rubber ball under it moves freely. Follow the mouse-cleaning instructions in your Mac manual.

- If this problem occurred right after a system software upgrade (System 6 to System 7, for example), you may have one or more incompatible extensions. Try turning off all your extensions to see if the problem goes away (see page 110). If you're using a non-Apple keyboard, see if the device has its own extension or Control Panel program and check with the manufacturer to make sure it's compatible with the new version of system software you've installed.

If a loose pin breaks off inside the mouse or ADB port after you've plugged a connector into the Mac, you'll probably have to have the port replaced by a technician.

- If none of the above solutions works, replace the system software (see page 112).

- If the problem continues, take the Mac in for service.

Some icons don't appear on the desktop, although the Mac starts up fine.

Problem: The desktop file is corrupted.

Solution: Hold down ⌘ Option while restarting your Mac. If you're using System 7 and this doesn't work, use a disk repair utility to delete the Desktop DB and Desktop DF files in your main disk directory (these are invisible in the Finder), then restart your Mac and rebuild the desktop.

The mouse button sticks down, and you have to click it again to release it.

Problem: It could be that the button is just sticking, or the microswitch is bad, or the screws holding the mouse case together are too tight.

Solution: Try taking the case apart, cleaning any dust from inside it, and then putting it back together without tightening the screws all the way. If this doesn't work, take it in for repairs.

You want to start up from a different partition on your hard disk drive, but the Startup Disk control panel won't let you.

Problem: The standard Macintosh software only recognizes disks by their SCSI addresses. If you've used a partitioning program to divide a physical disk into multiple partitions, the Mac defaults to the partition it has always used for startup.

Solution: Use the hard disk setup software that you used to partition the disk. It should have an option you can use to choose the startup partition.

Chapter 9

Installing Software

The Installer is the program Apple and many other manufacturers supply to make it easier for you to install the software on your disks. This chapter covers problems you may have while using the Installer.

About the Installer

In the old days, installing a program was a simple matter of dragging one or two files from a floppy disk. Now, however, most programs consist of a dozen or more files that belong in different places on your startup disk. The Installer handles installation chores automatically, reading a script that tells it where to put certain files. As a result, it has become the standard method of installing system software and most application programs on the Macintosh.

When you use the Installer, you choose a destination—a disk or folder where you want the software installed. The Installer then reads a script file that contains instructions about which file goes where, and creates folders and installs files accordingly. When you install System 7 software, for example, the Installer creates a System Folder, creates various folders inside it, and then copies all the Mac's system software files from a set of installation floppy disks or a hard disk or CD-ROM disk into the appropriate folders.

In order to work properly, the Installer needs four things:

- The Installer program itself

- An installer script that tells it which files go where

In some cases, the files being installed are compressed (so the software manufacturer can cram them onto fewer disks), and the Installer also takes care of decompressing the files once they're installed.

■ A set of files to install

■ A destination disk or folder that has enough room to contain the installed files

You can also choose either of two installation methods when you run the Installer:

■ *Easy Install* installs all the software files indicated in the script.

■ *Customize* lets you choose specific files from a list and install only those.

Installing system software

When you install system software from floppy disks, the Installer program and script come on a startup disk. (This disk has various names, depending on which version of the system software you're installing—we'll just call it the Installer disk here.) Along with the Installer disk, there are several other disks containing all the files to be installed. We'll refer to the whole group of installation disks as the Installer disk set.

Back up your Installer disks!

Many Installer problems occur because one of the files on the Installer disk or disk set is missing or has been damaged. The Installer expects to find a specific set of files on the disk it runs from and on other disks or folders it uses during the installation process. All those files, disks, and folders must have exactly the right names and creation dates. If one of the files is renamed, removed, or locked—or even if a new file is added—the Installer may not be able to run properly.

As a result, a lot of the solutions in this chapter involve using a different, undamaged copy of the Installer disk set. You'll save yourself a lot of trouble by making two or more backup copies of the Installer disk set, and using a backup copy to do each installation.

Running the Installer

When you start the Installer program (whether you start up from the Installer disk or not), the System Folder on the Installer disk takes over control of your Mac. This way, the existing System Folder on your regular startup disk can be replaced, if necessary. (You can't replace a System Folder while it's busy running your Mac.)

If you're running the Installer from a floppy disk, start up your Mac with that floppy. That way, the Installer disk's System Folder doesn't have to take over control of your Mac from another System Folder, because it's already in control.

If you're not running the Installer from a floppy disk, it's best to start your Mac from a disk other than the one on which you plan to install system software.

To run the Installer, double-click its icon, which looks like this:

 Apple now preinstalls system software on every new Mac it sells, and at this writing it no longer includes a set of Installer floppies with most Quadras, Performas, and some PowerBook models. I strongly recommend that you contact your Apple dealer to get a set of installation floppies as quickly as possible.

 If you're running a virus-checking extension or init, turn it off and restart your Mac before installing system software or any application. Virus checkers are notorious for interfering with software installations, because to them the installation process looks like something nasty is happening.

Installer

The Installer loads and displays its title screen. After you click the *OK* button, the Installer looks for a disk other than the one it's running from on which to install system software, and displays that disk name in its main dialog box. (You can't install files on the Installer disk itself.) Click the *Switch Disk* button in the dialog box to choose a different disk on which to install the software if you like, and then click the *Easy Install* button to install all the software. If you know exactly which files you want to install, you can instead click the *Customize* button and then select the files you want to install from a list.

For more information on using the Installer, consult the manual for the software you want to install.

System software installation problems

 Problem: You started your Mac with another startup disk, and your Installer disk contains an older version of the system software than

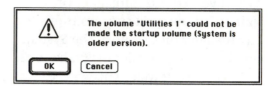

your startup disk does. The Installer disk's System Folder is trying to take over control of the Mac so the Installer can do its job, but the Mac won't give up control to an older version of the system software than the one it's currently running.

Solutions:

- Click the *OK* button and then eject the Installer disk. Restart the Mac with the Installer disk.

- If you want to install an older version of the system software than the one currently on your startup disk, drag the System or Finder file out of the System Folder on your startup disk, give the System Folder a different name, and then run the Installer to install a completely new System Folder (see page 112 for more details on this procedure).

 Problem: You started your Mac and are running under MultiFinder. Now you're trying to run the

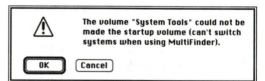

Installer from another disk. The System Folder on the Installer disk has tried to take control of the Macintosh, but your Mac can't switch control from one System Folder to another while running under MultiFinder.

Solution: Click the *OK* button to return to the Finder. Then restart your Mac with the Installer disk and run the Installer program.

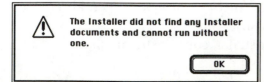

Problem: The Installer can't find any of the scripts it needs to install your system software. (This message is slightly different in System 6.)

Solutions:

- Click the *OK* or *Continue* button to return to the Finder. Then run the Installer from a disk that contains both the Installer and one or more Installer scripts. Any file or folder needed by the Installer must have the correct name and must be located at the same directory level on your disk as the Installer program itself. Just moving one of the folders or installation files into another folder will keep the Installer from finding it.

- If you're installing from a hard disk, make sure all your Installer files and folders are inside the same folder on that hard disk. If you're installing from floppy disks, make sure all the disks in the Installer disk set have the correct names and contain all the proper files.

Problem: The Installer isn't able to open an Installer script file, probably because the file is damaged. A similar message appears when the Installer can't find a particular script file.

Solutions:

- Click the *Continue* button to return to the Finder. Then restart the Mac with the same Installer disk and try the procedure again. It may be a one-time problem.

- If that doesn't work, use a different Installer disk to restart the Mac and then try the installation again.

Problem: If you're installing from floppy disks, this may just be a normal reminder that the Installer needs files that are on a particular disk (in this case, the disk named *Install 1*). But if you've renamed the required

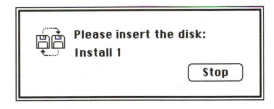

disk or have deleted or moved any of its files, the Installer won't recognize it and will display this message.

Solutions:

- Click the *Stop* button. You'll be asked if you want to stop the installation. Click the *Stop* button again, then click the *Quit* button in the Installer dialog box to return to the Finder.

- If you're installing from floppy disks, insert the disk you think is *Install 1* and make sure it's really named that. If the name is right, then one or more files is missing from the disk. You'll need to find another, complete copy of the *Install 1* disk and use it.

- If you're installing from a hard disk, make sure the *Install 1* folder is located inside the same folder as the Installer program itself and is named *Install 1*. If it's in a different place or has a different name, the Installer won't recognize it. If the name and the place are right, then the folder is missing some files. You'll have to replace it with a complete copy.

 Problem: You're installing new system software on a disk that already contains a System Folder. The existing System file contains 15 desk accessories, and the Installer program can't transfer that many DAs to the new copy of the System file it's installing.

Solution: Click the *OK* button to return to the Finder. Then use the Font/DA Mover program to remove at least one desk accessory from the existing System file. Once you've removed one or more DAs, try the installation process again.

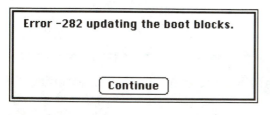

Problem: The Installer is having trouble writing information to your hard disk's boot blocks. Either there's a glitch in the Installer software or there's something wrong with that region of your hard disk.

Solutions:

■ Click the *Continue* button to return to the Finder, restart the Mac, and then try running the Installer again. The glitch may be temporary.

■ If you get the same message again, try using a disk diagnostic and repair program to repair your hard disk's boot blocks.

 Problem: You're trying to install a new version of the system software on a disk that already contains a System Folder. The Installer is trying to remove the old system files, but one or more of them is locked and can't be deleted. (System 7's alert message tells you that a file is locked and even names the locked file.)

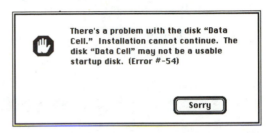

There's a problem with the disk "Data Cell." Installation cannot continue. The disk "Data Cell" may not be a usable startup disk. (Error #-54)

Sorry

Solution: Use the *Get Info* command to check each file in your System Folder and unlock them if necessary—just click the *Locked* checkbox in the Get Info window to remove the x from it. (If you're using System 7, the message tells you which file is locked.)

Problem: The Installer was unable to copy files to your destination disk (which is named Startup in the example at right). There could be any number of reasons for this, from a glitch in the Installer program to corrupted resource files to a problem with your hard disk.

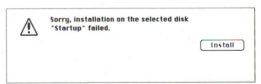

Sorry, installation on the selected disk "Startup" failed.

Install

Solutions:

■ Click the *Quit* button and then restart the Mac using the floppy disk that contains the Installer program. Try the installation again. If it still doesn't work, try using another Installer disk set.

■ If there were existing system software files on the disk, make sure they're all unlocked.

■ If the destination disk already contains a System Folder, move the System or Finder file out of it, give the folder a different name, then try the installation again (see page 112).

■ If the above solutions don't do the trick and you have a working System Folder on another disk, try dragging it onto the destination disk. If the Mac starts up okay after you drag-install a new System Folder, the problem is with your copy of the Installer or its script file.

■ If dragging a System Folder onto the disk doesn't work, your hard disk has a hardware problem and you'll have to call the disk's manufacturer.

Installing application software

When you use the Installer to install application software, the Installer usually doesn't come on a startup disk. You don't ordinarily have to start up your Mac from an application program's Installer disk in order to perform an installation. In fact, you usually can't anyway, since most application Installer disks don't contain a System Folder. On the other hand, there are a couple of problems unique to installing application software as opposed to system software. For example, some of the ancillary files that come with a program may already exist on your hard disk, and an alert message may ask if you want to replace them. If the Installer script is well written, it should take such contingencies into account, but some scripts don't. Another problem is damaged Installer disks or extension conflicts during the installation. Let's look at a couple of specific examples.

You get an Installer error message during the installation.

Problem: Assuming you're running the program's Installer after having started up from your regular startup disk, you may have an extension conflict; or there may be a problem with one of the installation disks.

Solutions:

■ Turn off all your extensions (particularly virus-checking extensions) and restart your Mac, then try the installation again.

■ If you still get the error message, there's probably something wrong with one of your installation floppies. If you're using the original installation floppies (not a good idea), try the backup set. (You did make one, didn't you?) If you don't have a backup set, call the software manufacturer for a replacement set.

■ If you're using a backup set of floppies, make another backup set from the original set of disks and try the installation again using the new backup set.

You're installing a program that uses networking or communications resources, and a message asks if you want to replace a file that already exists.

Problem: The program is trying to install a communications resource file such as AppleTalk, EtherTalk, or Apple Modem Tool, and a copy of that file was previously installed with some other program or your system software.

Solutions: The main thing is to make sure you end up with the most recent version of the file, whether it's the one that already exists on your disk or the new one being installed. Application developers don't always distribute the most recent versions of Apple system software files, and if you replace a newer version of a resource file with an older version, you can cause problems. What you do depends on your situation.

■ If you're using System 7 and there's only one file on your disk that has the same name as a file being installed, the alert message tells you which of the copies is older. If the Installer is trying to install a newer version, click the *OK* button and let the installation proceed. If the message tells you the existing file is a newer version than the one being installed, click *Cancel* to stop the installation, then make a copy of the existing file onto another disk. After you've copied the file, proceed with the installation and click *OK* when the message asks if you want to replace the file. This installs the older version of the file on your destination disk. Once the installation is done, drag the copy of the newer version of the file back to your destination disk, replacing the older one that was just installed.

■ If the message doesn't say whether the file being replaced is older or newer (or if there's more than one file with the same name), click the *Cancel* button in the alert box to stop the installation. Then you'll have to do some detective work. Examine each disk in the Installer disk set or check the program's manual for a list of the files being installed.

Compare the list with the contents of your Extensions folder or System Folder, looking for duplicate names. Then use the *Get Info* command to check each version of the file (the one on your hard disk and the one on the Installer disk set) to see which is the newer. If the one on your hard disk is newer, make a copy of it onto a floppy disk, then go ahead with the installation and click *OK* when the message asks if you want to replace the existing copy of the file. Once the installation is done, drag the copy of the file you made from the floppy disk back to your hard disk, replacing the one you just installed. If more than one file has the same name, you'll have to do this with each of them.

■ If the files on the Installer disk set are compressed and you can't select individual files to see whether they're older or newer than the ones you already have, you'll have to proceed with the installation. First, however, copy your System Folder files onto another disk. Then proceed with the installation and replace any existing files. Finally, compare the copies you made with the newly installed files and replace any that are older than the ones you had originally.

You're installing a program that doesn't need communications resources and a message tells you that a file already exists.

Problem: Some programs have so many resource files (spelling dictionaries, file format conversion files, Help files, and so forth) that their Installer scripts put them all into one or two folders with names like *Microsoft* or *Claris*. Some developers use such a resources folder with many of their programs, and the folder itself often has the same name no matter which program is being installed. When you install such a program, the folders are created inside the System Folder or the Preferences folder inside the System Folder. If you're installing a second program from the same developer, the Installer script may try to create new files inside that developer's resources folder. Some of the files (dictionary or file conversion files, for example) are the same as ones that already exist. In this case, you'll see an alert asking if you want to replace them.

Solution: Normally, you can click the *OK* button to replace any existing thesaurus, main dictionary, or format conversion resource files with the ones from the new program you're installing. These files will either be the same or they'll be newer versions. If the file in question is a custom spelling dictionary and you've already added some words to the existing dictionary, however, then you don't want to replace it. Click the *Cancel* button to stop the installation, rename your custom dictionary file so it's not replaced, then proceed with the installation.

Chapter 10

Working with Disks

In this chapter, we'll look at disk-related problems in three areas: setting up hard disks; inserting and ejecting disks; and working with disks on the desktop. If you're having problems logging onto an AppleShare file server or shared disk, see Chapter 15.

Setting up hard disks

A hard disk is only a dumb piece of hardware until you connect it to a Mac with a cable and install a device driver and Mac system software files on it. The device driver allows the Mac to recognize the disk as a standard storage device, and the system software lets the Mac start up from the disk. (Of course, if you don't want to be able to start up your Mac from the disk, you only need the device driver.)

Most Mac hard disks come set up and ready to use, with the necessary software drivers already installed. In some cases, however, you may have to set up the hard disk yourself. Even after the disk is set up, you may need to use the setup software to create *partitions* (discrete storage areas) on the disk, to test the disk's operation, to update the disk driver, or to reformat the disk.

Every hard disk comes with setup software provided by its manufacturer, and it would be impossible to cover all the error messages for every type and brand of software here. Fortunately, the procedure for setting up a hard disk is pretty consistent for all these products, so you might encounter several common problems with any setup program.

Some programs refer to the process of preparing a disk to store Macintosh files as *initializing,* and others call this process *formatting*. These terms are interchangeable in this chapter.

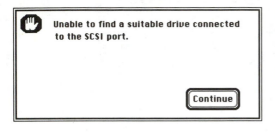

Problem: You usually get this message or one that says *Unable to select this drive* when you run your disk setup program and the Mac can't locate a SCSI disk. The disk drive is either not connected or not turned on, or the Mac is having trouble locating it.

Solutions: Make sure the drive is connected and turned on. You should be able to hear the disk running. If the disk is running, try these solutions:

- Shut everything off, turn the disk on first and let it run for 10 seconds, then turn on the Mac and start the disk setup program. It may be that the disk wasn't up to full speed when you started the Mac before, so it wasn't recognized.

- Turn off your Mac, the disk, and any other peripherals and check the SCSI chain (see page 111).

- Try zapping your Mac's PRAM (see page 115).

- Restart your Mac again and run a disk diagnostic and repair program. The repair program may be able to recognize and repair your disk.

- If you have other SCSI devices connected, try them to see if your Mac works with them. (Or, if you have a hardware diagnostic program like Snooper, run a test of the Mac's SCSI port.) If the SCSI port itself isn't the problem, your hardware is at fault and you'll have to call your hard disk's manufacturer.

You have a hard disk connected and running, but your hard disk setup software doesn't recognize it and there's no error message.

Problem: Many hard disk setup programs only recognize drives that have been set up with their own drivers. For example, Apple HD SC Setup won't recognize drives set up with software from other manufacturers, even though they're connected and working properly.

Solution: Either make sure you're using the hard disk setup program that came with the disk you want to work with, or use a third-party hard disk setup program (see Chapter 6).

Problem: You've tried to mount a hard disk volume to the desktop and you see this message. Either the drive isn't initialized, the disk driver software is damaged, or you have a hardware problem.

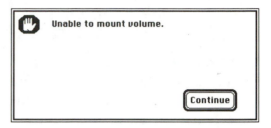

Solutions:

■ Try the procedure again. It may be a one-time glitch.

■ Use your hard disk setup program to update the hard disk driver, and then try the procedure again.

■ Restart your Mac, using a startup disk that contains a disk recovery program, and then try to mount and repair the drive. (See the disk recovery program's manual for instructions.)

■ Call the disk's manufacturer to see if they have any other ideas.

■ If none of these solution works, send the hard disk to a data recovery service. The service will recover your data and repair the drive, if possible (see page 99 in Chapter 6). If there's no data on the drive, use your hard disk setup program to reinitialize it.

Problem: The hard disk driver has probably become corrupted.

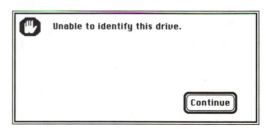

Solution: Shut down the Mac first and then the hard disk. Turn on the hard disk, and start the Mac with the floppy disk that contains your hard disk setup program. Then reinstall or update the hard disk's driver using the setup program.

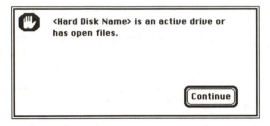

Problem: You're trying to update the driver software or change the partitions on a disk while files or programs on that disk are open. This is like trying to change a tire while you're driving the car.

Solution: Close all the files on the drive, shut down the Mac, and restart it with a different startup disk that contains your hard disk setup program. Then you'll be able to adjust the drive's partitions or update its driver.

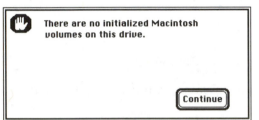

Problem: You've selected a hard disk with your setup program, and there's no Macintosh driver software on it. This message might also say *Can't find a Macintosh driver.*

Solution: Restart your Mac using a startup disk that contains the hard disk setup software; then initialize the hard disk and install a driver on it.

Problem: Either your hard disk setup program has a glitch or you have a hardware problem.

Solutions:

■ Restart the Macintosh with another startup disk and try initializing the disk with a different copy of the hard disk setup program.

■ If that doesn't do the trick, zap your Mac's PRAM (see page 115) and try the initialization again.

■ If the problem continues, restart your Mac with a startup disk that contains a disk recovery program and try initializing the disk with that program.

■ If these remedies don't work, call the company that sold you the hard disk.

Problem: There are various possible causes of this message or messages like it. It may be that one or more files on the disk are open (and you can't install or update the driver on a disk that has open files), or there may be more serious problems.

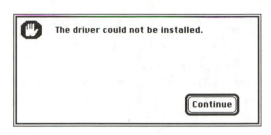

Solutions:

- Close any files that are open and restart the Mac using a startup disk that contains your hard disk setup program; then try installing the driver again.

- Check the SCSI chain (see page 111).

- Run the setup program and initialize or format the disk; then try installing the driver again.

- If you're still having problems, call the disk's manufacturer.

Problem: Either the disk hasn't been formatted properly or there was a minor glitch when you ran the verification routine.

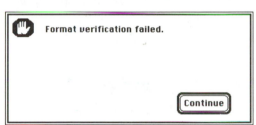

Solutions:

- Try running the format verification routine again.

- Reformat the hard disk and then run the verification routine again.

- If the problem persists, the disk itself may be malfunctioning. Contact the disk's manufacturer, or take it in for service.

Problem: Your disk probably has a bad ROM; if not, something else is wrong with the disk hardware.

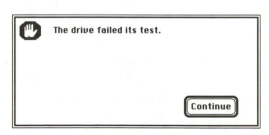

Solutions:

- Try the test again.

- Call the disk's manufacturer.

Some setup programs won't let you resize existing partitions once they're created, or will let you increase, but not decrease, their size. Also, some setup programs require that a partition be empty before you change its size.

A message says that you can't create or change a partition.

Problem: Either there isn't enough room on your disk for the partition you want to create or change, or you're not following the correct procedure for creating or changing the partition.

Solutions:

■ Check the manual for your setup software to be sure you're following the correct steps and observing the rules for creating or changing the partition. Pay attention to the size of the partition you're trying to create (and make sure there's enough space for it), and check to see whether or not your setup program allows you to change the size of partitions once you've created them.

■ If you've followed all the rules in the manual and you can't create the partition, you'll either have to live with the disk the way it is or reinitialize it and create a new set of partitions.

Inserting and ejecting disks

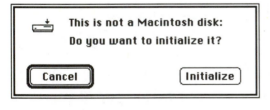

Problem: An alert message says the disk isn't a Macintosh disk or that the disk is unreadable. With older versions of the system software, the alert box has buttons called *One-Sided* and *Two-Sided*—you click the *One-Sided* button to initialize a 400K floppy disk, and the *Two-Sided* button to initialize an 800K floppy disk.

This error message is caused by one of four things:

■ The floppy disk you've inserted (or the hard disk your Macintosh is trying to recognize) hasn't been formatted for use by the Mac. It may be unformatted, or it may have been formatted under another operating system, like DOS.

■ The disk's desktop file is corrupted so the Mac doesn't recognize it.

■ The disk is physically damaged.

■ The floppy disk drive is dirty or out of adjustment.

Solutions: The solution you use depends on your situation.

 If the metal sliding door on a floppy disk is stuck, here's a last-ditch remedy: carefully remove the metal door (without touching the plastic disk inside), then insert the floppy and (assuming the disk is readable) immediately copy all of its files to another disk.

■ **If the disk has never been used**, or if you know it doesn't contain any information you want to save, click the *Initialize* or *Two-Sided* button. (The *One-Sided* button is only for old, 400K floppy disks, and you're probably not using them.) The Mac then initializes the disk. Any data on the disk is erased as part of this process, so if you think there's something on the disk you want saved, click the *Eject* (or *Cancel*) button.

■ **If the disk has already been formatted for the Macintosh** and you know it contains files, check it for physical damage. If it's a floppy, slide its metal door back and forth to make sure it moves freely. If the floppy's door does more freely, or if the problem is with a hard disk, try rebuilding the desktop file (see page 109).

■ **If the disk was formatted for use on a DOS computer** and you're trying to use it on the Mac, you must make sure your Mac has a high-density floppy disk drive. You also need to be running either Apple File Exchange or DOS Mounter. These are utilities that allow the Mac to read a DOS disk. (Apple File Exchange comes with older Mac system software; DOS Mounter is sold by Dayna Communications of Salt Lake City, Utah.) To work, they must be running *before* you insert the DOS disk in your Mac.

■ **If none of these remedies works and you're not trying to read a DOS disk**, then either the disk is damaged or the floppy disk drive is dirty or out of adjustment. If possible, try the disk in another Macintosh. If its icon appears on the desktop and you don't see an alert message, try cleaning the original Mac's disk drive with a drive cleaning kit (available from any Apple dealer or mail order house). If that doesn't work, take the drive to a service technician.

■ If you get the same message when you try the disk in a different Mac, try recovering files from the disk using a disk recovery program.

Problem: You've tried to initialize a disk but the Mac can't do it, probably because the disk is damaged.

Solution: Click the *OK* button to eject the disk. If it's a floppy you might try repairing the disk with a disk repair utility, but the damage is probably irreparable. If it's a hard disk, call the disk's manufacturer.

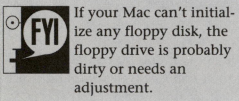

If your Mac can't initialize any floppy disk, the floppy drive is probably dirty or needs an adjustment.

Problem: A previous error in writing to the disk has caused a minor problem with the disk directory. Your Mac is asking for permission to repair the directory.

Solution: Click the *OK* button to repair the disk.

Problem: Either the desktop file on the disk you've inserted is so damaged that the Mac doesn't think it can be repaired, or the disk's directory is damaged, the disk is physically damaged in some way, or the Mac is having a temporary problem reading the desktop file. Under System 6, the alert says the disk is damaged and can't be used, and your only option is to click an OK button to eject it.

Solutions:

■ Click the *OK* or *Eject* button to eject the disk, and then check the metal sliding door on the floppy disk to make sure it slides freely.

If the metal sliding door won't move, try removing it (see page 147).

■ Reinsert the disk while holding down ⌘ Option to rebuild the desktop file. If the file can be rebuilt, you see the dialog box asking you to confirm that you want the desktop file rebuilt.

■ If the disk directory is damaged, rebuilding the desktop file won't work and you get the damaged disk alert message again. In this case, start up a disk repair program, then insert the disk again and try to repair it.

A floppy disk's icon doesn't appear on the desktop when you insert it into the floppy drive.

Problem: Sometimes you insert a floppy disk into a drive but its icon doesn't appear on the desktop so you can't work with it. This glitch usually crops up when the Mac is so busy doing other things that it doesn't realize you've inserted a new floppy. If you have this problem with an external floppy drive, it may also be the drive's connector cable.

Solutions:

■ Try ejecting the disk. If the disk is in the lower, right-hand, or only internal drive, press Shift ⌘ 1. If it's in the upper, left-hand, or external drive, press Shift ⌘ 2. If it's in a third floppy drive, press Shift ⌘ 0.

■ If you've been able to eject the disk this way, switch to the Finder (you may have to save your work and quit the program you're working in first). Then insert the disk again. This usually clears up the problem.

■ If the disk still isn't ejected, see the next problem.

A floppy disk won't pop out of the disk drive when you eject it.

Problem: You choose a command to eject a floppy disk, but it doesn't come out of the drive, or it only comes out part of the way and then seems stuck. Sometimes this is a temporary software glitch, but it could also be caused by a mechanical problem.

Solutions:

■ Try choosing the command two or three more times.

■ If the disk can't be ejected with a keyboard sequence, close any programs you have running and save your work. Then hold down the mouse button while restarting the Mac. The floppy should pop out during the startup sequence.

■ If these steps don't work, shut off the Mac. Then straighten out a paper clip and poke it carefully into the small hole at the right side of the disk drive opening. Be sure to insert the paper clip straight into the hole, not at an angle. You'll feel the paper clip pressing against a lever. Gently push the paper clip against the lever until the disk pops out. *Be careful!* If the disk only comes a quarter inch or so out of the opening, the metal sliding door on the floppy might be caught on the retaining tabs that hold the disk drive heads in place. If this happens, yanking the disk out by brute force will damage the drive. If the disk doesn't slide out easily after you press the internal lever, it's best to take the Mac to a service technician and have the disk removed there. It's a hassle, but an expensive disk drive repair is worse.

■ If the problem continues after you've taken the above steps and you have an external floppy drive, make sure the connector cable is plugged in firmly. If it seems to be plugged in okay, shut down your Mac and then unplug the connector and check it for missing or bent pins. If a pin is bent, try straightening it with a small needle-nosed pliers. (If the pin is loose, don't plug it back into the Mac—it could break off inside the port.) If the drive still doesn't work, or if its cable is damaged, you'll need to take it to a technician to be repaired.

You insert a CD-ROM or PhotoCD disk in your CD-ROM player, but the disk's icon doesn't appear on the desktop.

Problem: In order to use any disk in a CD-ROM player, you must have a CD-ROM driver installed in your System Folder. If you want to use a PhotoCD disk, you must also have the Apple Photo Access extension and the QuickTime extension (version 1.5 or later) installed in your System Folder. Finally, you need a foreign file format driver to read a High Sierra or other foreign format.

 CD-ROM drivers usually come with CD-ROM players. If you need copies of Apple Photo Access or QuickTime and they didn't come with your CD-ROM player, check with your Apple dealer.

Solutions:

- Press the eject button on your CD-ROM player to eject the disk. Make sure your System Folder or Extensions folder contains a CD-ROM extension for your model CD-ROM player, an Apple Photo Access extension, version 1.5 or later of the QuickTime extension, or a foreign file format driver if your CD is in that format. If all these files are present, restart your Mac to make sure they're all running.

- Check the SCSI chain to make sure the disk is properly terminated and connected and has a valid SCSI address.

A removable hard disk or other high-density removable storage disk's icon doesn't appear on the desktop when you insert it.

Problem: Removable cartridge storage devices such as a Syquest drive, Bernoulli box, floptical disk, or erasable optical disk aren't considered standard storage devices by your Mac. In order to have your Mac recognize such a device, your must install a special system extension for it in your Mac.

 Some third-party disk setup programs (like Drive 7) can install drivers on removable cartridge disks as well. See Chapter 6 for more information.

Solutions:

- Eject the disk from the storage device, locate the installation disk that came with the storage device, and install the device's system extension in your System Folder or Extensions folder. Then restart the Mac and insert the storage cartridge in the device.

- If the above solution doesn't work, use SCSI Probe or the setup program that came with your hard disk to scan your Mac's SCSI bus. The removable storage device should be present in the list of connected devices. If it isn't, shut everything down and check the SCSI cable and the SCSI address of the device. If it's the last device in the SCSI chain, make sure it's terminated properly. (Check the device's manual to see how to terminate it.)

Working with disks on the desktop

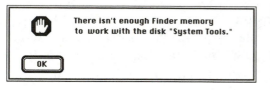

Problem: If you're using almost all of the memory available for your system software, there isn't enough memory left to read and store the desktop file of any new disk you insert. Or you may be able to insert the disk, but then you can't open its icon. You may see a message like the one above; or it may say *There isn't enough Finder memory to remember the image of this disk*, or *The disk <diskname> could not be opened, because there isn't enough memory available.*

Solution: Click the OK button to eject the disk, then quit one or more of the applications or DAs you have running and insert the disk or try opening it again. (In some cases, clicking the *OK* button just puts the alert away.) If you have this problem often, you should consider expanding your Mac's memory or eliminating some extensions, fonts, or sounds from your System file or System Folder.

Problem: With Macs that don't have a hard disk, you may often need to eject the startup floppy disk so you can insert a program or data disk. Under System 6, you can eject the startup disk and the Mac will automatically store enough of the system software instructions to let you work without it, as long as there's enough memory available. (You're not allowed to eject the startup disk at all under System 7.) If you get a message like the one above when you try to eject the startup disk, it means you have so many applications or DAs running that there's not enough memory left for the Mac to remember the instructions it needs.

Solution: Either forget about ejecting the startup disk, or close one or more applications or DAs to free up some memory and then try ejecting the disk again. If this is a frequent problem, you should consider adding a hard disk to your Mac (so you won't have to tie up a floppy drive with a startup disk). Another long-term solution is to expand your Mac's memory.

You can insert or mount a disk, but you get a "disk unreadable" or "Not a Macintosh disk" message when you try to open its icon.

Problem: A virus has infected the System Folder on your startup disk, or there's something wrong with the SCSI chain.

Solutions:

- Run a virus repair program to remove the virus (see Chapter 6).

- Check the SCSI chain (see page 111).

Problem: You've tried to eject a disk by dragging its icon to the Trash while one or more of its files were open. (If you use keyboard commands to eject a disk, the Mac lets you eject a disk

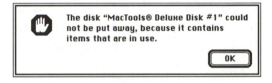

while its files are open, but it keeps a dimmed image of the disk's icon on the desktop.)

 Problem: Under System 6, any changes to the folders on a disk are recorded in its desktop file when the disk is ejected. In this case, the disk you're ejecting is so full that the changes can't be recorded. (System 7 doesn't have this problem because folder changes are recorded as they are made, and you can't make any changes once the disk is full.)

Solution: Click the *OK* button to eject the disk. Then insert it again and delete one or more of its files so that it has at least 1K of free space. When at least 1K of space is available on the

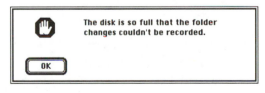

disk, eject it and then rebuild its desktop file (see page 109). After that, the desktop file will reflect the current contents and folder organization on the disk.

You're running System 7 and your Mac won't let you rename a 400K floppy disk or view folders it contains.

Problem: 400K floppy disks were designed for use with the old Macintosh File System (MFS), which was changed to the Hierarchical File System (HFS) with System 4.2 back when the Mac Plus was introduced in 1986. System 7 allows you to read and format 400K floppies, but it doesn't allow you to rename them. Also, System 7 doesn't recognize any folders created on a Mac running the old MFS system—these folders were just cosmetic adornments under MFS anyway, so newer Macs just show the files inside those folders and not the folders themselves.

Solution: Copy the files from any 400K disks to your hard disk or to an 800K or 1.4 MB floppy disk, and don't use 400K disks in the future.

You're running System 7 and you can't rename your hard disk.

Problem: You can't rename a disk when that disk is being shared over a network. If you're using an early version of System 7, there may also be a bug that prevents you from renaming a hard disk.

Solutions:

- Open the Sharing Setup control panel and turn file sharing off. (See Chapter 15 for more information.)

- Replace your system software with version 7.1 or later.

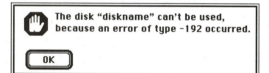

Problem: Your disk directory or driver has been corrupted.

Solutions:

- Run a disk diagnostic and repair utility to locate and repair the damage.

- Replace your hard disk driver.

Chapter 11

Working with the Finder

This chapter covers problems you may have when viewing, opening, printing, moving, copying, or erasing files in the Finder, or using other Finder commands. Because System 7 is far more adept at these things than System 6, several of the problems in this chapter relate to System 6 only. But since the new system also offers more Finder viewing options, it has its own set of specific problems.

If you're having trouble running a program or opening files from inside a DA or application, check Chapter 12. If you're having a printing problem that isn't mentioned here, see Chapter 14. Some other problems that occur when you try to open files from a disk being shared on a network are covered in Chapter 15.

Viewing documents

Some files or folders are missing from a window.

Problem: There are several possible causes for this problem, ranging from the item simply being misplaced or out of view in the window to a damaged desktop or directory file on your disk.

Solutions:

- Make sure the item is really missing. Use the Find File desk accessory (under System 6) or the *Find File* command (under System 7) to search for the item if you know its name. If you don't know its name, or if

FYI Early versions of System 7 had a bug that could cause files to disappear from windows. If this problem continues, upgrade to version 7.1 or later.

there are many items missing, try switching to different list views in the window (Name, Kind, Size, Date) to rearrange the window and see if the items show up. Next, open other folders and look for the items inside them. In most cases, the item is simply misplaced.

■ Close the window and open it again. Under System 7, window updates don't always happen immediately, so if you drag several items into a window while the Mac is doing other things (recalculating a spreadsheet in the background, for example), the window changes may not show up right away.

■ Restart the Mac and rebuild the desktop file as you do (see page 109). A corrupted desktop file can cause items to be hidden.

■ If you still can't find the item or items, choose the Name view for the window and look at the list of file names. If it seems that there's an alphabetical gap in the list that shouldn't be there (say, all file names between L and T are missing), use a disk diagnostic and repair program to check for and fix a problem with the disk's directory.

A System 7 list view window doesn't show the categories of information you need to see.

Problem: You're looking for a certain column of information in a list view window (such as Date, Size, or Kind), but it's missing from the window.

Solution: First, try widening the window on the desktop or scrolling it to the right—the column you need to see may just be temporarily out of sight. If this doesn't work, open the Views control panel in the Control Panels folder and click the checkbox in the List Views area next to the category of information you want to see. Then close the control panel. The missing information should now be showing (although you may still need to resize or scroll the window to see it).

You have a window view set to show dates, but the dates are missing or contain meaningless characters.

Problem: The PRAM is corrupted, or the date resource in the System file is corrupted.

Solutions:

- Zap the PRAM (see page 115).

- Replace the system software (see page 112).

- If neither of these works, you may have a logic board problem. Take the Mac in for a hardware diagnosis.

You can see the dates on items in Finder windows, but suddenly the documents you create or modify are dated January 1, 1904.

Problem: Your Mac's battery is dead or dying.

Solution: Take the Mac to a technician and have the battery replaced.

You set custom views or turn off the Trash warning in the System 7 Finder, but your custom settings are lost when you restart the Mac.

Problem: Your Finder Preferences file is corrupted, or your battery is dying.

Solutions:

- Locate the Finder Preferences file (it's inside the Preferences folder in the System Folder) and throw it away. Then restart the Mac to automatically rebuild this preferences file.

- If the settings are lost again after you rebuild the Finder Preferences file, take the Mac to a technician and have the battery replaced.

Windows open really slowly in the Finder.

Problem: Normally, the speed with which a window opens is directly related to the number of items in the window and (under System 7) to whether or not you have the Finder set to calculate folder sizes. A window that contains hundreds or thousands of items opens far more slowly than a window that contains only a few items. When you have the Finder set to calculate folder sizes it slows the Mac down even more, because it must calculate the size of

If you're calculating folder sizes and viewing the window by Size, this problem is even worse, because the Mac has to calculate the size of every folder in the window before it knows the order in which to display the window's items. In some cases, the window may take a minute or more to open, and in extremely severe situations, the window won't open at all.

each folder in the window before it can display that folder's icon. If your windows don't contain lots of items, your Mac may have a virus.

Solutions:

■ Choose a window view other than Size from the Views menu.

■ Open the Views control panel and uncheck the option to calculate folder sizes.

■ Run a virus detection and repair program to check for viruses.

■ If the window contains thousands of items, move a lot of them inside folders to reduce the item count.

■ If the window won't open at all under System 7, restart the Mac with a System 6 startup disk, then move the items into folders or into another window.

Opening and printing documents

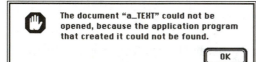

The document "a_TEHT" could not be opened, because the application program that created it could not be found.

OK

Problem: You've double-clicked a document, expecting the Mac to automatically load both the document and the program needed to work with it. But the file you've clicked has a generic or unknown document type so the Mac doesn't know which application to load, or the application that created the document isn't on your disk. (This message is slightly different under System 6).

Solutions:

■ If you know which application was used to create the document, install that application on your disk and then use it to open the document.

■ If you don't have the original application or don't know what it is, try using a different program to open the document. Use the program's import option, or try opening it as a text file.

■ Use Orphan Finder or Can Opener to open the file (see Chapter 6).

You double-click a document whose application you know is on your disk, but you get the "Application Busy or Missing" message.

Problem: Your desktop file is corrupted.

Solutions:

■ Rebuild the desktop file.

■ If you find you have to do this after each restart (in other words, documents revert to the generic "Document" kind in Finder windows after each restart), reinstall your system software.

 You can sometimes get this message when the application you used to create a document is on a different disk or hard disk partition than the document.

■ If the application is on another disk or in another hard disk partition, you'll have to open it first and then use it to open the document, or move it to the same disk or partition as the document.

Problem: Except for the System file it-self (under System 7), system software files like the Finder, Clipboard, preferences files, and Chooser extensions or device drivers can't be opened or printed. If you select one of these files and then choose the *Open* or *Print* command from the Finder's File menu, or if you double-click such a file to open it, you get this message (or a similar one under System 6).

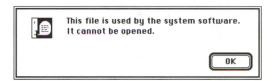

This file is used by the system software. It cannot be opened.

OK

Solutions:

■ Don't try opening or printing system files. You can avoid this message if you only open files whose Kind designation you recognize as belonging to a program you normally use. If a document's Kind information is missing or it says *document*, you won't be able to open it by double-clicking.

■ If you're trying to install fonts or DAs under System 6, you can't just double-click the System file to open it—you need the Font/DA Mover program. Refer to your Macintosh manual if you're not sure how to use the Font/DA Mover, or see page 54 in Chapter 3.

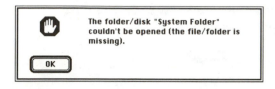

Problem: You occasionally see this message when you try to open a folder in the Finder. It's usually due to a temporary problem the Mac has reading the desktop file.

Solution: Try opening the folder again one or more times. The problem will usually go away. If it doesn't, rebuild the desktop file.

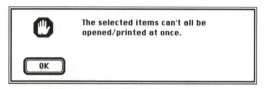

 Under System 7, you can select files to open or print from as many different programs as you want. The Mac will open them one at a time until it's out of memory. Any remaining documents or programs simply won't be opened or printed.

 Problem: You're running under System 6, and either you've selected files that were created by more than one application and are trying to open or print them all from the Finder at the same time, or you've simply selected too many files to be opened or printed at once. (This message may also say *Please open/print only documents of the same kind, Please open or print from only one application at a time*, or *There are too many items to print. Try again with fewer items.*)

Under System 6, you can only open or print from the Finder if the files you've selected were all created by the same program. But even if you select only files that belong to one application, there's a limit to how many files you can open or print at once. It depends on how much memory the Finder has available at the time.

Solution: Make sure all the files you select to open or print were created by the same version of the same application, or choose a smaller group of files and try again.

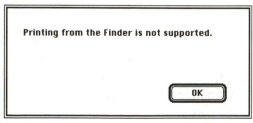

Problem: Some programs don't allow you to print documents from the Finder. Those programs display a message like this one.

Solution: Open the program itself and then open and print the document from inside the program.

Problem: There isn't enough memory available to allow you to open another window on the desktop, or to choose a command, or to keep all the current windows open. The message may also read *No more windows can be opened* or *The command could not be completed, because there isn't enough memory available.*

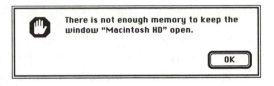

Solution: Close one or more of the windows you currently have open before trying to open any others. You may have to close several windows or even an application or a couple of DAs or control panels to free up enough memory. If closing everything doesn't work, restart the Mac to clear out the memory completely and then try again.

Problem: You've tried to open an item that's in the Trash, or you've tried to open an alias for an item and the item itself is in the Trash. You can't open or print anything in the Trash.

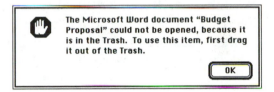

Solution: Drag the item out of the Trash and try opening it again.

Problem: You've tried to open an alias, but the item represented by the alias is damaged or isn't on the disk.

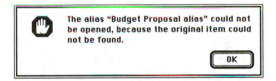

Solutions:

■ Select the alias and choose the *Get Info* command, then click the *Find Original* button in the information window. The Mac tries to locate the original item the alias represents. The item may have been damaged or renamed and moved into a deeply nested folder. In most cases, however, the item is simply no longer on the disk. If that's the case, you may as well delete the alias, because it no longer serves any purpose.

■ If the original item is found, the alias itself may be damaged. Delete it and use the *Make Alias* command to make a new one.

You try to open an alias and a message asks you to insert a disk.

Problem: The original to which the alias points is on a removable disk that isn't currently on your desktop. (If the original is on a network server or a hard disk that simply isn't mounted on your desktop, the disk will automatically be mounted.)

Solution: Insert the disk that contains the original to which the alias points.

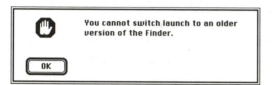

 Problem: You've tried switch-launching from the currently running Finder to another Finder under System 6, but the version you're trying to launch is older than the current one. (To switch-launch, you hold down ⌘ Option while double-clicking the Finder file on a disk. If the version of the Finder you double-click is as new as or newer than the one you're currently running, the Mac will run the new Finder.) This problem doesn't appear under System 7, because it doesn't allow switch-launching at all.

Solution: Whenever you switch-launch to another Finder, make sure it's a version as new as or newer than the one that's currently running. If you really must run your Mac under an older version of the Finder, you'll have to restart it with a disk containing that version.

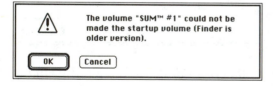

 Problem: You've tried to change the startup disk by switch-launching from the currently running System file to another System file. (To switch-launch using the System file, you hold down ⌘ Option while double-clicking the System file on a disk.) But the Mac won't change the current startup disk if the System file version on the new startup disk is older than the version of the System you're currently running.

Solution: Whenever you switch-launch to another startup disk, make sure both the System and Finder files on the new startup disk are versions as new as or newer than the ones on your current startup disk.

Problem: You've tried to switch-launch to a different System file from the one you started up with, but the Mac won't let you do that when MultiFinder is running.

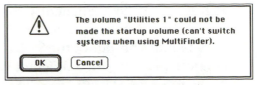

Solution: If you normally start up your Mac with MultiFinder and want to keep it that way, restart while holding down the ⌘ key. This starts your Mac with the Finder only for just that one time. (The *Set Startup* options you've set won't be affected—see page 39 in Chapter 3 for more information.) With the

 To switch-launch, hold down ⌘ Option while double-clicking the System file you want to use. For this to work, the version of the System file you want to switch-launch to must be as new as or newer than the one that's currently running.

Finder running, you can locate the alternate System file you want to use and then switch-launch to place it in control of the Mac.

 Problem: You've double-clicked another Finder program to open it while the Finder is running. The Mac will only let you run one Finder program at a time. (Under System 7, nothing happens when you try opening a second Finder.)

Solutions:

■ If you want to temporarily change the Finder you're running, you can switch-launch to a different Finder by holding down ⌘ Option while double-clicking the new Finder file.

 If the new Finder you try to run is a much older or much newer version than the corresponding System file, your Mac won't be able to run it. Rather than simply upgrading the Finder, you should upgrade all your system software at the same time.

When you do this, however, the version of the Finder you're trying to launch must be as new as or newer than the one that's currently running.

■ If you want to permanently change the version of the Finder you're running, restart the Mac with a different startup disk. Then drag the old Finder file out of the System Folder on your normal startup disk and replace it with a different version. The next time you start from your normal startup disk, the new version of the Finder will run.

Moving and copying disks, files, and folders

This section covers problems you may have when moving or copying disks, files, or folders in the Finder. If you're having problems copying or moving files to an AppleShare file server (or shared disk or folder under System 7), and your problem isn't explained here, look in Chapter 15.

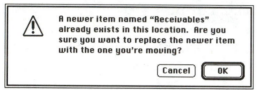

Problem: The Mac displays an alert like this whenever you copy something to a location where an item with the same name already exists. Under System 7, the alert message tells you if the item being replaced is older or newer than the item you're copying, based on the item's modification date and time.

But sometimes the Mac is wrong. Under System 7, information in Finder windows isn't always updated immediately, and you'll get a message like the one above when in fact the item being replaced is older than the one you're moving. For example, suppose you always save your working copy of a document to your hard disk, and then you switch to the Finder and drag a copy of the same document to a backup floppy. Let's suppose you did this yesterday, saving the original document at 3:25 PM and then drag-copying it at 3:26 PM. These modification dates and times are recorded in the Finder window. Now, the next day, you open the working copy of the document, make a few changes to it, save them, and then switch immediately to the Finder and drag the same document to the backup floppy disk. If the Finder hasn't had time to update the modification date on your working copy of the document, it still says 3:25 PM the day before, and an alert appears like the one above, saying that the document you're dragging is older than the one on the backup floppy.

Solution: If you know the Mac is wrong (and the item being replaced is really older than the one you're copying), click the *OK* button and replace the item. If you're not sure whether the item being replaced is older or newer than the one you're copying, click *Cancel* and then check the Date column in a list view window on the desktop. If you suspect that the Finder is just slow about updating window information, close the window and open it again to force an update. If the Date (or Last Modified) column isn't showing, use the Views control panel to display it or select the file or folder you want to know about and choose the *Get Info* command to check the modification date.

Problem: This isn't really a problem. Under System 7, there are folders within the System Folder that contain different types of system software files (see page 13 in Chapter 1).

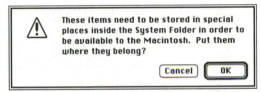

When you copy files to the System Folder by dragging their icons onto the System Folder's icon, the Mac offers to put things in their proper folders and displays an alert like this one. (If you're dragging only one item, it will name a specific item and folder).

Solution: Click *OK* to have the Mac put the files in their correct folders, or click *Cancel* to return to the desktop. If you want to copy items into other areas of the System Folder than the ones they'd normally be stored in, open the System Folder itself and then drag the items where you want them inside its window.

Problem: You're trying to copy files to a disk that's too full to hold them. (The System 6 alert text is a little different.) The alert message tells you exactly how much space you need to free up before making the copy.

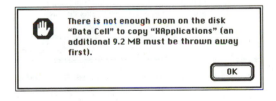

Solution: Either delete some files from the destination disk or copy fewer files to it. By viewing the files on the disk by Name, Kind, Date, or Type, you can see how large each one is and then figure out just how many you need to remove from the destination disk (or from the group you're trying to copy).

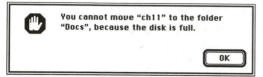

Problem: You're trying to move a file or folder into a different folder on the disk, but the disk is too full to make the change. (The System 6 message doesn't name the item.) When you get this message, a disk generally has no free space available.

Solution: Either forget about moving the file or folder to a new location, or delete one or more items from the disk and then try the move operation again.

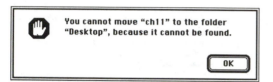

Problem: You've tried to move a file from a disk onto the desktop, but the disk you're moving the file from is too full to record where you're moving it to. Whenever you move an item from a disk to the desktop under System 7, the new location is saved to an invisible folder called *Desktop* on the disk. But if the disk is full, there's no room for the Desktop folder and the Mac has no place to store the item's new location. When that happens, it won't let you move any files to the desktop.

Solution: Delete some items from the disk to free up space, then move the item to the desktop. Or you can copy the item to another disk that does have room on it, and then move it to the desktop from there.

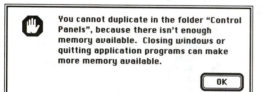

Problem: There's not enough memory available for you to duplicate or copy the selected item. (A similar message says that you can't copy an item.)

Solution: Close some windows, DAs, or programs to free up some memory, then try the operation again. If everything's closed and you still can't duplicate or copy the item, restart the Mac and try again.

Problem: You're trying to copy a file to a disk that is locked. (The System 6 message just says *The disk is locked).*

Solution: Unlock the disk. If it's a floppy disk, eject it and slide the plastic tab on its back away from the edge (so the hole is closed). If it's a hard disk, use its own setup/utility software to unlock it. Then try copying the file again.

Problem: The file or folder you've selected is either locked, busy, or copy-protected. (System 7 doesn't prevent you from duplicating or copying such files.)

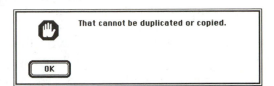

Solutions:

■ If the file or folder you're working with is on a disk inserted in or directly connected to your Mac, it has probably been locked by a program that's using it. Restart the Mac and try copying, duplicating, or moving the file again.

■ If you're working with a folder that's stored on a shared disk on a network, use the *Get Privileges* command to see if the folder is locked. If it is and you're its owner, you can unlock it. If you're not the folder's owner, you'll have to ask the owner to unlock it (see page 229 in Chapter 15).

■ If neither of the above solutions works, try restarting the Mac with another startup disk. It may be that the file is busy because it's being used by a system software file on the first startup disk. If that was the case, you'll be able to copy it now.

■ If that doesn't work, the file has probably been copy-protected by a software vendor. Try using a file-copying utility like Copy II Mac to copy it.

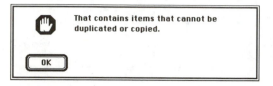

 Problem: You're trying to copy a folder that contains files that are locked, busy, or copy-protected.

Solutions:

■ Copy the files inside the folder one at a time. When you try to copy the locked file, you' get a warning message. The other files are copied properly.

■ To copy the locked file, you first have to close the file or quit the program using it. If you still get the same message, restart the Mac and then try copying the locked file again. Usually this unlocks it. If the file is needed by the System file on your startup disk, however, you'll have to restart using a different startup disk before copying it.

■ If these solutions don't work, the file has been copy-protected by a software vendor. Try using Copy II Mac or another file-copying utility. The utility may be able to overcome the copy-protection scheme. Make sure you can legally copy the file, though.

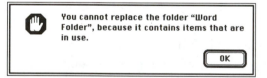 **Problem:** You're trying to completely replace the contents of a disk or folder, but it contains one or more files that are either locked or in use. (The System 6 message is slightly different.) These may be applications, System Folder files, or documents that are currently open.

Solutions:

■ Close any data files and quit any programs you have running and then try the copy operation again.

■ If you get the same alert again, restart the Mac using another startup disk and then try the copy operation. When you start up from another disk, the files in the original System Folder can be replaced because they aren't active anymore.

Problem: You've selected your startup floppy disk as the destination for the contents of another disk by dragging the other disk's icon onto the startup floppy's icon. To make the copy, your

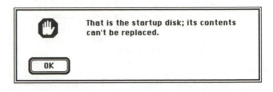

Mac would have to replace the contents of the startup disk from which it's currently running, and since it needs the files on the startup disk to operate, it can't replace them.

Solution: You probably selected the startup disk as your copy destination by mistake. If so, try the copy procedure again with a different disk selected as the destination. If you actually do want to replace the contents of your startup disk, you'll have to restart the Mac with another startup disk first. Then your Mac won't care if you replace the contents of the first startup floppy disk.

 Problem: You've dragged a disk icon onto a folder icon, and the Mac won't let you copy a disk into a folder. (System 7 simply creates a folder for the disk's contents and copies them into it.)

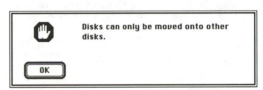

Solutions:

■ To copy the disk onto another disk, drag the icon of the disk you want to copy onto another disk icon. You see a message saying that a folder with the source disk's name will be created on the destination disk, and the contents of the source disk put inside it.

If a disk contains dozens of files, you may not be able to copy them all at one time—you may see a message saying there are too many items to copy. In that case, select smaller groups of files by shift-clicking them.

■ If you really want to copy the disk's contents directly into the folder you've selected, you have to copy the files themselves—rather than the disk icon—into the folder. The fastest way to do this is to open the disk's window so its files are showing, choose *Select All* from the Edit menu to select all the files at once, and then drag the selected files to the destination folder.

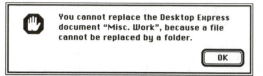

Problem: You've tried to copy an item (a file or folder) to a location that already contains an item with the same name. There are several variations on this text, but they all basically amount to the same thing: the Mac won't allow you to store two items with exactly the same name at the same level of a disk.

Solutions:

Depending on your inclination, you can do one of two things:

- Rename either the item you're trying to copy or the item with the same name in the destination folder.

- Copy the item to a different folder.

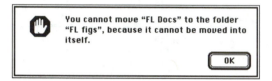

Problem: You've tried to move a folder inside the folder that contains it. This is an illogical operation, and the Mac won't let you complete it. A System 6 variation of this message says *That folder can't replace the folder that contains it.*

Solution: You probably selected the wrong destination by mistake. Just be careful about which folder you select as a destination next time.

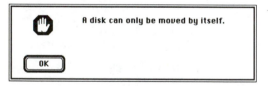

 Problem: You've selected a disk icon and a file or folder icon at the same time and are trying to move, copy, or trash them. You can't work with a disk icon and a folder or document item at the same time under System 6. (System 7 doesn't have this limitation.)

Solution: Select the disk icon by itself and then move it.

Problem: You've selected a group of files or folders and some of them are stored on a different disk than the others. This can happen when you've moved items from two different disks onto the desktop and have selected them there. You can only copy or move items from one disk at a time. (System 7 doesn't have this restriction.)

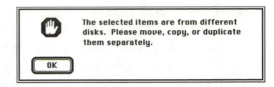

The selected items are from different disks. Please move, copy, or duplicate them separately.

OK

Solution: Copy or move items from different disks separately.

Problem: You've selected such a large group of files to copy or move that the Mac can't keep track of them all at once.

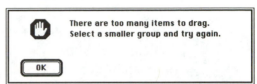

There are too many items to drag. Select a smaller group and try again.

OK

Solution: Select smaller groups of files and drag the smaller groups separately.

Problem: You've tried to copy a large group of files, or a large file by itself, and the Mac couldn't manage it.

The file "Foreign89" couldn't be written and was skipped (unknown error).

Cancel   Continue

Solutions:

■ If you're copying a group of files, click the *Continue* button to give the Mac a chance to copy the rest of the files in the group. You may see the alert message again as the Mac tries and fails to copy other

files in the group. Once the Mac has tried to copy all the files, check the destination disk and see how many were copied, and then try copying the ones that were skipped the first time. If you're copying a particularly large group of files, try copying the files in smaller groups, or remember the names of the files that are being skipped and copy them individually.

■ If you're copying only one file, click the *Cancel* button and then try making the copy again. You may have to try two or three times, but if you persevere, the Mac will finally do it.

■ If these remedies don't work, one of the disks or the file is probably damaged. Try copying the file to a different disk. If that doesn't work, try opening the file with the application that was used to create it. Then use the *Save As* command to save a copy of it to a different disk. If you can't open the file, use a disk repair utility to try salvaging it.

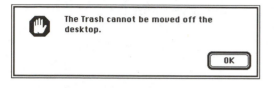

Problem: You've selected the Trash icon and are trying to drag it into a folder or onto a disk. The Mac won't let you duplicate the Trash or move its icon off the desktop. (The System 6 text is a little different.)

If you're using System 7, you can make one or more aliases of the Trash and put the aliases inside other disks or folders.

Solution: Don't try duplicating the Trash or dragging it into any disk or folder. You can move it to different places on the desktop, as long as you aren't moving it into a disk or folder.

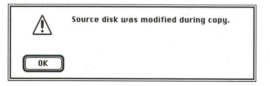

Problem: The disk you're copying from has been modified by a software error during the copying procedure. This isn't a good sign, because it means that one of the files or perhaps the disk directory was damaged.

Solution: Select the files on the source disk one at a time and copy them to another disk. If you get a message that a file can't be read or written, try copying that file again a couple more times. If you still get the message, the file is damaged and can't be copied. In that case, try opening it within its application. If that works, use the program's *Save As* command to save the file to a different disk. If you can't open the problem file with an application, use a disk repair utility to try recovering it and saving it onto another disk. When you've finished copying all the files on the modified source disk, don't use it again, or at least initialize it before you do.

There are extra Temp files on your disk.

Problem: Several applications create temporary files as insurance against power failures and system crashes. Theoretically, you're supposed to be able to open these after a crash or power outage and recover your data. Check your program's manual for information about how to recover data from these files. If you work with lots of different documents during a session, or if you have a lot of system crashes, you may end up with lots of temp files, in which case you can delete them to reduce clutter on your disk.

 Installer programs sometimes create their own temp files during the installation process. Normally these are deleted when you restart your Mac.

Solution: Delete the extra files.

Renaming or erasing disks, files, or folders

This section covers problems you may have when renaming or erasing disks, files, or folders in the Finder. If you're having problems doing these things with files or folders on an AppleShare file server or other shared folder or disk, see Chapter 15.

 Problem: You're trying to rename a file or folder on a disk that's locked. Since the disk is locked, no changes can be made to it. (Under System 7, you can't even select the name of a locked item.)

The file/folder could not be renamed.

OK

Solution: Unlock the disk. If it's a floppy, eject it and slide the plastic tab on its back toward the center of the disk so the hole is covered. (1.44 MB floppy disks have two holes, so the one without the tab always stays open.) If it's a hard disk, unlock it with its setup/utility software.

 You can also use keystrokes to throw away locked files. If you're using System 6, hold down Shift Option ⌘ while selecting and dragging the files to the Trash. If you're using System 7, hold down the Option key while choosing the *Empty Trash* command.

Problem: There are several variations on this message, but they all amount to the same thing: the Mac won't let you throw away an item that's locked or busy. You get such a message when you drag a system software file into the Trash, for example. Under System 7, you can drag such items into the Trash but you can't empty it—you get a message like the one above when you try. Under System 6, you sometimes see an alert as soon as you drag the item to the Trash.

Solutions:

- Click the *Continue* button (or the *OK* button) to delete other items in the Trash, then select the file and choose the *Get Info* command to see if it's locked. If it is, unlock it (see page 35 in Chapter 3). Once the file is unlocked, you can throw it away.

- If the file's information window doesn't show it to be locked, it has probably been locked by a program that's using it. Quit the program, if you know which program it is, then try trashing the file again. If this doesn't work, restart the Mac and try trashing the file again. If that doesn't work, restart with a different startup disk and then try the deletion again.

- If you're working with a folder that's stored on an AppleShare server or other shared disk, use the *Get Privileges* command to view the folder's privileges and see if it's locked. If the folder is locked and you're its owner, you can unlock it. If you're not the folder's owner, you'll have to ask the owner to unlock it. (See *Sharing disks or folders* or *System 6 file sharing* in Chapter 15.)

Problem: You're trying to move or delete a file from a disk that's locked. Since this requires making a change to the disk, you can't do it because the changes can't be recorded on a locked disk.

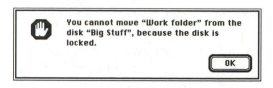

Solution: Unlock the disk. If it's a floppy disk, eject it and slide the plastic tab on its back away from the edge so the hole is closed. If it's a hard disk, use its own setup/utility software to unlock it.

Problem: You're trying to delete a folder from a disk that's very full. Under System 7, the Mac tries to maintain an invisible Trash folder on every disk. When you drag items into the Trash, they're stored in that folder. When the disk nears its capacity, the Mac automatically deletes the Trash folder to give you more file storage space. With the Trash folder gone, there's no place to store items you've dragged into the Trash, and the Mac must delete them immediately.

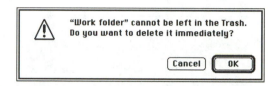

Solution: Either click OK to delete the item immediately or click *Cancel* to take it out of the Trash. If you want to store it in the Trash instead of deleting it right away, you'll have to delete enough items from the disk to make room for a new Trash folder. As you delete the items, you continue to see the above message—you have to keep clicking *OK* to delete them immediately until you no longer see the alert. When you stop getting the alert, the Trash folder has been recreated on the disk and anything you drag there will be stored until you empty it.

 Problem: You're trying to put a folder in the Trash and the folder may contain some invisible files. Your Mac is asking if you want to delete the folder anyway, even though you may be tossing out files you can't see. (System 7 doesn't alert you in this situation.)

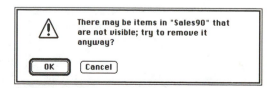

Solution: If you don't mind not knowing what you're throwing away, click the *OK* button. (Sometimes invisible files are locked or in use, though, so they can't be thrown away anyway even if you click *OK*.)

If you want to reconsider, click the *Cancel* button to take the folder back out of the Trash. If you open the folder with a disk diagnostic and repair utility, you'll be able to see any invisible items it contains and decide whether to save them.

 When you want to throw away a folder containing system-related files without seeing the above alert, hold down the [Option] key while selecting the folder and dragging it to the Trash. But remember—you can't ever throw away system files that are in use.

 Problem: You've dragged a folder into the Trash, and the folder contains one or more applications. (You see similar messages when you throw applications or system software files themselves in the Trash.) Under System 6, the Mac always double-checks before letting you throw away applications or system software files. (System 7 doesn't specifically alert you about applications when you drag them to the Trash, and it only warns you about system software files when you try to empty the Trash, not when you put such files in it.)

Solution: If you mean to throw the items away, click *OK*. If you don't want to throw them away, click *Cancel* and then drag them into a different folder before throwing the original folder away.

Using Finder commands

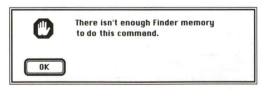

Problem: You have too many applications, DAs, or control panels running, or you have too many windows open on the desktop to allow the Finder to execute the current command. (The System 7 version of this alert tells you what to do about it.)

Solutions:

■ Quit one or more programs or close some windows, and try the command again.

■ If this is a recurring problem and your Mac will run under System 6, you might try assigning more memory to the Finder. Start up your Mac from a System 6 startup disk (like the *Disk Tools* or *Utilities 1* disk in the Installer set), select the Finder on your normal startup disk, and then use the *Get Info* command to give it more memory. (You can't assign more memory to the Finder while you're running under System 7, and some newer Macs won't start up under System 6.)

 Problem: You've tried to rebuild the desktop file on a full, locked, or damaged disk under System 6

The desktop file couldn't be created on the disk "Data Disk".

OK

(the "full disk" and "locked disk" messages are slightly different). The Mac needs to be able to write to the disk in order to rebuild the desktop file. (If you try to rebuild the desktop file on a locked or damaged disk under System 7, you won't see this warning—the disk icon simply appears on the desktop and the desktop file won't be rebuilt. If the disk is full, you'll still be allowed to rebuild the desktop file under System 7, because it always leaves enough room on disks for this.)

Solutions:

■ If the message says the disk is full, delete a file from it and try the procedure again. The desktop file is usually fairly small, so you should only need to delete one file.

■ If the disk is locked, unlock it by sliding the plastic tab away from the disk's edge (floppy disks) or using the hard disk setup software to unlock it.

■ If the disk isn't full or locked, use a disk recovery program to examine and repair the disk.

Problem: You've tried to make an alias, but the disk is locked. The Mac is giving you the option of putting the alias on the desktop.

Solution: Click *OK* to create the alias and have it appear on the desktop. If you want to create the alias on the disk, you'll have to unlock it first.

Problem: You've tried to set a startup application on a disk other than the one you used to start up your Mac. You can only select startup applications from among the programs stored on the startup disk you're currently using.

Solution: Choose a startup application from the current startup disk, or copy the application you want to use onto your startup disk.

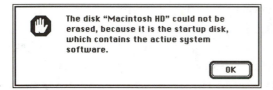

Problem: You've tried to use the Finder's *Erase Disk* command to erase your startup disk. The Mac needs the files on the startup disk to run, so it won't let you erase them.

Solution: You probably selected the startup disk by mistake. If you really do want to erase your startup disk, you'll have to restart the Mac with another disk first.

You're trying to change the icon for a document or folder under System 7, but the Mac won't let you paste the contents of the Clipboard to replace an item's icon.

Problem: You've probably selected a system software document or folder, and you're not allowed to change the icons on these items. Although you can select such an item's icon and copy it, you can't replace the icon.

If you haven't selected a system-related item and the Mac isn't letting you paste in a replacement icon, then you've selected the icon for an item that's currently open. You can't replace the icon of an item when it's open.

Solution: Choose a nonsystem item. If you know you've selected a nonsystem document or folder, make sure the item is closed on the desktop before you try pasting a new icon in its information window. If the item is an application program, you can't replace its icon while the program is running, so you'll have to quit it first.

You have more than 8 MB of RAM installed, but when you choose the _About This Macintosh_ command, it says all the memory above 8 MB is being used by the system software.

Problem: You don't have 32-bit addressing turned on. Without 32-bit addressing on, the Mac can only recognize 8 MB of RAM, and _About This Macintosh_ automatically shows everything over that as belonging to the system software.

Solution: Open the Memory control panel and turn on 32-bit addressing, then restart the Mac.

When you choose the _About This Macintosh_ command, the total of used and unused memory doesn't add up to the total installed in your Mac.

Problem: _About This Macintosh_ shows how much memory is used for the system software and for each application you're running, plus the largest unused memory block. Sometimes the largest unused block of memory is a lot smaller than the total of unused memory, because your unused memory is fragmented into several smaller blocks. On a 5 MB Mac, for example, 3.5 MB might be used by system software and applications, and yet _About This Macintosh_ reports the largest unused memory block as 1 MB or 800K, instead of 1.5 MB.

Solution: Quit all your applications and restart the Mac to defragment the memory.

 The best way to avoid memory fragmentation is to use a "first opened, last quit" approach. When you start working each day, first open the program you use the most—the one you're likely to have running all day—and then open any others after that. When you quit programs, quit first from the ones you opened the most recently.

The Mac beeps when you choose the *Find* command and click the *Find* button.

Problem: Either you haven't entered any find criteria, or the Mac has already found all the items matching your criteria. When you enter a name or other information for the Mac to search for, it finds all the items on your disk or disks that match those criteria, one item at a time. Once it's found the last item that matches your criteria, the Mac beeps if you click the *Find* button again.

Chapter 12
Running Programs, DAs, and Control Panels

This chapter covers problems you may have while running applications, DAs, or (under System 7) control panel programs. Obviously, special problems can crop up with each specific program (we'll cover the most popular programs in Part 4), but this chapter deals with problems that can occur with any program (other than the Finder or MultiFinder).

A DA name doesn't appear on the menu.

Problem: The DA names that appear on your menu are determined either by the contents of the System Folder you started up with or by the current settings in a resource manager program like Suitcase II or MasterJuggler. Either the DA isn't installed properly, the DA file is corrupted, or the DA file hasn't been opened by a resource manager program (if you're using one).

Solutions:

- If you started up from a different disk than usual, restart your Mac with your regular startup disk. The DA you want should appear on the menu. If not, try the appropriate solution below.

- If you're running System 7 and have started up from the disk you normally use, copy or move the DA program (or an alias for it) into the Apple Menu Items folder inside your System Folder. As soon as the DA or its alias is inside that folder, the DA name appears on the menu. If you're using a resource manager program, use it to locate the DA file and open it.

181

If you're not sure whether you're using a resource manager, look for the name Suitcase, Suitcase II, or MasterJuggler on the menu. If one of these doesn't appear, you don't have a resource manager installed in your system.

 If you're running System 6 and have started up from the disk you normally use, locate the DA file you want to use and then either install it with the Font/DA Mover or open it with a resource manager program.

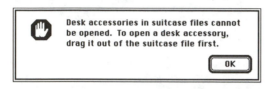

Problem: You're trying to open a DA by going into its suitcase file and double-clicking it, but under System 7, DAs must be taken out of their suitcases before you can use them.

Solution: When you double-click a suitcase file to open it, you see the DA file itself inside the suitcase file's window. To open the DA file, drag it outside the suitcase' window, then double-click it.

Problem: If you get this nasty message as you try to open a DA, it's probably because there are too many other files or DAs open, and the Mac is having trouble managing all those different items in its memory. (This happens most often on Macs with only 1 megabyte of memory.)

If you get the message while using a control panel or application, it's probably just a temporary glitch, possibly having to do with the order in which programs were opened (if you're running more than one at a time).

Another possible cause is trying to run Mac II class software on a Mac Plus or lesser model. This message may include other text, such as *Illegal instruction* or *Unimplemented core routine*.

Solutions:

■ Click the *Restart* button to restart your Mac, then try opening the program again. Unfortunately, you'll have lost any unsaved changes you made to files that were open at the time of the system crash.

■ If the program still won't load, check the manual for the program's hardware require-ments, and make sure your Mac is capable of running it.

■ If the problem continues, search your hard disk for mul-tiple System files or System Folders. If you find more than one, delete the one that isn't currently in use.

 You can tell which System Folder is in use by displaying your start-up disk's main folder in Icon view: the System Folder that's currently in use has a small Mac icon on it. (For more information, see page 64 in Chapter 4.)

Problem: The applications, DAs, or control panels you have open are taking up so much memory that there isn't enough left to open the DA or control panel you've selected. (The text of this message varies slightly, depending on what type of program you're trying to open and whether you're running System 7 or System 6.)

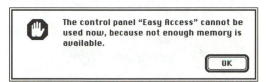

The control panel "Easy Access" cannot be used now, because not enough memory is available.

OK

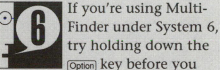 If you're using Multi-Finder under System 6, try holding down the Option key before you choose the DA from the menu. The Mac tries to use memory reserved for applications (instead of for the Finder) to open the DA.

Solutions:

■ If the Clipboard contains a lot of data, it may be using so much RAM that there isn't enough left for your program. Select a single character from an open document and copy it to the Clipboard twice (once to copy it, a second time to clear the Undo buffer of the stuff copied previously). This clears the Clipboard of the large amount of data and may free up enough RAM for you to run the program.

■ If the above solution doesn't work or doesn't apply to you, close one or more applications, windows, DAs, or control panels and try again until the program you want opens successfully.

■ If all else fails, restart the Mac and then open the item you want.

The Mac beeps when you try to open a DA or cdev under System 6.

Problem: The DA Handler file is missing from your System Folder, or it's corrupted.

Solution: Find the DA Handler file on your set of system software installation floppies and drag it to your System Folder; or replace the system software.

A control panel program or cdev isn't working properly—it won't retain its settings after a restart, you can't choose some settings, or option names are garbled.

 If you're using System 6, throw away the Control Panel DA and replace it with a new copy.

Problem: Either a system software file is locked, you have an incompatible extension, the control panel program is corrupted, or your Mac's battery is dead.

Solutions:

■ If you're getting a "write permissions" system error (-61) when you try to use the control panel, it means that one of your Mac's system software files is locked. Open the System Folder and use the *Get Info* command to see which of the files in it are locked and unlock them (see page 35).

■ Try turning off all your extensions and see if the control panel program works (see page 110). If it does, you have an incompatible extension.

■ If the control panel program or cdev still doesn't work, throw it away and replace it with a new copy.

■ If the problem relates to a Control Panel or cdev not retaining settings after shutdown (mouse settings, sound volume, or dates, for example), take your Mac to a technician and have the battery replaced.

■ If the problem persists, replace your system software (see page 112).

The General Controls control panel or Control Panel DA shows the current date as January 1, 1904. Even though you reset it, this date shows again each time you start up.

Problem: Your Mac's battery is dead or dying.

Solution: Take the Mac to a technician and have the battery replaced.

Problem: You've tried to open an application or a file, but there isn't as much memory available as the application or file normally needs to run. The Mac offers to try opening the program with less memory.

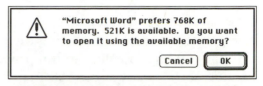

"Microsoft Word" prefers 768K of memory. 521K is available. Do you want to open it using the available memory?

Cancel   OK

Solution: The solution depends on whether you're running multiple programs or not.

If you try loading a program using less memory than it normally uses, the program may end up quitting unexpectedly some time later.

- If you're running multiple programs under System 7 or with MultiFinder under System 6, click the *Cancel* button, quit another program you have running, and then launch the program or open the file you originally wanted. If this doesn't work, you may need to quit all the programs you have running, restart the Mac, and then load the program you want. (Your Mac's memory may have become too fragmented to assemble a large enough block of RAM to store the program you want, even though there should theoretically be enough RAM available.)

- If your Mac has only 1 MB of RAM and you're trying to load just one program under MultiFinder, use the *Set Startup* command on the Special menu to restart with the Finder running, and then try loading the program. (MultiFinder itself takes up extra RAM; using the Finder instead may free up enough memory to run your program normally.)

- If you're not running multiple programs, your Mac's memory is being used up by your system software, or else the program you ran before hasn't been completely cleared from memory. This usually happens on Macs running System 6 with 1 MB of RAM or on Macs running System 7 with 2 MB of RAM. Try restarting the Mac and then loading the program you're trying to use. If this doesn't work, you can try reducing the size of the System file (see page 66). The best long-term solution is to expand your Mac's RAM.

The program quits or the Mac restarts itself spontaneously while you're working.

Problem: If too many programs, files, and DAs are open at the same time, the Mac may have trouble managing them in its memory, or the System file may not have enough memory to run properly. Both problems can result in a spontaneous restart, or the Mac may display an alert message saying that the program has unexpectedly quit.

Two other explanations for this problem, although far less likely, are a virus or a defective or failing power supply in your Mac.

Solutions:

■ Try running your Mac with fewer applications, DAs, or control panels open at once. If the problem goes away, you can be sure that memory usage was the problem.

Use the Font/DA Mover to remove any DAs or fonts you don't use regularly, or remove your DAs and fonts from the System file and run them using a DA management program like Suitcase II or MasterJuggler. If the problem continues, check to see how many inits are loading when you start up your Mac. If you have too many of them loading at once, they can cause your Mac to run low on memory. Try dragging some of the larger ones outside of the System Folder (or turning them off with an extension manager program—see Chapter 6), and then restart the Mac. If the problem goes away, you may have to live with fewer inits, increase your System heap with a utility like HeapFixer, or add more RAM to your Mac.

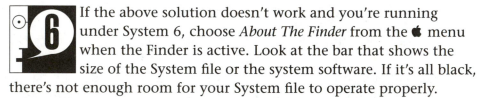 If the above solution doesn't work and you're running under System 6, choose *About The Finder* from the menu when the Finder is active. Look at the bar that shows the size of the System file or the system software. If it's all black, there's not enough room for your System file to operate properly.

■ If the problem only occurs with a specific combination of programs, they may be incompatible with one another. Try running the programs one at a time. If the problem occurs while one of them is running, try reinstalling it from its master disk, or ask the manufacturer if it needs to be upgraded for the version of system software you're using.

■ Run a virus detection and repair program to check for viruses.

■ As a last resort, try replacing the system software (see page 112). You may have a defective System file.

■ If, after trying all these remedies, the problem continues, you probably have a bad power supply. Take the Mac in for repairs.

Problem: Your Mac is having a temporary problem. It's usually an isolated event.

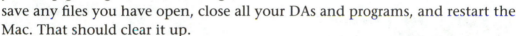

Solution: Try the operation again. If you keep getting the same message, save any files you have open, close all your DAs and programs, and restart the Mac. That should clear it up.

Problem: The Mac is having a memory management problem that's preventing it from reading the Clipboard file. Usually this problem is caused by having too many programs, DAs, or control panels open. More often than not, the contents of the Clipboard will be lost.

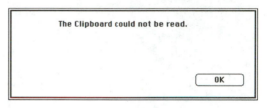

Solution: Close all the applications, DAs and control panels you have open. Then reopen the programs and documents you were using to copy and paste the data, and try it again. If that doesn't work, restart the Mac and try again.

A directory dialog box appears instead of the DA screen when you choose the DA name.

Problem: Some DAs need data storage files to work. If you choose a DA you've just installed, or if you've moved the data file, the DA displays a dialog box like this so you can find the data file and open it.

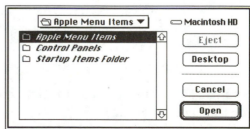

Solution: Use the dialog box to locate the DA's data file, then click the *Open* button. If you can't remember the name of the data file, try files with names similar to the DA itself. For example, choosing a file named Scrapbook or New Scrapbook would be a good bet if you're using the SmartScrap DA. If you're using WordFinder, it would make sense to look for a thesaurus file. Don't be afraid to guess—if you're wrong, the DA simply won't open the file.

You're trying to open a different DA storage file, but you can't open it; or when you do, it doesn't open in the format you're used to seeing it in.

 Problem: You're probably using the wrong *Open* command to open the DA file. Because DAs run at the same time as other programs, other program menus are still on the screen when you're working with them. (Under System 7, DA menus appear by themselves,

because DAs work just like standard applications.) If the DA has file management commands of its own, they're located on a separate menu like the one in the illustration at left.

The commands shown on this menu have nothing to do with the commands on the File menu, which belong to another application.

Solution: Make sure you use the *Open* command on the DA's menu to open files for that DA.

You made changes to a DA's storage file and you thought you saved them, but the changes weren't saved.

 Problem: You probably used the wrong *Save* command to save the changes. Because DAs run at the same time as other programs, other program menus are still on the screen when you're working with the DA. See the previous problem description for further discussion.

Solution: Make sure you use the *Save* command on the DA's menu to save files for that DA.

Problem: These messages nearly always occur when you don't have enough application memory specified for the program you have open, or when the

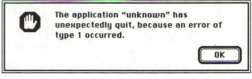

Mac is having trouble managing its memory. (The System 6 message says *unknown error*.)

Solutions:

- If you're running the program under System 7 or under MultiFinder in System 6, click the OK button and then use the *Get Info* command to make the application memory size or current memory size at least 128K larger than it is now (see page 35).

- If that doesn't work, or if you're not running multiple programs, restart the Mac and then run the program again. If it's a temporary problem, that should clear it up.

- Try reinstalling the application from its original program disks.

- If that doesn't do the trick, try replacing the system software (see page 112).

- If this doesn't fix things, call the program's publisher for technical support.

You expect to see a file name in the list that appears when you use a program's *Open* command, but the name isn't there.

Problem: Either you're looking in the wrong folder or on the wrong disk, or the file isn't the program's standard type. When you use the *Open* command with some applications or DAs, you're only able to see the files that were created by that particular program, or that have compatible formats, even though there may be other files inside the folder. To see other files that can be imported, you may have to select an *Import* or *All Files* option or use a separate *Import* command.

Solutions:

- Check the disk name at the right of the dialog box. If you have the wrong disk selected, click the *Desktop* or *Drive* button or insert a different floppy disk.

■ Check the folder name above the list of files to see if you're looking in the right folder. If you're in the wrong folder and you can't remember the name or location of the folder you need to look in, use the *Find* command (in System 7) or a file-finding DA like *Find File* to locate the file you want.

■ If you know you're looking in the right folder and disk, the file may not be the program's standard type. If the dialog box has an option called *All Files, Import,* or something similar, select it. If there's no such option, click *Cancel* and then look for an *Import* command on the program's File menu. You should see a list of files you can import that includes the name of the file you need. If the file name doesn't appear, it can't be opened with the program you're using.

You get an error message when you try to save a file.

Problem: Different programs display different error messages when there's a problem saving a file. The file could be damaged, the disk may be full, or there may be a temporary glitch with the program itself. Whatever the problem is, there are a few basic remedies to try when you run into a file-saving problem.

Solutions:

■ Try the save operation a couple more times. It may be a temporary glitch.

■ If the problem continues, check to see whether the disk to which you're saving is full. In some programs, the amount of available disk space is shown right underneath the disk name in the dialog box that appears when you choose the *Save As* command. If the disk is full, you obviously need to save the file to a different disk or delete some unneeded files from the current disk to make room.

■ If the disk isn't full, try saving the file under a different name—this will create a new copy of the file. If this remedy works, the original file is probably corrupted and you should delete it from the disk after saving the new copy.

■ If none of these remedies works, check your disk for viruses.

■ Reinstall the program. The program itself may be corrupted.

■ Try saving a file from a different program. If you have a problem with it too, check your SCSI chain (see page 111).

When you save new documents, they always end up in the same folder where the application is located.

Problem: The Mac defaults to the folder from which you last opened an application.

Solution: If you're using System 7 and want to save documents to a particular folder most of the time, put the real program in that folder and make aliases and put them in other folders where you'd normally look for the program itself to launch it. For example, many people keep all their applications in a folder called Applications. If you do this, however, the Mac will default to the Applications folder when you save new documents, and you'll have to navigate to a different folder to save documents elsewhere. Now, suppose you always use Excel to work with documents stored in a folder called Budgets. To avoid having to navigate out of the Applications folder and into the Budgets folder when you save each new document, store Excel in the Budgets folder and put an alias for it in the Applications folder. Then you can launch Excel from the Applications folder just like any of your other programs, but since the real program is located in (and launched from) the Budgets folder, all new documents will automatically be saved there.

A program seems to run more slowly than usual.

Problem: The Mac may be handling a lot of different tasks (such as running other programs or sharing files) and can't devote as much time as usual to running your program. Another possibility is that the program has become fragmented in memory so it's taking longer for the Mac to locate and execute certain program instructions.

Solutions:

■ If you have file sharing on and lots of other users are accessing files on your disk, ask them to copy the files to their own disks. As long as a user has a file open from your disk, your Mac has to devote some of its energy to supporting that open file. Once a file is copied to another user's disk, the file-sharing task is done.

■ If you're running several other programs and you don't need to have them running, quit them. If you must have other programs running and you're doing background tasks like transferring files, sorting databases, or recalculating spreadsheets, you have to expect a performance slowdown.

- Try turning off all your extensions or inits and running the program. If you have lots of extensions running, they may be slowing down your Mac.

- If you've opened and closed several other programs, control panels, or DAs during the current session with your Mac, or if you've copied a particularly large selection to the Clipboard, your program may have become fragmented. Try selecting one or two characters and copying them twice. If this doesn't help, save your documents, quit the program, and launch it again. If that doesn't help, restart the Mac and then launch the program again.

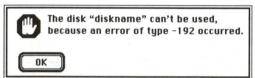

Problem: Your Mac displays this message when you quit any program. Your hard disk driver or directory is corrupted.

Solution: Run a disk diagnostic program and check for directory damage. If this doesn't solve the problem, update the hard disk driver.

Your Mac displays an "illegal instruction" or "unimplemented core routine" error message when you try to launch a program.

Problem: You're probably trying to launch a program that wasn't designed to run on your model Macintosh.

Solution: Check the program's manual to see if the program was designed to run on your Mac, or call the manufacturer to find out if you can switch to a version that you can run.

Your Mac displays a system error -90 when you try to run a program.

Problem: The program expects to find a floating point processor in your Mac, and your Mac doesn't have one.

Solutions:

- Run the program on a Mac that has a math coprocessor, or is based on the 68030 or 68040 chip.

- Check with your local user group or the Macintosh software library on an online service like CompuServe or America OnLine for a program called SoftFPU, then install it on your Mac. This program simulates the presence of a floating point processor.

Chapter 13

QuickTime, Video, and Sound Problems

This chapter covers general problems you may have with the Mac's visual and audio display software. (Not all problems are software related, however. You'll find some CPU- and monitor-specific hardware problems in Part 3.)

Before we get into the problems, however, let's take a quick look at the way the Mac handles QuickTime, video, and sound information.

About QuickTime

QuickTime is an extension to Macintosh system software that allows you to manage and play time-based information. (Time-based information can be sounds, animated sequences, or movies, but for the sake of simplicity, we'll refer to QuickTime files as movies.) With QuickTime installed, you can play movies in a small window on your screen, and you can also copy and paste movies or frames from movies just as you would text or graphics.

In order to use QuickTime, you must be using a Mac with a 68020 or newer processor with at least 4 MB of RAM and System 6.0.7 or later. You must also have the QuickTime extension installed in your Extensions folder. (If you're using system software version 6.0.7, you put QuickTime in the System Folder and must also install the 32-bit QuickDraw file from inside the Apple Color folder on the Printing Tools disk that came with your set of installation floppies.)

If your set of system software installation floppies doesn't include the QuickTime extension, you'll have to obtain it separately from your Apple dealer.

Because they incorporate sounds, images, and motion, movie files tend to be huge. It's not at all uncommon for a QuickTime movie to be 5 MB or larger. There are three basic ways QuickTime manages large files:

1. QuickTime movies are displayed as small images: a movie is only about 2 inches square on your screen, and you usually can't resize it.

2. QuickTime incorporates automatic data compression, so files are stored in less space on your disk. When you play a QuickTime movie, QuickTime automatically decompresses the data so it can be played and viewed properly.

3. QuickTime uses pointers. When you paste a QuickTime movie into a document, you paste only a copy of the movie's first frame and an invisible pointer that tells the Mac where the actual movie file is located. When you click a movie to activate it, the Mac finds the actual file, decompresses it, and plays it.

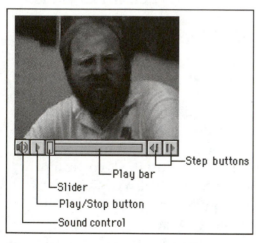

Playing movies

When you have QuickTime installed and you select a QuickTime movie, a set of controls appears below it, as in the figure at left.

The controls work like the buttons on a tape recorder, allowing you to play, stop, advance, and rewind the movie. You can advance the movie a frame at a time by clicking the step buttons, or you can drag the slider to advance proportionally through the whole movie. When you click the sound control at the left, a slider appears like the one in the Sound control panel, which you can drag up or down to change the sound volume.

Each movie is made up of individual frames, and along with selecting or playing a whole movie, you can also select individual frames or groups of frames and copy them elsewhere.

This brief introduction to QuickTime covers only the basics. To learn more, consult your QuickTime user's guide.

About video

Different Macs support video differently. The Mac Plus, SE, and Classic support only black-and-white video (except for the new Color Classic), while the LC and other Mac II-class machines support color. Although you can buy an external video adapter for monochrome machines like the Plus and SE so you can plug in a larger external monitor, any monitor you plug in will still display only black-and-white images.

Color Macs, on the other hand, can display different colors or shades of gray. The number of colors or gray shades a Mac can display depends on its own video capabilities. Macs can display 4, 16, 256, 32,768, or 16.7 million different colors, depending on your video circuitry.

Built-in video versus video expansion cards

Color Macs are divided into two classes: those that have built-in video support and those that require video expansion cards. Machines that have built-in video (such as the IIci, IIsi, IIvx, LC, PowerBook, Centris, and Quadra) can display video right out of the box. To use a monitor, you simply plug it into a port on the back of the Mac. Depending on the machine, the amount of RAM installed, and the monitor you're using, these Macs can display from 16 colors to 16.7 million colors on the screen at once, and you can add more RAM or video RAM (VRAM—pronounced V-RAM) to support more colors if you like.

If a Mac model doesn't support built-in video, you must plug a video expansion card into a slot inside it, and then connect a monitor cable to a port on the video card that sticks out of the Mac's back panel. These machines include the Mac II, IIcx, IIx, and IIfx. Video expansion cards can support either 256 colors or up to 16.7 million colors, depending on the card.

Built-in color video is less hassle to use, but on some Macs, displaying more colors can reduce the memory you have available for running programs. Here's the deal:

■ If you use a video expansion card, the card itself contains its own memory, so displaying more colors doesn't affect your available RAM.

■ If you use a Mac LC, IIvx, Centris, or Quadra, the Mac has separate VRAM to support the video output. Application and system software is kept in regular RAM and isn't affected by the number of colors you display.

Most Macs that support built-in video can also accept video expansion cards. For example, you could use the built-in video to drive one monitor and add an expansion card to support a second monitor.

■ On a Mac IIsi or IIci, however, the built-in video runs in a portion of the Mac's regular RAM. The more colors or gray shades you display, the less RAM you have left for running your programs. Displaying 256 colors requires over 300K of RAM, for example, while displaying 16 colors requires only about 64K of RAM.

Selecting colors and monitors

On color Macs, you use the Monitors control panel to select color or monochrome video output, and to choose the number of colors or gray shades you want the Mac to display. The Monitors control panel determines what type of video support your Mac and monitor can provide, and then displays appropriate options. (If your monitor can't display more than 16 different colors or gray shades, for example, you won't have a 256-color option.)

If you have more than one monitor connected to your Mac, you also use the Monitors control panel to select the startup monitor. The startup monitor is the one with the menu bar icon on it in the Monitors control panel, and you can change startup monitors by dragging the menu bar from one monitor icon to another (see Chapter 3).

If you use a third-party monitor, it may also have come with a control panel program or system extension that gives you additional video configuration options.

About sound

As discussed in Chapters 1 through 3, sounds are stored in the System file, and the Sound control panel lets you select which beep sound you want for your Mac and how loud it plays.

If you have a Mac IIsi, LC, or another model that has a sound input port, you can connect a microphone to the Mac and use the Sound control panel to record new sounds of your own and add them to the System file.

If your Mac doesn't support built-in sound recording, you can buy a MacRecorder from Macromedia in San Francisco and connect it to another port on your Mac.

Now that we've taken a quick tour of the Mac's video and sound capabilities, let's look at some common problems you may run into.

QuickTime problems

You click a QuickTime movie but the controls don't appear.

Problem: You don't have QuickTime installed on your Mac, or the item you're clicking isn't really a QuickTime movie.

Solution:

■ Check inside your Extensions folder to see if the QuickTime extension is there. If you just dragged the extension there, you need to restart your Mac to activate it.

■ If the QuickTime extension is installed and active, then the item you've clicked isn't really a QuickTime movie. If the item was copied from a Mac that doesn't support QuickTime, the Mac only copied a graphical representation of the movie's first frame, not the pointer QuickTime needs to locate the movie itself. You'll have to find the movie and copy it again.

You click a QuickTime movie and a message asks you to insert a disk or says the movie can't be found.

Problem: The movie file for the item you're clicking is no longer on a disk available to your Mac. It may have been deleted or renamed.

Solution: If you know which disk contains the movie you're trying to play, insert it. Otherwise, you're out of luck.

A movie plays jerkily, the sound is distorted, or there are gaps in the sound.

Problem: This is a very common problem with QuickTime, and it varies with the specific content of each movie. Because there's so much data contained in a movie, your Mac may simply not be able to play it back smoothly. The problem may be your Mac's processing speed, the speed of the disk from which the movie is being read, the version of QuickTime you're running, or the movie's contents.

Solutions:

- Make sure you're running the latest version of QuickTime (1.6 at this writing). Newer versions are significantly faster than older ones and also use less memory.

- If you're playing the movie from a CD-ROM disk, try copying the movie to your Mac's hard disk. The hard disk's faster access time may make enough of a difference to eliminate the jerkiness or distortion.

- Upgrade your Mac with a QuickTime accelerator card (check a Mac magazine for different products), or play the movie on a faster Mac model.

Video problems

You want your Mac to display color and it's only displaying black and white.

Problem: Either your Mac or your monitor is incapable of displaying color, or you have the Monitors control panel set wrong.

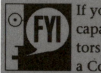 If you're using a color-capable Mac, the Monitors control panel shows a Colors option even if you're not using a color monitor.

Solutions:

- Open the Monitors control panel and click the Colors button. (There won't be a Colors button if your Mac can't display color.)

- Make sure you're using a color monitor, rather than a grayscale or monochrome one.

The Monitors control panel only has options to display 4 or 16 colors, and you'd like to display 256, 32,768, or 16.7 million colors.

Problem: Your Mac isn't set to display more than 16 colors, or it isn't capable of displaying more than that.

Solutions:

- Open the Monitors control panel or cdev and see if there are options to display more than 16 colors. If so, click the one you want.

■ If there are no options to display more than 16 colors in the Monitors control panel, then your Mac can't currently display more than this many colors. If you're using a Mac that has built-in video, you may not have enough VRAM installed to support more than 16 colors on the monitor you're using, or you haven't assigned enough of your regular RAM to support more than 16 colors. If you own a Mac IIci or IIsi, open the Monitors control panel, click the Options button, and then click the button to assign more RAM to the video functions. If you're not using a Mac IIci or IIsi, you should be able to add more VRAM to the Mac so it will support more colors.

■ If you know your Mac can display more colors and you still can't find the option you need, try zapping the PRAM (see page 115). If this doesn't work, try restarting from another disk. If you can see the color option when you start up from a different disk, replace the system software on your normal startup disk.

■ If none of the above solutions works, take your Mac in for service.

You've connected an external (or second external) monitor to your Mac, but you can't move the mouse pointer to the new monitor, or the menu bar and other desktop features still show up on the original monitor.

Problem: You need to install the new monitor in the Monitors control panel, or reset the startup monitor.

Solutions:

■ To install the second monitor, open the Monitors control panel and click the icon for the monitor you've just installed (it should have a 2 on it if it's the second monitor). Then restart the Mac. You should now be able to move the pointer to it or drag windows onto it.

■ To make the menu bar appear on the second monitor, open the Monitors control panel and drag the menu bar from the monitor it's currently on to the other monitor icon, then close the control panel and restart the Mac. The menu bar and other desktop elements should now be on the second monitor.

Window or dialog box colors seem to change randomly as you use different programs.

Problem: Either an application or control panel program is changing your system's color settings, or the color table resource in your system is corrupted.

Solutions:

■ If you're using a desktop customizing control panel program like Kolor (which allows you to customize the colors of window titles, scroll bars, and other desktop elements), try turning it off. It may be conflicting with color settings in the applications you run.

■ If the colors change in one particular application, check with the manufacturer to see if there's a newer version of the program.

■ Reinstall your system software. The color table may be corrupted.

■ If none of the above solutions works, take the Mac in for service.

Sound problems

There's no sound coming out of your Mac's speaker.

Problem: You probably have the sound level set at zero in the Sound control panel, or a speaker wire is disconnected or corroded.

Solutions:

■ Open the Sound control panel and drag the slider up from the zero setting. If the control panel is already set to a value other than zero, try increasing the volume. If that doesn't work, try selecting a different sound.

■ If the above solution doesn't work, try replacing the system software (see page 112 in Chapter 7). The Sound control panel you have installed may be corrupted.

■ If none of the above solutions works, your Mac's speaker wire may be disconnected. (This is particularly likely if you have a Mac Plus or other compact Mac and this problem occurs just after you've had the Mac opened up.) If you have a Mac II model, you can open up the lid and check the speaker connections. If you don't have a Mac II model or you're skittish about doing this, take the Mac to a technician for a diagnosis.

The sound volume on your Mac is low, even though you have it turned up in the Sound control panel.

Problem: Your Sound control panel or the Mac's PRAM is corrupted.

Solutions:

- Zap the PRAM (see page 115 in Chapter 7). If this doesn't solve the problem, replace the Sound control panel.

- If neither of these solutions works, replace the system software.

You want to select a particular sound but its name doesn't appear in the Sound control panel.

Problem: The sound isn't installed in your System file.

Solutions:

- If you're using System 7, locate a copy of the sound file and drag it inside the System file's window, then restart your Mac.

- If you're using System 6 or earlier, use a sound management utility to install the sound.

You've chosen a particular sound in the Sound control panel, but the sound doesn't play, it doesn't play properly, or a different sound plays.

Problem: The sound resource is corrupted.

Solutions:

- Replace the sound file with a fresh copy.

- If this doesn't solve the problem, or if the problem recurs, replace the Sound control panel itself.

- If the sound still doesn't play properly, replace the system software.

Sounds don't play smoothly no matter which sound is selected.

Problem: An extension or cdev is probably interfering with the sound functions on your Mac. Extensions that deal with the clock or timing functions of your Mac, such as menu clocks, sound management programs, appointment reminder programs, and the like can interrupt sound playback.

Solution:

■ Turn off any extensions that use your Mac's clock. If you don't know which ones these are, turn off all your extensions and then turn them on one at a time until the problem recurs (see page 110).

■ If turning off all your extensions doesn't solve the problem, replace your system software (see page 112).

Chapter 14

Printing and Font Problems

Printing from a Macintosh can be a complex affair, especially if you're using a program that produces PostScript files or combines PostScript commands with standard text. Printing with non-Apple printers has its own problems as well. This chapter will get you through most of the printing problems associated with basic business applications. If you're having printing problems with a particular program or printer, check Parts 3 and 4 of this book, or get help from the program's publisher or the company that made the printer.

This chapter covers problems related to selecting printers with the Chooser and viewing or printing fonts. Before we get into them, however, let's take a quick look at how you spot problems when you're using PrintMonitor.

Spotting PrintMonitor problems

PrintMonitor only works with printers that use one of the LaserWriter printer drivers or a recent version of the StyleWriter driver. If you're using an ImageWriter, you should skip this section.

Many of the errors discussed in this chapter appear as alert messages, but if you're running PrintMonitor you may not see the messages right away.

If you've never changed PrintMonitor's preferences and you're using System 7, the Mac notifies you that there's a printing problem and asks you to switch to the PrintMonitor program's window. Once the PrintMonitor window is showing, you see a message that tells you the specific problem.

Using PrintMonitor's preferences settings, you can have the program simply flash its icon in the menu bar to notify you of a problem. If you've set that preference, you won't see an error message until you choose Print-Monitor from the Application menu (or the menu, under System 6).

To change PrintMonitor's preferences, double-click the PrintMonitor icon in the Extensions folder (or the System Folder, under System 6) to open the program, and then choose *Preferences* from the File menu. You see a dialog box like the one above.

By clicking buttons in this dialog box, you can choose whether or not to have the PrintMonitor window show immediately when you print something. You can also choose the method PrintMonitor will use to notify you of problems and decide to have it remind you to insert a sheet of paper when you choose a manual feed printing job.

Now let's get onto some specific printing problems.

Printer access and Chooser problems

Nothing happens when you try to print a document.

> ✋ Can't open printer.
>
> [OK]

Problem: You may or may not see this alert message, but in any case you don't get any results when you try to print a document. Either the printer driver you need isn't installed, the printer isn't ready to print, you haven't chosen a printer driver for the Mac to use, or you've selected the wrong printer port.

Solutions: Choose *Chooser* from the menu and see if there's an icon for the printer you want to use.

■ If there's no icon, you need to install the driver for your printer. Close the Chooser window and see the instructions in the next section, *The printer icon doesn't appear in the Chooser window.*

- If the printer icon appears in the Chooser window, click it and then (if necessary) select the specific printer of that type (see page 42 for more information).

- If you can see the printer icon and the above solution doesn't work, make sure the printer is on and that its Select or Ready light is lit.

- If the printer is on and ready, make sure you have paper inserted in the manual feed tray if you've chosen the *Manual Feed* option in the Print dialog box. If you choose the *Manual Feed* option and there's no paper in the manual feed tray, the printer waits about a minute for you to insert paper, and then gives up.

- Try replacing the printer driver.

- Replace the system software.

- If none of the above solves the problem, call the printer manufacturer's technical support line.

The printer icon doesn't appear in the Chooser window.

Problem: The Chooser extension that produces the icon isn't installed.

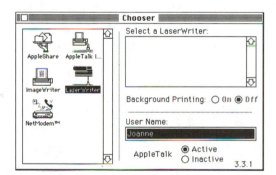

Solution: Close the Chooser window and quit any programs you have running to return to the Finder.

- If you're using a non-Apple printer, locate the disk that contains the printer driver and drag the driver file (or files) onto the System Folder icon on your startup disk. (If you're running under System 7, you see a message asking if you want the items placed in the right folder; click the *OK* button.) The driver then appears in the Chooser window and you can select it there.

- If you're using an Apple printer, use the Installer to install the printer software. Start up the Installer program, then click the *Customize* button on the main Installer screen. Choose the printer software option from the list of items you can install, then click the *Install* button.

Once the installation is complete, quit the Installer and select the correct printer in the Chooser. (If you're not sure how to do this, see page 42.)

You've selected a printer icon in the Chooser window, but the name of the printer you want doesn't appear.

Problem: You've tried to select a printer by clicking its icon in the Chooser, but its name doesn't appear in the list of printers at the right. There are four possible problems:

- The printer isn't turned on or ready.

- The printer or your Mac has become unplugged from the network.

- There's some network interference that's preventing your Mac from "seeing" that printer on the network.

- There's something wrong with the printer's internal electronics.

Solutions:

- Make sure the printer is turned on and warmed up. If a laser printer was in the process of starting up, it might not have warmed up in time to appear on the network as a working printer at the time you opened the Chooser. Once the printer is initialized (the Ready light stops flashing and stays lit), you can print your file.

- If the printer is on and ready, check the network cable at the back of the printer and the one plugged into the Mac's printer port to make sure they're plugged in firmly. If the network cable on your Mac is plugged into the phone port, move it to the printer port and make sure the *AppleTalk Active* button is selected in the Chooser window.

- If you're still having the problem, try selecting and using a different network device. If you can, then there's something wrong with the connection between your Mac and that particular printer, or with the printer itself. If you can't select any network devices, the problem may be with your network connection cable. Try using a different network connection cable.

- If there are several other network devices (like printers or modems) plugged into the same branch of the network as the printer you want to use, heavy use on one of them may be blocking the signals that have to travel from your Mac to the printer. This is especially a problem with network modems, because using them involves transferring a lot of data over the network.

 A network troubleshooting program can help you detect traffic problems on your network and figure out how to solve them. See Chapter 6.

■ If a network modem or other device is daisy-chained to the same network interface as your printer, try turning it off and selecting the printer again. If the printer appears in the Chooser, select it again and try printing again. If this works, the other device is the culprit, and you'll have to move it to a different network location. If this doesn't work, try moving the printer itself to a different network location.

■ If none of the above remedies works, there's something wrong with your printer. Try restarting it. If that doesn't clear up the problem, call its manufacturer. You may need to take it in for repairs.

Problem: Your Mac is expecting to print your file on a printer that's been selected with the Chooser, but the printer can't be found on the network, or it's not responding as the type of printer you selected. (The message text varies.) There are five possible causes for this:

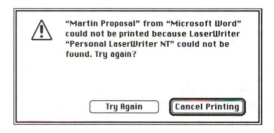

■ You've selected the wrong type of printer with the Chooser, so the Mac isn't finding the one you specified.

■ The printer isn't turned on or ready.

■ The printer or your Mac has become unplugged from the network.

■ There's some network interference that's blocking the Mac's electronic access to that printer.

■ There's something wrong with the printer's internal electronics.

Solutions:

■ Click the *Cancel Printing* or *Cancel* button. Then open the Chooser and select the printer driver for the type of printer you're using.

■ Try the other solutions offered for the preceding problem (starting on page 206).

Your document prints on the wrong printer.

Problem: You've selected the wrong printer with the Chooser. Remember, the Chooser indicates which printer will be used for any printing job you send from your Mac, so if you chose a different printer for another program or file you were printing before, that printer will continue to be used for all future print jobs until you select another printer.

Solution: Choose the Chooser from the menu, click the icon representing the type of printer you want to use, and then (if necessary) select the specific printer of that type (if you're on a network and there is more than one printer of that type connected). See page 42 for more information.

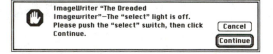

Problem: The printer either isn't connected properly, isn't selected, or isn't turned on.

Solution: Check that the printer is on and has paper in it. Then make sure the printer's Select or Ready light is lit. If the light isn't on, press the Select button on the printer, then click *Continue* to finish printing the file.

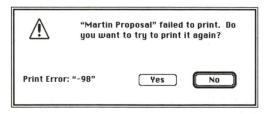

Problem: You're trying to print to a network printer, but you have AppleTalk set to Inactive in the Chooser window. (The System 7 message tells you that this is the problem and what to do about it.)

Solution: Open the Chooser DA and click the *Active* button next to the word *AppleTalk* in the lower right corner. If you don't see these buttons, select the LaserWriter or network printer's icon first to make them appear.

Problem: Someone else on your network is using a different version of the Laser Prep or LaserWriter file than the version you have. (System 7

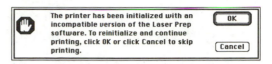

did away with the Laser Prep file.) After a laser printer is turned on, it's initialized by the Laser Prep file or LaserWriter file located on the Mac that first prints to it. From then on, the LaserWriter expects every print job to be sent from a Mac with the same version of the Laser Prep file or LaserWriter driver installed. If your Mac has a different version, you'll be given the above option to reinitialize the printer (which takes a couple of minutes) before the file can be printed.

Solutions:

■ If you're in a hurry, click *OK*. The printer is reinitialized for your version of the Laser Prep file and then your file is printed. But when someone who's using a different version of the Laser Prep file tries to print, they'll get this message too and will have to initialize the printer again.

■ The best solution to this problem is to make sure that everyone on the network is using the same (and preferably the latest) version of the Laser Prep file and/or LaserWriter printer driver. You can find out the version number of each of these files by selecting them one at a time and then using the *Get Info* command on the Finder's file menu. (Under System 7 the files are in the Extensions folder inside the System Folder; under System 6 they're just in the System Folder itself.)

■ Once you've determined which of the Laser Prep and/or LaserWriter files is the newest version on your network, copy that version into the Extensions folder inside the System Folder (under System 7) or into the System Folder (under System 6) on the startup disk of each Mac on the network. Even if two Macs on the network are using different versions of the system software, they can both use the same version of the LaserWriter files.

Problem: Your printer driver, PrintMonitor, or Chooser is not properly selected or is corrupted.

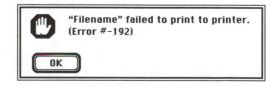

Solutions:

■ Open the Chooser and reselect the printer, then try printing again.

- Throw away the printer driver and install a fresh copy from your system software installation disks.

- If you're using PrintMonitor, throw away the PrintMonitor application from your System Folder or Extensions folder and install a new copy from your system software installation disks.

- Replace your system software entirely.

The laser printer stalls in the *preparing data* sequence.

Problem: You're trying to print to a laser printer, but the *preparing data* message on your screen (or in the PrintMonitor dialog box) doesn't go away. Some print jobs, particularly those that use lots of graphics or different fonts, require several minutes to prepare on a laser printer. But sometimes the printer can become stalled in this sequence.

Solution: Press ⌘ . to cancel the printing job. It will probably take a few minutes. If the job isn't canceled, or if you get impatient, shut off the laser printer, wait one minute, and then turn it on again to clear its memory buffer. Then press ⌘ . again. Once the laser printer is ready to go, try printing again.

A message says that there isn't enough memory to print a document when you're using PrintMonitor, or PrintMonitor crashes when you print something.

Problem: PrintMonitor doesn't have enough memory to work with, the PrintMonitor Documents folder is corrupted, or PrintMonitor itself is corrupted.

Solutions:

- Quit PrintMonitor if necessary, then use the *Get Info* command to increase PrintMonitor's memory size (see page 35).

- If this doesn't work, throw away the PrintMonitor Documents folder in your System Folder. PrintMonitor automatically creates a new one the next time you print.

- If this doesn't work, throw away the PrintMonitor application from the Extensions folder or your System Folder, and install a new copy by dragging it from one of your system software installation floppies (it's on the Printing floppy disk in system software version 7.1).

General printing problems

The print doesn't begin at the top of the page.

Problem: Either the top margin is too big in the document or (with continuous-feed printers) the top-of-form setting is wrong.

Solutions:

- Use the appropriate formatting command to check the size of the top margin in the document, and specify a smaller margin if necessary.

- If you're using an ImageWriter or another printer that can use continuous-feed paper, advance the paper until the top of one page is underneath the print head, then press the *Top of Form* button if there is one. If there's no *Top of Form* button, advance the paper until the top of the page is underneath the print head, and then shut the printer off and turn it on again.

Print and/or graphics are chopped off at the left or right side of the page.

Problem: Either you're trying to print something wider than the printer is capable of printing, or the page setup is wrong. It's possible to set a very small paper size with the *Page Setup* command and then to print on larger paper. When you do, however, the Mac acts as if the physical paper is the size you set, and it won't print outside the theoretical edges of that page.

Also, every printer has a maximum printable area that's about ½" in from the edges of the paper. Most programs warn you when you try to set margins wider than can be printed, but if you have the margins set properly and paste in a graphic that's wider than the printable area, the printer tries to print the entire graphic and won't succeed.

Solutions:

- Choose the *Page Setup* command and make sure the paper size setting matches the paper you're using.

- If you're using a LaserWriter, click the *Options* button in the Page Setup dialog box and then choose the Larger Print Area option.

- Make sure you leave at least ½" of blank space at all four edges of a document, because most printers can't print within a half inch of the paper's edge.

- If you're using an ImageWriter, try using a different font or size.

Label data doesn't print properly onto each label.

Problem: Either you have the paper size set wrong or the label data isn't formatted properly with the program you're using.

Solutions:

- Choose the *Page Setup* command and make sure the paper size is set to the size of one label in your printout, not to the size of the whole sheet of labels. The height and width of a label is measured from the top or left edge of one label to the top or left edge of the next label, including any space between labels.

- Use the program from which you're printing labels to make sure you don't have data printing too close to the edge of a label and that blank lines aren't being eliminated. Label paper sometimes slips a little in printers, so it's best to leave at least 1/8" of space between the edge of the data and the edge of the label. (Use a smaller font size or larger label stock if necessary.)

- If your label data contains some blank fields (such as a blank Company Name field in some records), make sure the program is set to maintain the same record height even when fields are blank. If the program is set to eliminate any blank lines, some labels will be taller than others, and it will be impossible to print properly on a sheet of labels where all the labels themselves are the same size.

Words overlap one another when you print on an ImageWriter II.

 Problem: Some programs don't handle spacing well when you use larger sizes than normal in bitmapped versions of "city" fonts like Geneva and New York.

Solutions:

- Upgrade your system software to version 7.1 or later, or install TrueType versions of the same fonts on your Mac.

- If the document or paragraph where the problem occurs is set to justified text, try printing it with left-aligned text instead.

- Try choosing a different font or font size.

Spacing between words or letters is uneven, or there are odd-sized gaps between words.

Problem: Your document is set to justified alignment, or you've set the fractional character widths option.

Solutions:

- Change the paragraph alignment in your document to left-aligned instead of justified (consult the program's manual for instructions).

- If your document isn't set for justified alignment, choose the *Page Setup* command, look for a *Fractional Widths* or *Fractional Character Widths* option, and turn it off.

The LaserWriter spends a lot of time downloading the same fonts at the beginning of each printing job.

Problem: If a document uses nonresident fonts, it tells the LaserWriter to download them at the beginning of the print job. When the job is done, the fonts are flushed out of the LaserWriter's memory to make room for any new ones needed by the next job. (Of course, the LaserWriter has a few dozen resident fonts that it maintains in ROM and that never go away.)

Solution: Use the LaserWriter Utility that came with your LaserWriter to download the fonts you need before you begin printing documents. When you use this utility to download fonts, the fonts aren't flushed out at the end of a print job.

A StyleWriter or Personal LaserWriter LS or SC won't print shadowed text.

Problem: The Mac prints shadowed text by printing a character's "shadow" one pixel offset from the character itself. On higher-resolution printers like the StyleWriter or non-PostScript LaserWriters, one pixel is only $\frac{1}{360}$ or $\frac{1}{300}$ of an inch (respectively), so while it's easy to see the shadow on the screen (where a pixel is $\frac{1}{72}$ of an inch), the shadow is hard to see on the print-out.

Solution: There's no way to change the way the Mac prints shadowed characters on a non-PostScript printer, but you can try using different fonts or font sizes to make the shadowing more pronounced.

Font problems

This version of Font/DA Mover is out of date. To install a font, drag it to the System file. To put a desk accessory in the Apple menu, drag it to the Apple Menu Items folder.

OK

Problem: You're trying to launch the Font/DA Mover on a Mac that's running under System 7, but you need a newer version.

Solution: First of all, you don't need the Font/DA Mover to install or remove a font under System 7 (see page 54 in Chapter 3). If you use a resource manager program, however, it's handy to be able to combine various font or DA files into one suitcase. You can use Font/DA Mover version 4.1 or later under System 7 to create or change suitcase files.

Fonts on the screen look jagged at certain sizes.

Problem: You're using bitmapped (or fixed-size) fonts and you've specified a size for which you don't have a bitmap installed. As a result, the Mac tries to scale a smaller size that you do have installed, and the results aren't always elegant.

Solution: Use a TrueType font (or a PostScript font if you have ATM installed). Both of these font setups produce smoothly scaled characters at any size.

A font name you expect to see on a menu has been replaced by a different font name.

Problem: You're using a different Mac or a different System file than the one you used before, and the new Mac (or System file) has a different font with the same ID number as the font you expected to see.

Solution: Install a copy of the font you want to see, or go back to using the Mac or System file you were using originally.

Your document prints with the wrong font, or the characters don't look right.

Problem: If your document includes fonts that aren't built into the LaserWriter, and you've selected the *Font Substitution* option in the LaserWriter's Page Setup dialog box, the LaserWriter substitutes some of its built-in fonts for the ones that were in your document. (If your document contains the Geneva font, for example, the LaserWriter substitutes Helvetica.

If your document contains the New York font, the LaserWriter substitutes Times.)

If the LaserWriter can't come up with a suitable substitute, or if you haven't selected the *Font Substitution* option, it creates a bitmap of the font you're sending from your Mac. Bitmapped fonts don't look as good as the built-in ones from your LaserWriter.

If you're printing a document that was originally created on another Mac (or with a different System file), the font specified in the document may have the same font number as a

 In System 7, font number conflicts are automatically resolved as fonts are moved into the System file or Fonts folder. Under System 6, font number conflicts are resolved as fonts are moved into the System file with the Font/DA Mover program. But if you're printing a document from a Mac with a different System file, or if you're using a resource manager program and have font suitcases stored in other locations, the conflicts may not be resolved.

different font stored in the current System file. The LaserWriter selects fonts by number, so if a font specified when the document was created has the same number as a different font in the current System file, the LaserWriter uses the font with that number. This problem is most likely when you use custom fonts, rather than those that come with every Mac or are built into LaserWriters.

Solutions:

- Make sure you have a copy of the printer font you want to use in the System Folder of your startup disk. That way, the LaserWriter can download it and use it if necessary. If you don't want any font substitutions, deselect the *Font Substitution* option in the LaserWriter Page Setup dialog box.

- If you plan to print a document from a different Mac than the one on which you created it, take along suitcase files for the fonts you want to use, along with a copy of the System file you used to create the document, and install them on the Mac you will use to print the document.

- If you're using a resource manager program, use the font reconciliation utility that came with it to check for and resolve any font ID conflicts between suitcase files.

■ If you're printing large sizes (18 points or larger) on a non-PostScript printer, you may need to upgrade your printer driver. Drivers for these printers that were released before March, 1991, had problems with large characters being chopped off. Upgrade your printer driver to a TrueType-compatible version, or upgrade your system software to System 7, which includes the newer drivers.

Your document prints with the right font, but the spacing between characters isn't what you expect.

Problem: The document has probably been created with a PostScript font, and the Mac you're using doesn't have that font and has substituted a TrueType version of the font instead. TrueType fonts aren't exactly the same as PostScript fonts with the same names. Another possibility is that you have your program's *Fractional Character Widths* option set wrong.

Solutions:

■ Choose the *Print* command from your program and see if the *Fractional Character Widths* box is checked in the dialog box. This option makes characters slide closer together. Check or uncheck the box to obtain the results you want.

■ Check the Fonts folder or System Folder on your Mac and see if there's a PostScript version of the font you need. If not, you'll have to obtain one or reformat the document.

Some characters are garbled, or are different than what you expect.

Problem: In smaller point sizes, some TrueType fonts don't produce accurate characters. For example, a "3" in 6-point Geneva looks like a dollar sign ($).

Solution: Use a larger size or try a different font.

You have Adobe Type Manager installed, but it doesn't recognize fonts in your Fonts folder under system software version 7.1.

Problem: You need version 3.0 or later of ATM to recognize fonts in the Fonts folder.

Solution: Upgrade your version of ATM, or move the fonts you want recognized to the System Folder itself.

Some of the fonts in your Fonts folder aren't available.

Problem: The Fonts folder under version 7.1 and later can store as many suitcases as you like, but the Mac will only open 128 of them at startup. It opens the first 128 suitcase files it finds (in alphabetical order).

Solution: Combine some suitcase files to reduce the number of suitcases to 128 or less.

Chapter 15
File Sharing and Network Problems

If you're connected to an AppleTalk network and are working with Apple-Share servers or hard disks being shared by other users on the network, you may run into some problems specific to accessing or using files over the network. In this chapter, we'll discuss file sharing in general, see how you can use the Mac's system software to access shared files on a network, and then look at the most common problems you might have when doing so.

File sharing basics

Sharing files on an AppleTalk network means being able to access disks connected to other Macs on the same network. Those disks may be connected to an AppleShare file server (a Mac specifically set up to share files) or to a Mac running System 7 whose owner has decided to share files. When you're connected to a remote disk, its icon appears on your desktop just like a disk that's directly connected to your Mac.

The person who controls each file-sharing Mac is called the Mac's *owner* or, if the Mac is an AppleShare file server, the *AppleShare administrator*. Apple-Share disks are always available on the network as long as the AppleShare server is running. Under System 7, a Mac's owner must specifically make disks available for sharing on the network.

Each Mac on a network must have a unique name so that users can distinguish among them. The AppleShare administrator names a server when he or she sets it up; individuals name their Macs when they first share files under System 7 (see page 223.) Disks connected to these Macs must also have

If you're using System 6, you can't make your own disks available for sharing. unique names so you can tell which is which from your remote location on the network.

Even if a disk is available on the network, though, you can't necessarily access it. Before you can access a Mac's disks, its owner must grant *access privileges* to you.

In addition to the Macs themselves, each folder on a shared disk has an owner—the person who created that folder or copied it to the shared disk. On most disks shared under System 7, the Mac's owner owns the majority of folders because he or she created them before deciding to share the disk. Once the disk has been shared, however, other network users who have access to it may create folders on it, which they then own.

The owner of any shared folder can control access to it by assigning it specific access privileges. In some folders you may grant full access (so other users can open or modify existing files or create new ones); in other folders you might grant more restricted access (the ability to see files but not to create new ones, for example) or no access at all.

If you're an AppleShare administrator or the owner of a Mac running System 7, you give individual network users access to your disks either by making them *registered users* of that Mac or by allowing them to connect as *guests*. A privilege assigned to a specific user only applies to that user, while one assigned to guests applies to anyone who connects to that Mac as a guest; thus the privileges you have depend on which name you use to connect to a particular Mac.

These are the basics of file sharing on the Mac. Now let's look at how you connect to a network file server.

Choosing a network file server

When choosing a network file server, you have to enter a user name and sometimes a password to connect to the remote disk. This is true whether you're using System 6 or System 7, and whether you're connecting to an AppleShare file server or to a disk being shared from a System 7 Mac. If you're using a different type of networking software, the procedure is entirely different. Consult the manual that came with the software for more information.

To choose a network file server:

1. Choose the Chooser from the 🍎 menu.

2. Click the AppleShare icon. The names of all AppleShare servers and individual Macs that are currently sharing files appear at the right.

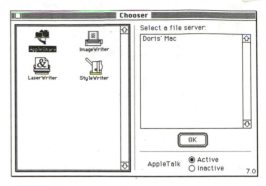

 If you're using System 6 and you don't see an AppleShare icon, your Mac hasn't been set up for use with AppleShare. Ask your network administrator for help.

3. Click the name of the file server to which you want to connect. You see a dialog box in which you can register as a user of that file server.

   If you're a registered user of the file server, type your name (and password, if necessary). Otherwise, click the Guest button to register as a guest. (If you're not sure whether you're registered or if you have a password, ask the remote Mac's owner or your AppleShare administrator.)

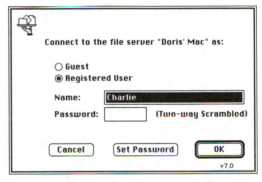

4. Click the *OK* button to connect to the server you've selected. A list of all the disks or shared folders currently connected to the server appears. If only one disk is connected, it is selected automatically, as in the example on the next page.

5. Select the disk or folder you want to access, and then click the *OK* button. The item's icon appears on your desktop and you are returned to the Chooser window, which you can then close.

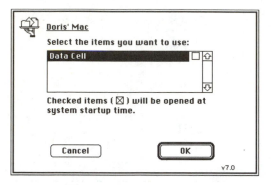

Doris' Mac

Select the items you want to use:

Data Cell

Checked items (⊠) will be opened at system startup time.

Cancel   OK

v7.0

 The checkbox following each disk name gives you the option of connecting to the remote disk automatically each time you start your Mac. Once you've checked the checkbox, you'll see options for storing your user name and password so they're supplied automatically at startup when your Mac connects to the remote disk. For a full explanation of these options, consult a general System 7 or System 7 file sharing user's guide, or—if you're using System 6—an AppleShare user's guide.

AutoRemounter

Remount Shared Disks :

◉ After Sleep

○ Always

○ Off

Connect To Disks By :

○ Automatically Remounting

◉ Always Entering Passwords

1.0

Using the Auto Remounter control panel (for PowerBooks)

If you own a PowerBook, you can use the Auto Remounter control panel to set up your Mac so it automatically reconnects to shared network disks. The Auto Remounter control panel is shown at the bottom of this page.

You have the option to reconnect to shared disks After Sleep (only when the PowerBook wakes up from sleep) or Always (whenever you turn the PowerBook on or wake it up from sleep). When you select the *After Sleep* or *Always* option in the top of the dialog box, the two options appear below. Click one of the buttons to either reconnect automatically or only when you enter a password. Use the password option if security is a problem and you don't want others to have access to any disks you've set up to automatically remount.

Using shared disks

Once you've connected to a remote disk or folder, you can access it as if it were directly connected to your own Mac; however, your ability to open files or make new folders on the shared item may be restricted, depending on how you registered as a user and which access privileges are assigned to that user name.

As a registered user, you can create folders of your own on the shared disk or folder and then control who can access them by setting access privileges. If you connect to a remote Mac as a guest, you can still create folders on the remote disk, but you can't control access to them.

Although the method for connecting to a remote server is the same under both systems, the specifics of sharing files and setting access privileges differ significantly, depending on whether you're using System 7 or System 6. In the sections that follow, we'll cover the two versions separately.

System 7 file sharing

If you're running System 7 and you're on a network, you can make any hard disk or CD-ROM disk on your Mac available to other people on the network. (You can't share floppy disks because it takes too long to access them.) With System 7's built-in file sharing capabilities, you can share an entire disk or just the folders you specify.

Sharing files from your Mac involves five types of activities:

- Setting up your Mac for file sharing

- Registering users (to specify who can connect to your Mac)

- Sharing disks or folders (specifying which disks or folders you want to share)

- Setting access privileges (to restrict access to shared items)

- Managing connected users (seeing who's connected and/or disconnecting people)

Let's look at these one at a time.

Setting up your Mac for file sharing

To set up your Mac for file sharing and turn file sharing on, the first tool you use is the Sharing Setup control panel.

The Network Identity section is where you type your name (in the Owner Name box), your password

```
┌─────────────────────────────────────────────────┐
│ ▦□       ══  Sharing Setup  ══                   │
│ ┌───────────────────────────────────────────────┐│
│ │ ▣  Network Identity                            ││
│ │                                                ││
│ │ Owner Name:    [                            ]  ││
│ │ Owner Password:[          ]                     ││
│ │ Macintosh Name:[                            ]  ││
│ ├───────────────────────────────────────────────┤│
│ │ ▢  File Sharing                                ││
│ │        ┌─Status──────────────────────────────┐ ││
│ │ [ Start ]  File sharing is off. Click Start to││
│ │        │  allow other users to access shared  ││
│ │        │  folders.                            │ ││
│ ├───────────────────────────────────────────────┤│
│ │ ◈  Program Linking                             ││
│ │        ┌─Status──────────────────────────────┐ ││
│ │ [ Start ]  Program linking is off. Click Start││
│ │        │  to allow other users to link to your││
│ │        │  shared programs.                    │ ││
│ └───────────────────────────────────────────────┘│
└─────────────────────────────────────────────────┘
```

(in the Owner Password box), and a name for your Macintosh (in the Macintosh Name box).

To turn on file sharing, click the *Start* button in the File Sharing area. After a few seconds, the button name changes to *Stop* and the Status area reports that file sharing is on. You can then close the control panel.

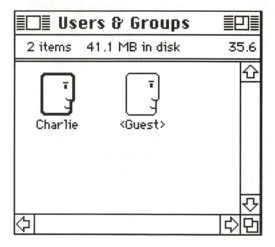

Registering users

In order to assign different access privileges to different people on your network, you need to register them by name. For this purpose, you use the Users & Groups control panel, as shown at left.

To register a new user, choose the *New User* command from the File menu or press ⌘ N. A new user icon appears in the control panel with the name *New User*. You can then change the icon's name to one that identifies the person you're registering.

To give a user a password, double-click his or her icon. A dialog box appears in which you can enter a password.

Groups are collections of users who all have the same access privileges for a given shared item. Granting privileges to a group gives more than one user, but not all users, access to an item. For example, everyone in a group called Marketing might have access to a folder called Sales, while users who weren't in that group would not.

To register a new group, choose *New Group* from the File menu. A *New Group* icon appears in the Users & Groups control panel. You can rename the icon if you like. To add users to a group, just drag their icons onto the group icon.

To delete users from a group, double-click the group icon to open it and then drag the user icons from the group's window into the Trash. To delete an entire group, just drag its icon to the Trash.

Once you've registered users or groups, you can assign them specific access privileges with the *Sharing* command.

Sharing disks or folders

As we've mentioned, System 7 lets you share individual folders or whole disks. Before you can share disks or folders from your Mac, you must turn on file sharing using the Sharing Setup control panel (see page 224). Once file sharing is on, follow these steps to share an item from your Mac:

1. On the desktop, select the item you want to share.

2. Choose *Sharing* from the File menu. You see a window like the one in the illustration shown above.

   The sharing window has the name of the folder or disk you selected. The item's type is indicated by an icon at the top left corner of the window (in this case, a folder).

If you've never assigned access privileges to folders or disks, the default is for everything to be available to everyone on your network. To limit access, you must register users and then assign specific privileges. See *Setting access privileges*, next.

3. Click the *Share This Item And Its Contents* checkbox. The access privileges options in the middle of the window become active, and you can change them if you like. (See *Setting access privileges*, next.)

4. If you want all the folders within the current folder to have the same access privileges it had, click the *Make All Currently Enclosed Folders Like This One* checkbox. Otherwise, items inside the current folder retain whatever privileges were originally assigned to them.

5. Check the *Can't Be Moved, Renamed or Deleted* checkbox if you want to lock the folder or disk so other users can't rearrange or rename it or throw it away. It's a good idea to check this box so that you're the only person who can make such changes.

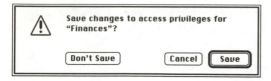

6. Once the access privileges and other checkboxes are the way you want them, close the sharing window. You see an alert asking you to confirm changes to the folder's access privileges.

7. Click the *Save* button. The folder is now available to other users on the network.

Setting access privileges

When you first share an item, the access privileges options in the middle of the sharing window default to full access for everyone, as shown below.

You can set separate privileges for three groups of users:

- The item's Owner (yourself).

- A particular User or Group name. (You must register groups or users to do this, and then choose the group or user name from the pop-up menu).

- Everyone, which means anyone who connects to your Mac, either as a registered user or as a guest.

When someone connects to your Mac over the network and selects this item to share, the privileges they have depend on whether they've connected to your Mac as a registered user or as a guest, and on how the checkboxes are set for that user or class of users.

The checkboxes in the See Folders, See Files, and Make Changes columns of the sharing window grant different types of access to the shared item.

Only a shared item's owner can change its access privileges. If you're an item's owner, however, you can also reassign ownership of the item to another registered user by choosing a different user name from the Owner pop-up menu.

- See Folders allows others to see any folders contained in the current folder.

- See Files allows others to view, open, and copy items in the folder.

- Make Changes allows others to add, change, or delete items in the folder.

 Make sure you uncheck boxes in the Everyone row if you're going to limit access to a particular user or group. If you only uncheck boxes in the User/Group row, everyone on the network will still have access, because the Everyone boxes are still checked.

You can use the checkboxes in any combination. When a box is checked, that privilege is granted; when it is unchecked, the privilege is withheld.

For example, if only the Make Changes boxes are checked, others on the network will be able to save new files to the folder, but they won't be able to open the folder and see its contents. (You might use this setup when you want others to save new files to a folder that contains private items.) If you check only the See Files boxes, others will be able to see and open files in the folder but they won't be allowed to save new files to it. (You could use this option if your folder contained standard documents that you wanted others on the network to use but not change.)

Viewing a shared item's status

You can also use the *Sharing* command to view a shared item's status at any time, whether the shared item is on your own disk or on one you've accessed over the network. To see a shared item's information, select it on the desktop and choose the *Sharing* command. If you own the shared item, you'll see a sharing window like the one in the previous section, and you can make changes to the access privileges. If someone else owns the item and it's located elsewhere on the network, its sharing window looks something like the one in the illustration above.

This window shows you where the shared item is located (in this case, on the *Data Cell* disk connected to *Doris' Mac)*; the user name you've used to connect to that Mac (as Guest in this case); and the access privileges you have for that item. Because you don't own the item, all the access options in the window are dimmed and you can't change them. Also, there are no checkboxes for sharing or locking the item because only the item's owner can set these options.

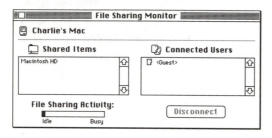

Managing connected users

To find out which other network users are connected to your Mac, or to disconnect a user, use the File Sharing Monitor control panel.

If other users are connected to your Mac, their names appear in the Connected Users list on the right. (In this example, the only user who is currently connected has registered as a guest.)

In addition to seeing who's connected to your Mac, you can use this control panel to disconnect users. Just select the user's name in the Connected Users list and click the *Disconnect* button. Before this change takes effect, you'll be given a chance to notify users that they're about to be disconnected.

 # System 6 file sharing

Under System 6, you can't share files from your own disk on the network. You can connect to remote file servers, but your Mac must have AppleShare workstation software installed. This software comes with system versions 6.0.4 and later, and with the AppleShare server software package. It adds the Access Privileges DA to the menu and the *Get Privileges*

AppleShare's access defaults are the opposite of System 7's file sharing defaults. When you create a new folder using AppleShare, it's not available to other users and you must use either the *Get Privileges* command or the Access Privileges DA to grant access to others.

command to the File menu in the Finder. It also puts the AppleShare driver in the System Folder so you can select it in the Chooser window.

Once your Mac has been set up as an AppleShare workstation, you can connect to AppleShare file servers or to disks or folders that have been shared on the network from Macs running System 7. If you connect to a shared disk as a registered user, any folders you create on that disk will be available only to you—no user on the network will be able to open these folders or change their contents except for the administrator of the AppleShare server or the owner of the System 7 Mac that's sharing the disk. (These people have full access privileges for your folders and can even reassign ownership of them to someone else.) If you connect as a guest, folders you create will be available to anyone on the network and you won't be able to restrict access to them.

Using the Get Privileges command

To view a folder's or disk's privileges, select it and then choose *Get Privileges* from the File menu. If you're the folder's owner, you see a dialog box like the one shown here.

This example shows the default privileges for an item that has just been created on a shared disk. Notice that only the item's owner has access to it. You can click the other checkboxes to assign privileges to a particular group of users or to everyone on the network.

If you don't own the folder, the *Get Privileges* command displays a smaller dialog box that shows the folder's location, identifies its owner, and explains what your access privileges in it are.

The options for locking folders and setting access privileges in the Access Privileges dialog box are the same as those described for the *Sharing* command under System 7. See *Sharing disks or folders* on page 225 and *Setting access privileges* on page 226 for more information.

When you're finished, click the *Save* button to reset the folder privileges and click the close box to put away the Access Privileges dialog box. The changes you've made take effect immediately.

Using the Access Privileges DA

If your Mac is set up to use AppleShare, you also have an Access Privileges DA on your ⌘ menu. This DA serves the same purpose as the *Get Privileges* command. The main difference between the two is that the Access Privileges DA only works under the Finder—you can't use it with MultiFinder. When you're using MultiFinder, you must switch to the Finder from whatever other program you're running and use the *Get Privileges* command.

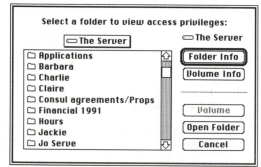

To use the Access Privileges DA:

1. Choose *Access Privileges* from the ⌘ menu. The Mac displays a file navigation box that lets you select the folder whose privileges you want to view.

2. From the list in the box, select the folder whose privileges you want to view.

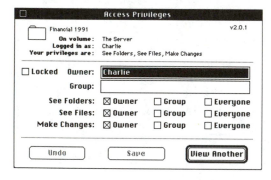

3. Click the *Folder Info* button to view or change the folder's privileges. The Mac displays a dialog box like the one shown to the left.

   (If you aren't the folder's owner, you see a smaller dialog box that won't let you reset the access privileges.)

4. Reset the folder's access privileges by clicking the options you want to change, and then click the *Save* button to save the changes.

5. Click the *View Another* button to view or change the privileges on another folder, or click the close box to close this dialog box.

As with the *Get Privileges* command, any changes you make with the Access Privileges DA occur immediately.

Now that we've covered the Mac's software tools and options for working with shared files, let's look at some common error messages and problems you're likely to encounter as you use shared files on a network.

Common networking problems

Problem: You've chosen the *Sharing* command in order to share a selected disk or folder under System 7, but you haven't turned on file sharing with the Sharing Setup control panel.

Before you can share anything you must turn on file sharing, so the Mac is giving you a chance to do so.

Solution: Click the *OK* button to open the Sharing Setup control panel so you can turn file sharing on.

Problem: You've tried to turn on file sharing in the Sharing Setup control panel under System 7, but you haven't entered an Owner Name in the Network Identity area of the dialog box. (A similar alert appears if you don't enter a Macintosh Name.)

Solution: Click the *OK* button, type names in the Macintosh Name and Owner Name boxes, and then click Start to turn on file sharing.

Problem: You've entered a Macintosh Name and Owner Name in the boxes in the Sharing Setup control panel and have clicked the *Start* button to turn on File Sharing, but you haven't entered a password in the Password box.

Solution: A password isn't required for you to start up file sharing. Click the *Continue* button to turn on file sharing without a password, or click *Stop* to go back and enter a password in the Password box. The password protects your Mac so nobody else can share disks or folders when you're not there (they'll need a password before they can turn on file sharing). If you don't care about this, you don't need a password.

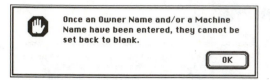

Problem: You've deleted the Owner Name and/or Mac Name from the Sharing Setup control panel and now you're trying to close it. Once you've entered a Mac Name and Owner Name, the names can only be changed—they can't be eliminated.

Solution: Click the *OK* button and type a name of some sort in the Owner Name and Macintosh Name boxes; then close the control panel.

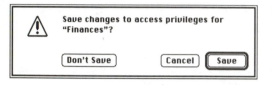

Problem: You've made a change to the access privileges for a shared folder or disk, and you're trying to close the sharing window (in System 7) or the Access Privileges dialog box (in System 6). The Mac is asking if you want to save the changes you've made.

Solution: If you want to save the changes you've made, click *Save.* If you want to close the dialog box or window and return to the desktop without making any changes in the item's access privileges, click *Don't Save* or *No.* (The text varies slightly in the System 6 alert.) If you want to return to the Access Privileges dialog box or window to view the current settings or make more changes, click *Cancel.*

You've set access privileges to prevent a certain user or group from accessing a folder or disk, but that user or group still has access.

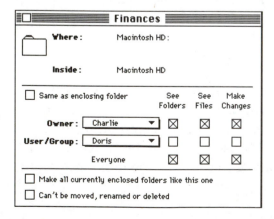

Problem: When you set access privileges to restrict access to a shared item, denying privileges to one particular user or group doesn't do any good unless you also deny them to Everyone in the sharing window. See the example in the illustration on the left.

In this sharing window, none of the access boxes is checked for the user named Doris. At first glance, you might think that Doris wouldn't have any access to this folder. But since all the access options are checked for Everyone, Doris can access the folder just like anyone else. The Everyone category of privileges is the lowest common denominator, so these privileges must be at least as restrictive as those for any user or group whose access you want to limit.

Solution: When using the sharing or access privileges window to restrict the access of a particular user or group, make sure you also restrict the privileges for the Everyone category.

Problem: You've shared disks or folders from your Mac, and now you're trying to shut down, turn off file sharing, or disconnect users. This dialog box and others like it give you the chance to warn other users on the network that your Mac is about to become disconnected as a server.

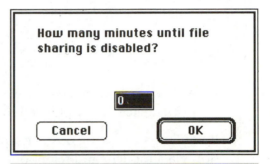

How many minutes until file sharing is disabled?

    0

    Cancel   OK

Solution: Type in the number of minutes you want to elapse before your Mac shuts down and then click the OK button. Other users on the network will see a message on their screens telling them that your Mac is about to shut down. Once your Mac or its file sharing feature actually turns off, the other users will see a message saying that this has happened.

 As a matter of network courtesy, give other users at least a minute's warning before you disconnect them, shut off file sharing, or shut down your Mac. That way, they can save any open files they're using and remove any shared items from their desktops by dragging them into the Trash.

Problem: You're trying to access an AppleTalk device but you don't have AppleTalk set to Active in the Chooser window. You can also get a message like this when you've clicked the *AppleTalk Active* button in the Chooser but you have something

An AppleShare system error occurred. (Please run the Chooser to activate AppleTalk.)

    OK

other than a network cable (like a StyleWriter cable) connected to your printer port, so the Mac won't let you activate AppleTalk.

Some communications products that allow remote connections to an AppleTalk network over telephone lines, such as AppleTalk Remote Access, the Shiva Net-Modem, and the Hayes Interbridge, work by fooling the Mac into thinking its printer port is connected to AppleTalk when it actually isn't. Sometimes the Mac gets really confused by this software.

Solutions:

■ Click the *OK* button. If you're not returned to the Chooser window, open the Chooser and then click the *AppleTalk Active* button to turn on AppleTalk. If you still get the error message, try one of the following solutions.

■ If you're not trying to connect to a shared device from a remote location via a modem and telephone line, make sure you have an AppleTalk network cable or the interface cable for an AppleTalk network device firmly plugged into your printer port.

■ If you're trying to log onto an AppleTalk network from a remote location via a modem and telephone line, make sure the software for the AppleTalk network bridge is correctly installed in your System Folder. If it is, disconnect anything that is currently connected to your printer port, restart the Mac, open the Chooser, and then select the *AppleTalk Active* option again.

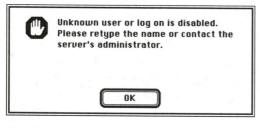

Problem: You've tried to log onto a shared disk with a user name that isn't registered on that server or file-sharing Mac.

Solutions:

■ If you know you're registered as a user on the server, try typing the name again. Make sure you don't add any extra spaces or punctuation—the Mac is particular about these things.

■ If you don't have a registered user name, choose the option to connect as a guest. You'll be able to create folders and save files to the server, but you won't be able to restrict access to folders you create.

Problem: You've typed an incorrect password while trying to connect to a shared disk.

> ✋ **Sorry, your password is incorrect. Please reenter it.**
>
> [OK]

Solutions:

- If you know the password, be sure you type it exactly as it was given to you. Don't add any extra spaces or punctuation. Also, make sure you're using the correct password for the user name that appears above the Password box on the screen.

- If you've forgotten the password, ask the AppleShare server's administrator or the owner of the remote Mac to tell you what it is.

- If you don't know the password and nobody will tell you what it is, you can log onto the shared disk as a guest. You'll be able to create folders and save files to the server, but you won't be able to restrict access to folders you create.

- If you set the password yourself and you don't remember it, you'll have to ask the AppleShare administrator or the owner of the remote Mac to delete your user name and then register you as a user again, so you can enter a new password.

The shared disk's icon doesn't appear on your desktop.

Problem: You haven't connected to the shared disk from your Mac. To have access to a shared disk, you must first connect to it (see page 220).

Solution: Follow the instructions on page 220, or ask your AppleShare administrator or the local network guru to show you how to connect.

You've set up AppleShare to automatically connect you to a server when you start up the Mac, but sometimes this doesn't happen.

Problem: Either the server isn't running or connected, the network isn't working properly, the AppleShare resources on your Mac are corrupted, or your disk directory is damaged.

Solutions:

■ Make sure the network server is up and running, and that it's properly connected. Ask the AppleShare administrator or the owner of the file-sharing Mac to help.

■ Try installing a different Mac at the same network location and see if the problem continues. If possible, use a network troubleshooting utility to make sure there aren't any signal problems on the network.

■ If the network is okay, replace the system software.

■ If the problem continues, run a disk diagnostic and repair program and check your disk for directory damage.

Problem: You're trying to drag a folder or file from a shared disk's window onto your desktop. The Mac doesn't allow you to do this. If you're using System 7, the Mac offers to copy the item to your startup disk.

Solutions:

■ If you want to put a file or folder from a shared disk onto your desktop, you must first copy that file or folder to a disk directly connected to your Mac.

■ If the Mac won't let you copy the file or folder, it's because you don't have the access privileges required to do so. In that case, select the file or folder, choose the *Sharing* command (in System 7) or the *Get Privileges* command (in System 6) to find out who owns the file or folder, and then ask that person to change the privileges so you can copy it.

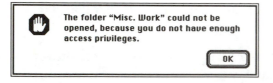

Problem: This message and others like it mean you're trying to open a folder or disk, and you don't have the See Folders or See Files privileges that you need to open it.

Solution: Ask the folder's owner to change the disk or folder's access privileges so you can open it. You can see who owns the item by selecting it and then choosing the *Sharing* command (in System 7) or the *Get Privileges* command (in System 6) from the File menu in the Finder.

Problem: You're trying to copy a shared folder for which you have only See Folders privileges. With these privileges, you can't see any files stored within the folder. The

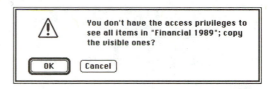

Mac won't let you copy files that you aren't allowed to see, so it's asking you if you want to copy only the folders you can see.

Solution: Click the *OK* button to copy the folders you're allowed to see, or click the *Cancel* button to cancel the copy operation.

Problem: You're saving some folders and files to a shared folder (Misc. Work in this case) for which you don't have See Files privileges. Without these privileges, you won't be

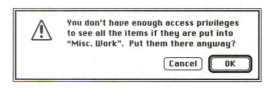

able to see the files you save to that folder.

Solution: If you don't care that you can't see the files you save to that folder, click the *OK* button. If you want to be able to see the files, click the *Cancel* button to return to the desktop, and then ask the folder's owner to change your access privileges to See Files.

Problem: When you're trying to move, copy, or duplicate inside a shared folder or disk for which you don't have Make Changes privileges, you see a message like this one. (The text

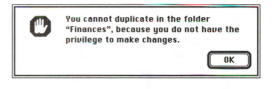

varies, depending on exactly what you're trying to do.)

Solution: Either give up the operation or ask the folder's owner to change its privileges so you can make changes. You can find out who owns the folder by selecting the folder and choosing the *Sharing* command (under System 7) or the *Get Privileges* command (under System 6).

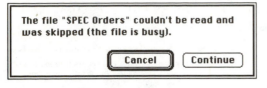

Problem: You've tried to copy a file from a shared disk, but the file is in use and the Mac can't copy it. This problem occurs with files that lock themselves upon being opened to prevent more than one user from using them at a time.

Solution: If you're only copying one file, click the *Stop* or *Cancel* button, wait until the file is closed by whoever's using it, and then copy it. If you know who's using the file, ask him or her to close it. If you're copying a group of files, click the Continue button to copy the other files in the group, and wait until later to copy the file that's busy.

Problem: You've tried to copy a file from a shared disk, but for some reason the Mac can't manage the copy. This usually happens when you're copying a particularly large file (or a large group of files) over a busy network. It's a temporary problem.

Solutions:

■ If you're copying a group of files, click the *Continue* button to give the Mac a chance to copy the rest of the files in the group. You may see the alert message again as the Mac tries and fails to copy other files in the group. Once the Mac has tried to copy all the files in the group, check the destination disk and see how many of them were copied; then try copying those that were skipped. If you're copying a particularly large group of files, try copying them in smaller groups, or remember the names of the files that are being skipped and copy them individually.

■ If you're only copying one file, click the *Cancel* button and then try the copy again. You may have to try it two or three times, but if you persevere, the Mac will finally make the copy.

Problem: You've selected the Access Privileges DA, but you aren't connected to an AppleShare file server. You must be connected to a server to use this DA.

Solution: Use the Chooser to locate and log onto an AppleShare file server (see page 220 for more information).

Problem: You were connected to a shared disk, but the disk has become disconnected. There are several possibilities—the Mac's network cable may have come loose, the file-sharing

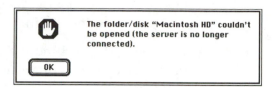

Mac's owner may have turned off file sharing or has disconnected you as a user, or the file-sharing Mac or AppleShare server may have been shut off.

Solution: Report the problem to the owner of the file-sharing Mac or the AppleShare server administrator. If you want to try fixing it yourself, check the cable connecting your Mac to the network and make sure both ends are plugged in securely. The network cable for your Mac should be plugged into your Mac's printer port. If you still can't see the shared disk when you click the AppleShare icon in the Chooser window, ask the shared disk's owner or administrator to check its connections and operation, to make sure you're allowed to connect to that Mac, and—if it's a file-sharing Mac under System 7—to verify that file sharing is on.

Problem: You're trying to share an entire disk with System 7's *Sharing* command, but you've already shared a folder inside that disk.

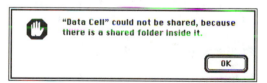

Solution: Select the folder inside the disk that's currently being shared, choose the *Sharing* command, and uncheck the *Share This Item and Its Contents* checkbox in the Sharing window. Then select the disk icon itself and share it (see page 225). If you're not sure which folder on the disk is being shared, you'll have to check them out individually by selecting them one at a time and then choosing the *Sharing* command.

Problem: You're trying to drag a disk icon into the Trash while the disk or a folder inside it is currently being shared.

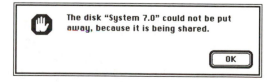

Solutions:

■ Select the folder inside the disk that's being shared, choose the *Sharing* command, and uncheck the *Share This Item and Its Contents* checkbox in the Sharing window. Then drag the disk icon into the Trash.

■ If you're trying this technique with a CD-ROM disk and it fails, try turning file sharing off completely with the Sharing Setup control panel. If this doesn't work, you'll have to restart the Mac before you can eject the disk.

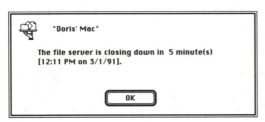

Problem: You see this message on your Mac when another Mac that's sharing files on the network (either a System 7 Mac or an AppleShare server) is about to disconnect or shut down.

Solution: Click the *OK* button to make the message go away, then save or close any files from the shared disk that you have open and drag the shared disk's icon into the Trash to break the connection from your end.

Your networked Mac automatically mounts several disks when you start it up, and you don't want it to.

Problem: You have the automatic mounting options set for these disks.

Solutions:

■ Select the AppleShare resource in the Chooser to display each shared network volume, double-click each volume's name, and then uncheck the *Mount at Startup* box.

■ If you're using a PowerBook, use the Auto Remounter control panel to turn off automatic remounting.

Chapter 16

Publish and Subscribe Problems

In this chapter, we'll look at System 7's Publish and Subscribe technology and some common problems that can occur when you use it.

About Publish and Subscribe

Publish and Subscribe creates an automatic link between a selection of data in one document (the publisher) and a selection of data in another document (the subscriber). Although Publish and Subscribe is built into System 7, each application must support it (many applications don't).

If an application supports Publish and Subscribe, it has commands on its Edit menu, usually called *Create Publisher, Subscribe To, Publisher Options,* and *Subscriber Options.* These names can vary, however.

To publish data, you select the data and then use the *Create Publisher* command to create an *edition* file. Once you do this, the published data is sent to the edition file whenever you save the document. (You can also save the data at any other time by using the *Publisher Options* command.)

To subscribe to data, you move the insertion point or selection to the place where you want the data to appear, then use the *Subscribe To* command to locate and subscribe to the edition file. Once you've done this, the subscriber's data is updated each time the document is opened; or you can subscribe manually at other times by using the *Subscriber Options* command.

Data is linked specifically to one edition file. If you move the edition file or rename it, the Mac maintains the data link to the publisher and any subscribers. If you copy an edition file, the copy doesn't receive any data updates from the original publisher. If you delete an edition file, the data link is broken, but the publisher will automatically create a new edition file when the document is next saved.

You can also open an edition file by double-clicking it. When you do, you see a window that shows the data in the edition, along with a button you can click to open the publishing document. An edition file can have more than one subscriber, and the edition file can even be located on a shared network disk or server so it can be subscribed to over a network.

Publishers and subscribers are identified in documents by gray borders. Usually a subscriber can't be modified, because it's automatically modified by updates from the edition file. However, some programs have subscriber options that allow you to modify a subscriber to change the data's style or format, for example.

For more details about Publish and Subscribe, consult your program's manual.

Publish and Subscribe problems

Problem: You've opened a document containing a subscriber or you've tried to manually update a subscriber with the *Subscriber Options* command, and the edition file you subscribed to has been deleted.

Solutions:

■ If the edition was accidentally deleted, open the publishing document and save it again. The edition is automatically recreated at its old location, and the subscriber should now be able to find it.

■ If the edition was moved to a shared network volume that you don't have mounted on your desktop, use the *Subscriber Options* command to cancel the subscriber, mount the shared volume on your desktop, and then use the *Subscribe To* command to subscribe to the edition on the shared volume.

Problem: Subscribers are typically changed by updates from an edition file, and you can't edit a subscriber as long as it's linked to an edition file.

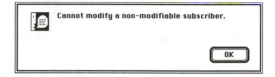

Solutions:

■ Some programs have a subscriber option that lets you modify a subscriber if it contains numbers or text. Check your program's manual to see if it has such a feature. However, any changes you make to the subscriber's data will be overridden by changes sent from the edition file. For example, if you change a number or a character format by editing a subscriber, the number or format may change again due to an update from the edition file the next time you open the document.

■ If your program doesn't allow you to edit a subscriber, you'll have to break the link to the edition file. Select the subscriber, choose the *Subscriber Options* command, and click the *Cancel Subscriber* button to break the link. Then you'll be able to edit the subscriber.

You change data in a publisher but it doesn't change in the subscriber.

Problem: The subscriber may have been canceled. However, subscribers don't update immediately when you change a publisher, so you shouldn't expect that. Normally, a subscriber is only updated when the publisher is saved or when the subscriber is opened.

Solutions:

■ Select the publisher, choose the *Publisher Options* command, and click the *Send Edition Now* button. The latest information is published immediately. If the subscriber still doesn't update immediately, then select the subscriber, choose the *Subscriber Options* command, and click the *Get Edition Now* button.

■ If the above solution doesn't work, the subscriber has been canceled or the edition file is corrupted. Publish a new edition and subscribe to it.

When you subscribe to data, it overwrites existing data in your document.

Problem: Subscribing to data is just like entering it by hand, and the subscribing program treats incoming data just as it would treat anything you type at the keyboard. Incoming subscriptions may or may not overwrite data in the document, depending on the type of program. For example, if you select a group of spreadsheet cells containing existing data and subscribe to an edition, the data from the edition overwrites what was in the cells originally. On the other hand, if you place the insertion point between two paragraphs in a word processing document, the subscription is inserted between the two paragraphs.

Solution: There's no solution for this problem. Assume that subscriber data will affect your document the same way data you type or paste in would.

Data in a subscriber isn't in the same format as surrounding data in the document.

Problem: Publish and Subscribe maintains the data format from the publishing document. Fonts, sizes, and styles are the same in a subscriber as they were in the publisher.

Solutions:

■ Open the publisher and change the font, size, or style of text to match what you want in the subscriber.

■ If your program allows subscriber modifications, you can choose this feature with the *Subscriber Options* command and then reformat the data in the subscriber. When the subscriber is next updated from the edition file, however, the old formatting from the publisher will return.

■ If your program doesn't allow subscriber modifications or you want to make a permanent change in the data format, use the *Subscriber Options* command to cancel the subscriber and then reformat the data.

You copy an edition file to a different disk and delete it from the original disk, but instead of updating the edition you moved, your program creates a new edition file on your original disk.

Problem: When you publish an edition, the Mac knows where the edition is located. If you move an edition to another location on the same disk, the publisher and any subscribers can still find it. However, if you copy the edition file to another disk and then delete it from the original disk, the Mac assumes that the edition is gone and automatically creates a new one on your original disk.

Solution: To create an edition on a different disk, choose that disk as the location for the edition when you first publish it.

Chapter 17
Communications Problems

In this chapter, we'll look at general problems you may have when using modems and communications programs, along with a couple of more specific problems you may have with Apple-supplied communications programs. Before we do, however, we'll run through the basics of Macintosh communications.

About Mac communications

Communications between any two personal computers involve several levels of interaction, each with has its own potential problems. In this section, we'll go through what happens during a communications session between your Mac and another computer. Some of the techniques and concepts covered here are referred to in the problem/solution part of the chapter.

In order to communicate properly, you must have a physical means of establishing a connection, software to manage the communications session, and a computer at the other end of the line that is set to communicate properly with your Mac. Let's look at these one at a time.

The physical connection

Other than using a network (discussed in Chapter 15), your Mac can communicate via a cable directly connected between one of its serial ports and another computer, or over a telephone line. When you use a telephone line, you must use a hardware device called a *modem* to convert the digital information being exchanged by the two computers into sounds.

247

Modems range in price from less than $100 to over $1000, depending on the speed with which they can send or receive data, whether or not they can also handle facsimile transmissions, and other features. You can buy a modem from any computer dealer.

Direct cable connections are used when two computers are in the same room, but most commonly you use a modem. You connect a modem to your Mac either by plugging it into an internal slot or by plugging it into your modem port with a cable. You must also plug a telephone line cord into your modem, and (if it's an external modem) connect it to an AC power source. Internal modems turn themselves on automatically, but you must switch on an external modem before it will work.

Even when your modem is connected properly, the quality of the telephone line can determine communications success. If a connection is filled with static, it may not be able to accurately carry the sounds generated by your modem, and the remote computer's modem won't understand them properly. As a result, what left your computer as deathless prose may end up on the remote computer's screen as garbage.

Communications software

Once you've got the physical connection worked out, you need software that handles the communications process—the interaction between the Mac, modem, phone line, and remote computer. Programs like MicroPhone and the communications modules in integrated programs like Microsoft Works and ClarisWorks allow you to send or receive data, dial telephone numbers with a modem, and determine how data is displayed on your Mac's screen.

Every modem responds to a set of commands from your communications program. Most modems use a standard set of commands called the *Hayes command set.* (Hayes was one of the first big makers of personal computer modems, and nearly everyone else has adopted its command set.) When you buy a communications program for general use, make sure it supports Hayes-compatible modems.

Before you make a connection, you use the communications software to choose the *communications method*, the *terminal settings*, and the *file transfer settings*. Let's look at these more closely.

■ **The communications method.** This is the type of connection, usually a choice between a direct serial cable and a modem, although some programs have different modem connection settings. Along with the type of connection, you identify the serial port to which the direct cable or modem cable is connected. When you choose the method, you also set the transmission speed—called the baud rate or bps (bits per second)—and communications protocols (parity, stop bits, and data bits). All these settings must match those on the other computer you're connecting to, or else the communication will fail. If you're using a modem, you can also choose whether the modem uses pulse (rotary dial) or tone dialing.

 Some online computer services, such as America OnLine, Prodigy, and CompuServe, have their own communications programs that make it easier to connect to and use them. If you're using one of these services, it's much easier to use that service's communications software than to use a generic program, and in many cases you *must* use the service's software.

- **Terminal settings.** Whenever you're connected to another computer, you can send text by simply typing it on your screen. When the other computer sends text to your Mac, you see it on your screen. The terminal settings control how data is displayed on your Mac's screen. These settings can include the size of text and the width of each line, the size and shape of the screen cursor, and the *local echo* setting, which determines whether or not text you send to the other computer is also displayed on your screen.

- **File transfer settings.** Instead of typing text to send it, you can transfer entire files. Because you're sending a whole file, the file can contain text, graphics, or program instructions. To make transfers of entire files more reliable, file transfer settings let you send data in larger blocks, using error-checking routines that detect transmission errors and resend data blocks when necessary. In addition, these settings let you decide how and where incoming files are stored on your disk. When you transfer entire files, you don't see the contents of the file on your screen

In the old days, it was up to each software developer to create its own way to select the communications, terminal, and file transfer settings. In 1991, however, Apple released the Apple Communications Toolbox, which provides lots of key communications software modules ready-made for developers. These days, most communications programs use the Communications Toolbox.

If your program uses the Communications Toolbox, you'll see files like XModem Tool, Apple Modem Tool, Kermit Tool, and Serial Tool in your Extensions folder or (under System 6) System Folder. These tools are components of the Communications Toolbox.

The remote computer

Like your Mac, the remote computer needs a physical connection and communications software to connect properly. Most importantly, the remote computer must use the same communications and file transfer settings as your Mac does. If it doesn't, you won't be able to send or receive text or files properly, and you may not be able to connect at all.

Before beginning a communications session, therefore, make sure you're using the same settings as the remote computer. If you're connecting to another person's computer, call that person and agree on which settings you'll use. If you're connecting to an online service or to another large computer used by many other people, consult the manual for the online service or contact the computer's system operator to find out which settings you should use.

This overview gives you a general idea of what's involved in Macintosh communications. For the specific steps you take to connect with the software and modem you're using, consult the manuals for those products. Now let's look at some common problems you may run into.

General communications problems

Some of the problems in this section occur when you're not connected to another computer, and others happen when you are connected. In some cases you need to break the connection to fix the problem, in others you don't. The solutions specify whether you need to disconnect before fixing the problem.

You want to connect a modem cable to your Mac's serial port, but it's already being used by another device.

Problem: All your Mac's serial ports are in use.

Solution: Buy a switch box or serial port expander. A switch box connects to one of your serial ports and has a knob on it that lets you manually select one of two or three serial devices connected to it. A serial port expander works the same way, except that you use a Control Panel program to select which of the connected devices you want to use. Switch boxes and serial port expanders are available at computer stores and through computer mail-order houses, and cost from $35 to about $150.

 Although a switch box or serial port expander lets you connect several devices through one of the Mac's serial ports, your Mac can only communicate with one of the connected devices at a time. Serial port expanders come with software that automatically switches the connection from one device to another if you're using devices that use the Apple Communications Toolbox. Apple's own Serial Port Arbitrator software does the same thing when you use AppleTalk Remote Access.

The modem doesn't work at all.

Problem: Modems are pretty reliable, but occasionally they die, and some are even "dead on arrival," right out of the box. More likely, though, it's a problem with your modem cable or software.

Solutions:

- Make sure the modem itself is operating. If it's an internal modem, shut off your Mac, open the case, and make sure the card is properly seated in the expansion slot. If it's an external modem, a steady power light or status lights should come on momentarily when you turn it on. If these don't come on, make sure the AC power cord is plugged in securely or (if it's a battery-operated modem), that the batteries aren't dead.

- If it's an external modem and the power or status lights come on, check the data cable between the modem and your Mac's serial port. Are both ends plugged in securely? Are you using the right cable? (Some printer and modem cables have the same connectors, but the pins inside them are different.) Are any pins bent in the cable connectors? Are you sure you plugged the cable into the Mac's modem port? Try using a different data cable, if necessary.

■ If the cable seems all right, make sure commands are getting from your software to your modem. Start your communications program and check the communications method to make sure you've selected one for your modem. Some programs have specific settings for different models of modem, and others have general settings like "Hayes Compatible Modem" or "Apple Modem Tool." Consult your communications software manual for information about which setting to select.

■ If you have the right setting and the modem lights are on, display the terminal window in your communications program and type a direct modem command. If you have a Hayes-compatible modem, type *ATA* and then press ⌐Return⌐. This is a modem wake-up call: it should make your modem's status lights blink (on external modems), and you should see *OK* on your screen as the modem acknowledges the command.

■ If you don't see the *OK* message or the status lights don't blink, recheck your communications method setting and your cable connections. These are the most likely problems. If you're really sure these aren't the problem, check your modem's manual to see if there are any DIP switches on the modem that need to be set before it will work properly with your Mac. The modem may have been set up for use by a different type of computer.

■ If possible, try the modem and cable on another Mac. If it works, then you you're either doing something wrong with your software, you're plugging the modem into the wrong port, or there's something wrong with your Mac's serial port. If you know your software settings and port connection are okay, try using the printer port instead (resetting your communications program's communications settings to let the Mac know you've switched ports, of course). If the modem works when connected to your printer port, there's something wrong with your modem port. Take the Mac in for service.

■ If the modem doesn't work on another Mac, take the modem in for service (be sure to take the cable with you). Most modems have fairly lengthy guarantees, so if the modem is broken, you can probably get it fixed or replaced for free.

The modem appears to work, but you can't dial out or receive a call.

Problem: There's something wrong with your phone line or phone line connection.

Solutions:

- If your modem has two modular connectors, you may have the phone line plugged into the wrong one. (Some modems have a connector for the phone line and a second one where you can plug in a telephone handset, and they're not interchangeable.) Try plugging the phone line cord into the other connector.

- Make sure the phone cord is plugged securely into the modem and into the wall jack.

- Try plugging the phone cord into a regular telephone and then lift the handset to see if you get a dial tone. If you do, then your modem isn't responding properly to commands from your communications software.

- Check your software's communications settings and make sure you're using the proper communications tool for your modem. There may be a tool for your specific brand and model of modem, or there may be a generic tool such as Apple Modem Tool or Hayes Compatible Modem. Try the different generic tools one at a time if there isn't one for your particular modem.

- Your modem may not be fully compatible with the modem commands your software is sending out. Call the software manufacturer for help.

The modem connects but then disconnects immediately, or the screen is filled with meaningless characters.

Problem: You aren't using the same communication settings as the remote computer.

Solutions:

- Disconnect if you're still connected, then call the remote computer's operator (or if it's an online service, consult the service's manual) to determine the proper baud rate, parity, stop bit, and data bit settings. Then choose those settings in your communications program. If there are other settings than these in the communications settings options for your software, ask the other computer's operator about them, check the software manual, or check the online service's manual to see what to do about them.

■ If you've chosen the proper settings, the phone line may be very noisy. Try redialing the remote computer. If that doesn't work, connect a telephone handset to the phone line and call information or some other number and listen to see if there's a lot of static on the line. Usually you can obtain a clear connection if you redial a few times, but there may be an equipment problem in your telephone service area.

You can connect and most of the characters make sense, but there are still some meaningless characters once in awhile.

Problem: The telephone line is probably noisy, but you may also be receiving characters your Mac can't interpret.

Solutions:

If you're connected to a non-Mac computer, it may be sending characters your Mac can't interpret. However, if the garbage characters are obviously meant to be ordinary text, disconnect and redial. You can usually get a clearer connection by redialing. If the line doesn't clear up and you're aware of adverse conditions (a thunderstorm or telephone equipment problems in your area, for example), try calling when the conditions are better.

Each character you type appears twice on the screen, or what you type doesn't appear on your screen at all.

Problem: You have the wrong local echo or duplex setting in your communication software.

Solution: Go to the Terminal Settings dialog box in your software, and change the local echo or duplex setting. There are only two settings (usually a checkbox or an on/off button), so just choose the other one. You shouldn't have to disconnect to do this.

You want to choose a communications tool, but it doesn't appear on the menu in your communications program.

Problem: The tool probably isn't installed in your Extensions folder or System Folder. Every software developer who uses the Communications Toolbox from Apple is required to include a basic set of tools such as the XModem Tool, the Serial Tool, and the Apple Modem Tool, but you may be trying to choose one that isn't part of the basic set. For example, you may want a terminal setting tool that makes your Mac act like a particular type of mainframe or minicomputer terminal, and your software developer hasn't provided it.

Solution: Call your software developer to see if they offer such a tool. If they don't, contact your Apple dealer.

You get a "low memory" or "out of memory" message as you send or receive text.

Problem: The communications buffer (also called the scrollback area in some programs) is too large, and it's taking up too much memory.

Solutions:

■ If you're still connected to the remote computer and you want to stay connected, you need to clear the buffer immediately. Select the contents of the communications buffer, copy them, open a word processing document if possible, and paste the data into that document. Then clear the communications buffer, either by selecting and deleting its contents or by choosing a Clear Buffer command in your program (consult your software manual). If you can't open a word processing program, you'll have to simply clear the buffer and lose the data. Next, use your program's *Capture Text* command and begin capturing the contents of your screen to a file on disk.

■ If you're disconnected and you want to prevent this problem in the future, use your program's communications or terminal settings to reduce the size of the buffer, or capture the text to a file on your disk instead of storing it in the buffer. Consult your software manual for details.

If you've changed the document margins and you still find that lines are chopped off or wrapped improperly, it's probably because the text only has a carriage return at the end of each paragraph, and there are more than 80 or 132 characters in a paragraph. Try saving the file using the *Text with Line Breaks* option rather than the plain Text option. Using the line breaks option adds a return character at the end of each line.

When you receive text, it doesn't wrap down to the next line properly.

Problem: You've chosen the wrong line wrap setting under your program's terminal settings options, or you've chosen the wrong terminal tool.

Solutions:

■ Make sure you're using the correct terminal tool for the computer you're connected to. If you're connected to a minicomputer or mainframe, you may need to use the terminal settings option to choose a specific terminal tool, such as VT320. If you're calling an online service or another Mac, the TTY Tool or VT102 Tool should work.

■ If you've chosen the correct terminal tool, use the terminal settings options to choose a different line wrap setting. There's usually a setting like *Auto Linefeed On Return*, or *Auto Wrap to Next Line*. If this setting isn't on, turn it on.

When you transmit text, the lines don't end in the same place as they did in your original document, or (if you're transmitting to an electronic mail service), a message says that lines are too long to be transmitted properly.

Problem: Most electronic mail services have a maximum line width they'll display (usually 80 characters), and another line width they'll accept (usually 132 characters). If your lines are longer than this, they'll be chopped off or wrapped around to the next line.

Solution: To stop lines from being chopped off, reformat the text in your word processor before you send it by changing the margins so lines are shorter than the limit allowed by the electronic mail system. To eliminate line wrap at odd places, reformat the text so lines are shorter than the maximum line display width.

When you receive a file and open it in your word processor, there are carriage returns in odd places or at the end of each line.

Problem: When some programs convert files to text before they're transmitted, they add a carriage return at the end of each line.

Solution: Use the search and replace feature in your word processor to search for carriage return characters and replace them with nothing. Use the command to search for and replace the returns individually, however, because using the "replace all" feature eliminates all the carriage returns from the document, and there will be some (those separating paragraphs, for example) that you want to keep.

You're trying to receive a file using the *MacBinary* option with the XModem tool, and a message says there isn't enough disk space to receive the file.

Problem: If you're using an early version of the XModem tool and the file you're trying to receive isn't actually in MacBinary format, the Mac tells you that there isn't enough disk space, when in fact this isn't the real problem.

Solutions:

- Make sure there actually is enough disk space on your disk to receive the file.

- If you have enough disk space, switch to the Straight XModem file transfer method and then receive the file again.

- Contact your communications software vendor or an Apple dealer and upgrade to version 1.0.2 or later of the XModem Tool. It will automatically switch to the Straight XModem method when you try to receive a non-MacBinary file.

Apple-specific communications software problems

You've just installed AppleTalk Remote Access or MacTCP, and a message says it isn't correctly installed when you first try to open it.

Problem: You need to turn AppleTalk on in the Chooser.

Solution: Open the Chooser and turn AppleTalk on.

AppleTalk Remote Access has stopped working on your Mac.

Problem: You probably installed some other networking software since you installed AppleTalk Remote Access (ARA), and that software's Installer replaced your AppleTalk file with an older version (56 or earlier) that doesn't work with ARA. If you're using a PowerBook and running System 7 with the System 7 Tune-Up Kit, your system isn't loading AppleTalk at startup.

Solutions:

- Reinstall AppleTalk Remote Access.

- If you're using System 7 Tune-Up Kit and a PowerBook, use the Chooser to select the *AppleTalk Active* button. ARA should work then.

You're trying to use AppleTalk Remote Access and a message says the serial port is in use.

Problem: You're using an early version of the Serial Tool along with the Serial Port Arbitrator.

Solutions:

- Hold down the Option key to override the dialog box.

- To fix the problem permanently, upgrade to version 1.0.2 or later of the Serial Tool.

Chapter 18
Desktop CPUs

In this chapter, we'll look at problems that are specific to certain desktop Macintosh models. The problems are organized by Mac model in roughly chronological fashion, from the Mac Plus and earlier models to the Quadras and Performas.

Your Mac Plus won't recognize an external hard disk, or it crashes when you shut off an external hard disk.

Problem: The Mac Plus doesn't provide SCSI termination power through its SCSI port and has trouble recognizing some SCSI devices. SCSI devices themselves must provide the termination power, so if a SCSI device is turned off when the Mac Plus is still running, the SCSI bus gets screwed up and the Mac crashes.

Solutions:

- If the drive has an external terminator and the Mac Plus won't recognize it, remove the terminator. If the drive is internally terminated, you may have to turn off termination using the drive's set-up software. In extreme cases, you may need to have the drive opened up to have the terminator removed.

- It's normal (but annoying) for the Mac Plus to crash when you shut off the external hard disk. Don't turn off external SCSI devices while the Mac Plus is running—shut down the Mac first and turn it off, then turn off the external devices.

You want to change the startup device on your Mac Plus, but there's no Startup Disk control panel under System 7 (and no Startup Device cdev in the Control Panel under System 6).

Problem: The Mac Plus and earlier models don't support the Startup Disk control panel or Startup Device cdev.

Solution: The Mac Plus scans down the SCSI chain from addresses 6 to 0, and starts up from the first device it comes to that contains a valid System Folder. To make a disk the startup device on a Mac Plus, change its SCSI address to one that's higher than the current startup disk. For example, if you're starting up from an internal hard disk (SCSI address 0), attach an external hard disk and give it address 1. If you're starting up from an external hard disk with SCSI address 3, change the SCSI address on a second external hard disk to 4, 5, or 6.

Your Mac can't read 800K disks.

Problem: The Mac Plus and older models, as well as some Mac SE models, can only read 400K disks because they don't have a high-density disk drive.

Solution: Transfer the data to a 400K disk using another Mac, or upgrade your Mac to a high-density disk drive.

Your Mac Plus freezes at startup without a sad Mac or question mark icon.

Problem: You have a SCSI peripheral connected to the Mac, but it's not turned on. This problem occurs only in the earliest Mac Plus models.

Solution: Shut off the Mac, then either disconnect the SCSI peripheral or turn it on. Restart the Mac.

You created a color document on a Mac II, but when you print it from a Mac Plus or SE the colors are different.

Problem: The Mac SE and earlier models support only 8 colors, while Mac II and newer models support 256 or more.

Solution: Print the document from a Mac II or newer machine.

Your Mac SE30, IIcx, or IIx won't access more than 8 MB of RAM.

Problem: These machines don't support 32-bit addressing. Use Apple's 32-bit system enabler in your System Folder (if you're using system software version 7.1) or get the MODE32 extension (available on online services or from user groups) for any version of System 7.

If you're using an original Mac II, you must either use MODE32 or get the Mac IIx logic board upgrade.

 Once you set your Mac up for 32-bit addressing, make sure your hard disk driver software is 32-bit compatible (or "32-bit clean"), and that the ROMs on any add-in cards are also 32-bit clean (they may need upgrades). You can use Help! or Alert! to determine whether any applications need to upgraded to 32-bit clean versions (see page 95 in Chapter 6).

Apple's 32-bit system enabler requires the Mac IIx ROM chip, which is only available with the high-density floppy disk drive upgrade for the Mac II.

Solution: Don't fiddle with 32-bit addressing unless you're sure you need to use more than 8 MB of RAM. If you do, install the MODE32 extension or Apple's 32-bit system enabler.

Your Mac LC or LCII doesn't show more than 8 MB of RAM installed when you choose the *About This Macintosh* command, even though you have 10 MB installed.

Problem: These models don't recognize RAM over 8 MB unless 32-bit addressing is on.

Solution: Use the Memory control panel to turn on 32-bit addressing.

The speaker on your Mac IIsi doesn't seem to work.

Problem: Either the sound volume is set at zero, the wire connecting the speaker with the logic board has come loose, or the contacts on the speaker are dirty.

Solutions:

- Open the Sound control panel or cdev and make sure the volume is set to a number other than zero.

- If the sound volume is set correctly, shut off the Mac, open the lid, and make sure the speaker wires are connected (look at the plugs on the back of the speaker).

- If the wires are connected, remove the speaker wire connectors, clean them with a rubber eraser or electrical contact cleaning spray, and replace them. (If you're skittish about doing this, take the Mac in for service.)

Sound fades in and out intermittently on a Mac LC or IIsi.

Problem: Some extensions, inits, or cdevs that work with time events can interfere with the sound functions of these machines.

Solutions:

- Try turning off any extensions, cdevs, or inits like Pyro, SuperClock, SoundMaster, and other screen-saver, clock, or appointment reminder programs (see page 110 in Chapter 7), and see if the problem clears up. If it does, activate the extensions one at a time until the problem recurs—then you'll know which extension is causing it.

- If the above solution doesn't work, check the speaker wires (see the previous problem).

Your Mac Classic II won't recognize 400K disks.

Problem: The Classic II just won't recognize these older disks.

Solution: Use another Mac to move the files to an 800K disk.

Your Mac IIsi's keyboard periodically goes nuts—it acts as if one or more keys is being held down, so the character or command is repeated over and over. You have to press the "stuck" keys again to unlock them.

Problem: Although it sounds mechanical, this is probably a software or electrical problem. Either the keyboard file in your system software is corrupted or there's a bad circuit in either the keyboard or the logic board.

Solutions:

- Replace the system software (see page 112).

- Try using a different keyboard or keyboard cable.

- If the problem doesn't clear up, there's probably a bad circuit on the logic board. Since the failure is intermittent, however, it will be difficult to

 I swapped keyboards and keyboard cables and had my IIsi's logic board replaced in an attempt to solve this problem, and the problem persists. I've had to simply live with it.

detect. If you can't have the logic board replaced under warranty (which is unlikely at this point), you'll have to learn to live with the problem or spend a lot of money to replace the logic board in the hope that this will solve the problem.

The Launcher doesn't appear when you start up your Macintosh Performa, or it appears and you don't want it to.

Problem: The Launcher's appearance depends on whether or not it (or an alias for it) is located in the Startup Items folder inside your System Folder.

Solutions:

- To make the Launcher appear, select the Launcher control panel in the Control Panels folder, choose *Make Alias* from the File menu, and then drag the Launcher alias into the Startup Items folder inside your System Folder. When you restart the Mac, the Launcher will appear.

- To make the Launcher disappear, open the Startup Items folder in your System Folder and drag the Launcher alias out of it. You can either throw the alias away (by dragging it to the Trash) or simply move it out of the Startup Items folder into another folder. The next time you restart the Mac, the Launcher won't appear.

When you start up your Mac Performa with At Ease, it keeps asking you to insert a removable hard disk cartridge, even after you do so.

Problem: You've used the At Ease control panel to automatically save documents to a removable hard disk cartridge, and the removable cartridge has an incompatible SCSI driver.

Solution: Contact the removable hard disk's manufacturer for an upgrade to its driver software, or use a compatible third-party utility like Drive 7 to format the removable device (see page 91 in Chapter 6).

Applications crash when you load them on your Mac Quadra, or they run more slowly than usual, even though the same programs work fine on another Mac.

Problem: The programs are probably incompatible with the Quadra's internal cache.

Solutions:

- Use the Cache Switch control panel to turn the Quadra's internal cache off, and see if this resolves the problem. (If the Cache Switch isn't in your Control Panels folder, copy it from the Tidbits disk in your set of system software version 7.1 installation floppies.)

- Contact the developer for an upgrade to the program that is compatible with the cache.

You set up your Performa to start up with At Ease, but you've forgotten the password you defined for it so you can't get to the desktop.

Problem: At Ease requires a password, and if you don't enter the password, you can't get to the desktop.

Solution: Start up your Mac with another startup disk, then open the Preferences folder inside the System Folder on your Mac's internal hard disk and drag the At Ease Preferences file to the Trash. After this, you should be able to restart your Mac from the internal hard disk. Since you threw away the At Ease Preferences file that contained your password, At Ease should no longer require one.

Chapter 19

PowerBooks and Portables

This chapter covers problems specific to Macintosh Portable and PowerBook models. We'll cover Portable-specific problems first, then move into problems that can occur on either Portable or Powerbook models, and finish with PowerBook and PowerBook Duo problems. Some of these problems occur only on specific models, so look for model numbers in the problem description headings.

You locked down the Caps Lock key on your Mac Portable, but after the machine wakes up from sleep it acts as if Caps Lock isn't down.

Problem: The Macintosh Portable always reverts to lowercase mode when it wakes up from sleep, even if you have the Caps Lock key locked in the down position. This is normal (if somewhat annoying) behavior.

Solution: Unlock the Caps Lock key and then lock it again after the Portable wakes up.

It seems to take forever to print from a Mac Portable.

Problem: "Forever" is, of course, subjective. It always takes longer for any Mac to print documents horizontally, to print with many different fonts, or to print from some graphics programs. If none of these is the case, however, there's also a Portable-specific feature that slows printing down. When you print to a printer that requires the Mac Portable itself to do the print processing, the processing can be delayed by this model's power-saving features. The

Portable falls into a "rest" mode (which slows down the processor to a crawl to help preserve battery life) whenever the Mac thinks nothing is going on. The Mac Portable checks the screen to determine activity, so even though it may be processing a print job in the background, it can fall into rest mode because there's nothing happening on the screen. This only happens with certain applications (certain versions of Word, Excel, and MacDraw, for example) that don't display an animated cursor or something else that moves on the screen during printing.

Solution: Turn off the Portable's Rest mode. Open the Portable Control Panel (or the Portable cdev in the Control Panel DA under System 6), hold down the Option key while clicking the *Minutes Until Automatic Sleep* option, then turn Rest off in the dialog box that appears.

Your PowerBook or Mac Portable won't go into sleep mode, even though you've it set to do so.

Problem: There are several possible reasons.

- You have the unit plugged into AC power and have the *Don't sleep when plugged in* option clicked in the PowerBook control panel (or the *Stay awake when plugged in* option clicked in the Portable control panel).

- You're connected to an AppleTalk network and have volumes mounted on your desktop (Mac Portable only).

- You have an open serial port (you're running a communications program, for example, or have a modem set to auto-answer).

- You're running an extension or init that makes the Mac think it's busy when it really isn't.

Solutions:

- If you're running under AC power, check the PowerBook or Portable control panel to make sure you haven't set the Mac to stay awake.

- If you're using a Mac Portable, unmount any network volumes.

- If you have a communications program running, quit it.

- If your internal modem is set to auto-answer, cancel this option.

- If the above solutions don't work, turn off all your extensions or inits and see if the problem clears up. If it does, you know that one of the extensions is the problem (see page 110 in Chapter 7).

- If turning off extensions doesn't fix the problem, reinstall your system software.

Your Mac Portable or PowerBook won't recognize an external SCSI device, or it crashes when you shut off an external SCSI device.

Problem: The Mac Portable and PowerBook don't provide SCSI termination power—they rely on external SCSI devices to provide it. As a result, they're particularly sensitive to proper device termination. If you shut off a SCSI device while the Portable or PowerBook is still running, the SCSI bus gets screwed up and the Mac crashes.

Solutions:

- If the PowerBook won't recognize the drive, check the termination. If the drive has an external terminator, remove it. If the drive is internally terminated, use the drive's setup software to disable its termination. In rare cases, you may have to have the drive opened up to have the terminator removed.

- Always shut down the Portable or PowerBook before turning off any SCSI peripherals, and always turn any such peripherals on before starting up the Portable or PowerBook.

The battery on your PowerBook 100 doesn't seem fully charged when you use the Battery control panel.

Problem: The Battery control panel was designed for the batteries in other PowerBook models, and doesn't accurately show the charge on PowerBook 100 batteries.

Solution: Ignore the inaccuracy, or buy a collection of PowerBook utilities that can accurately report the charge level (see Chapter 6).

You can't seem to connect with AppleTalk Remote Access when you use an external modem on a PowerBook 100.

Problem: You have the Network control panel set wrong.

Solution: Open the Network control panel and choose the *Remote Only* option.

Your PowerBook won't run on battery power, although it works okay on AC power.

Problem: The storage switch on the back of the PowerBook 100 may be in the wrong position, or (on any PowerBook) there may be a blown fuse on the logic board.

Solutions:

- If you have a PowerBook 100, make sure the storage switch on the back of the PowerBook (next to the AC power plug) is up (closest to the top of the PowerBook). In the down position, this switch disables battery power.

- If this isn't the problem, it's probably a blown fuse on the logic board. Take the PowerBook in for service. Make sure the technician checks the AC power adaptor plug for damage—if the insulator at its tip is defective, the plug could be shorting out and blowing the fuse.

You upgraded your PowerBook's internal hard drive and now it crashes when the drive wakes up after sleep.

Problem: The hard disk's driver is incompatible with the PowerBook.

Solution: Contact the drive's manufacturer for an upgraded driver that is compatible, or buy and use a third-party hard disk setup program like Silver-Lining or Drive 7 to install a PowerBook-compatible driver see Chapter 6).

You can't get your PowerBook to work with a LaserWriter SC.

Problem: Assuming you've checked all the obvious things (the cables are connected, the power is on, there's paper in the printer) and you don't have another device like an external hard drive on the SCSI bus, it's probably because the SCSI bus power fuse inside the LaserWriter SC is blown. The PowerBook doesn't provide SCSI termination power through its SCSI port, and if the LaserWriter SC's SCSI power fuse is blown, it can't provide termination power. As a result, the PowerBook can't "see" your printer on the SCSI bus.

Solution: Either add another device to the SCSI chain that does provide termination power (a hard disk would do it), or have the LaserWriter's SCSI bus fuse replaced.

You can't select a printer port in the Chooser on your PowerBook Duo with an internal Express Modem, even though nothing is connected to either port. A message says the port is in use when you try to select it.

Problem: The Serial Port Arbitrator is or was installed in your Extensions folder, and this has the Chooser fooled into thinking the ports are in use.

Solutions:

■ Remove the Serial Port Arbitrator from your System Folder completely—drag it to a folder outside the System Folder and restart.

■ If the problem persists, zap the PRAM (see page 115).

You can't get your PowerBook Duo to work with an external modem directly connected to it, even though the modem works fine when connected to a Duo Dock.

Problem: Assuming the modem is on and correctly plugged into your Mac's modem port, you probably have AppleTalk set to on in the Chooser.

Solution: Open the Chooser and turn AppleTalk off.

The battery on your PowerBook Duo won't charge fully.

Problem: Sometimes the power manager in the PowerBook Duo goes on the blink, and you need to reset it.

Solution: Hold down the *Reset* button on the back of the unit for at least 5 seconds, release it, then hold the button in again for another 5 seconds and release it. When you release the button the second time the Duo restarts, and the battery should charge normally. If this doesn't work, repeat the procedure.

Your PowerBook's speaker makes intermittent clicking sounds, and turning down the volume with the Sound control panel doesn't help.

Problem: Some PowerBook models make this noise each time they shut down their sound amplifiers (to conserve battery power) or power them up again.

Solution: Plug an earphone jack into the sound output port to disable the speaker completely. Of course, you won't be able to hear any sounds at all, but if the click really bugs you, this is the answer.

The screen gets dimmer as you use your PowerBook 170 or 180.

Problem: The active matrix display on these models is very sensitive to the voltage level supplied by the battery. The display is brightest when you run the PowerBook off AC power. As the voltage level drops during normal use, the display dims slightly.

The PowerBook's hard disk disappears when you run under AC power.

Problem: Either the power adapter is defective or there's something wrong with the logic board.

Solution: Take the PowerBook in for service.

Your PowerBook's trackball isn't working properly—it's not moving the pointer properly, it's hard to roll, it rolls and then stops, or the buttons don't work properly.

Problem: Either the rollers inside the trackball are dirty, the retaining ring is too tight, or the internal cables or switches in the trackball need to be tightened or replaced.

Solutions:

- First, try removing the retaining ring, removing the trackball itself, and then cleaning the rollers inside the ball housing. Replace the ball and retaining ring.

- If that doesn't work, take the PowerBook to a technician and have the connections between the trackball and the logic board checked. If the connections are okay, the trackball probably needs to be replaced.

Your PowerBook's keyboard seems stiff. You really have to punch the keys to get them to register.

Problem: The keyboard is probably screwed down too tight, restricting the movement of the its keys.

Solutions:

- Loosen the screws that hold the keyboard in place.

- If loosening the screws doesn't work, call Apple and see if you can get a replacement keyboard.

Your PowerBook's screen has lines on it no matter which application you're running.

Problem: In most cases, this means that the cable connecting the screen with the lower half of the PowerBook is cracked or damaged.

Solutions:

- If the PowerBook is under warranty, you should be able to get it fixed for nothing by an Apple dealer.

- If the PowerBook isn't under warranty, send the machine to a component-level repair service and have the cable replaced (see Chapter 6).

Your network slows down when you have one or more PowerBooks or PowerBook Duos connected.

Problem: If you have the Auto Remounter installed in the Control Panels folder and you're running the PowerBook off AC power, the PowerBook sends packets out over the network every few seconds to confirm the presence of mounted network volumes.

Solutions:

- Remove the Auto Remounter from your System Folder. If the problem persists, remove it from your hard disk completely.

- Run the PowerBook on battery power.

You get an error message when you try to install a new fax cover page using the Fax Cover application.

Problem: The Fax Monitor Pref file is corrupted.

Solution: Throw away the Fax Monitor Pref file from inside the Preferences folder in the System Folder, then run the Fax Cover application again to install new pages into the Fax Cover Library and re-create the Fax Monitor Pref file.

Your PowerBook can connect to a fax machine, but then it won't send a fax.

Problem: The PowerBook's hard drive is probably waking up from sleep. You can connect to a fax machine before the hard drive is up to speed, but you can't send or receive until the hard drive is fully up to speed.

Solution: Use the PowerBook control panel to prevent the PowerBook from sleeping, or make sure the hard disk is completely up to speed before you connect to the fax machine.

Chapter 20

Monitors

This chapter covers problems specific to monitor hardware. The organization of problems moves from the general to the specific, from problems that can occur with any monitor to problems that occur only with certain monitors, video cards, or software combinations.

The monitor doesn't come on when you turn on the Mac.

Problem: The monitor is either off or unplugged, or its power supply has gone bad.

Solutions:

■ Move the mouse or press a key on the keyboard to make sure the screen hasn't been temporarily blacked out by a screen saving utility.

■ Make sure the brightness control on the monitor isn't turned all the way down. (The monitor may in fact be on, but it's not showing anything because the brightness is turned all the way down.)

■ Check the power switch to see that it's on. You can hear the picture tube energize when the power comes on.

■ Make sure the monitor's power cord is securely plugged in at both ends, and that the power source is okay (see page 112 in Chapter 7.)

■ If none of these solutions works, take the monitor in for repairs.

The monitor's power light comes on, but the screen is black.

Problem: The most likely problem is that the brightness and contrast controls are turned down. If not, there's a hardware problem with the monitor.

Solutions:

- Turn up the monitor's brightness and contrast controls.

- If turning up the brightness and contrast controls doesn't work, try running the video tests in Snooper to get an idea of what's wrong and how to fix it. If you don't have Snooper, have the monitor checked by a service technician.

The monitor's power light comes on and the screen lights up, but there's nothing on it.

Problem: The video input cable connecting your Mac or video output board isn't plugged in correctly.

Solution: Turn the whole system off, check the video cable plugs to make sure they're tight, and try starting up again.

The monitor shows colored or gray shadows, double images, or a shrunken or distorted image, or it has a blue, green, or red tint.

Problem: The monitor isn't adjusted properly, or one of its circuits is bad.

Solution: Take the monitor in for service.

Your monitor makes a buzzing or crackling sound when you turn it on.

Problem: Every color monitor has one or more *degaussing coils* that neutralize magnetic fields inside the picture tube. The coils can make a slight buzzing or crackling sound as they're energized when you turn the monitor on. If the buzzing is really loud, the coil may be vibrating against the monitor case.

Solution: Have the monitor checked out by a technician.

Your monitor periodically pops, goes blank, and then comes back on right away.

Problem: The monitor tube or flyback transformer is arcing. Sometimes this happens because a piece of coating has come loose from inside the monitor tube. This problem is usually more annoying than it is dangerous.

Solutions:

- If the problem doesn't happen very often, try to ignore it.

- If the problem occurs frequently (a couple of times a day or more), take the monitor in for repairs.

The monitor's image is rippling, or the edges of the image aren't square.

Problem: Your monitor may be getting electromagnetic interference from another device, or it may need to be adjusted.

Solutions:

- If you have a second monitor or another electronic device next to the monitor with the problem, try turning it off. If the problem goes away, electromagnetic interference is the problem. Move the second device farther away from the monitor.

- If you're using two monitors, you can't move them farther apart, and you need to have both on at once, you can get an electromagnetic shield that will block the interference. Call NoRad Corporation, 800-262-3260.

- If you aren't using two monitors and don't have another large electrical device next to your monitor, the monitor needs to be adjusted. Take it in for service.

Your monitor isn't showing the correct number of colors or shades of gray, or isn't showing color at all.

Problem: You probably have the Monitors control panel set wrong. Of course, if your monitor can't display color, changing a software setting won't make any difference.

Solution: Open the Monitors control panel and check the number of colors or gray shades you have set. See page 45 in Chapter 3 for more about the Monitors control panel.

You're using two monitors, but your Mac keeps displaying the desktop and menu bar on the wrong one.

Problem: You have to reset the Monitors control panel to make the Mac display the menu bar on a different monitor.

Solution: Open the Monitors control panel and drag the menu bar from the current monitor's icon to the second monitor's icon, then restart your Mac. See page 45 in Chapter 3 for more about the Monitors control panel.

 Your Mac crashes with a system error -25 when you use two or more monitors.

Problem: There's not enough memory to maintain applications, data, Clipboard information, and other data on two or more screens. When you use a monitor that has a high resolution mode (say 2000 x 2000 pixels), the problem is worse because more memory is required to display all those extra pixels on the screen.

Solution: If you're using the Finder, try eliminating anything from your System file that uses extra memory, such as extra inits, fonts, or sounds.

If you're using System 7 or MultiFinder, try increasing the application memory for each of the programs you want to run (see page 35).

Your color monitor has one or two thin horizontal lines running across the screen about a third of the way from the top and/or the bottom.

Problem: The lines are support wires that are part of the design of the Sony monitors that Apple uses. There's no way to make them go away.

 Your Mac crashes when you open the CloseView utility.

Problem: The CloseView utility isn't compatible with Mac II models that use Apple's display card 4•8, 8•24, or 8•24 GC.

Solution: Upgrade your system software to System 7. The version of CloseView that comes with that version is compatible with Apple's display cards.

You're running System 7 and the Mac freezes when the CloseView extension is loaded during startup.

Problem: Either the extension is incompatible with others you're running, or you're using a third-party monitor whose own software is incompatible with CloseView.

Solutions:

■ Restart the Mac with all extensions off and see if it starts okay. If it does, restart with only the CloseView extension running. If it still starts okay, you have an extension conflict. See page 110.

■ If you're using a third-party video card and the Mac locks up when CloseView is the only extension loaded, there's probably a conflict between it and some software in the card's ROM. Restart the Mac without CloseView running. If it starts okay, contact the video card's manufacturer about the problem. You may not be able to run Close-View with that video card, or there may be a ROM upgrade that fixes the problem.

Your Mac IIvx crashes occasionally with a Radius video card installed.

Problem: Assuming you've eliminated potential causes like insufficient memory and incompatible extensions or applications, some Radius video cards made before the IIvx came out are incompatible with this model Mac.

 Other third-party monitor makers may have video cards that are incompatible with newer Mac models as well. If you've eliminated other possible causes of system crashes, call the monitor company and ask about possible problems with their card.

Solutions:

■ Check other possible causes first (see Chapter 7).

■ Contact Radius for a software upgrade that fixes the problem.

You plugged a VGA monitor into your Mac, but it doesn't work.

Problem: Standard Macintosh video has different vertical and horizontal scan rates than standard VGA video. However, some Macs can deliver VGA-standard video if you plug the right adapter into them. Depending on the Mac model you have, you either need a specific type of VGA monitor or you have the wrong connector.

 James Engineering of El Cerrito, California, specializes in connecting VGA monitors to Macs, and they sell several types of adapters. Their number is 510-525-7350.

Solutions:

■ If you have a Mac II, IIx, IIcx, IIfx, IIsi, or IIci, you must have a
multiscan, multisynch VGA monitor and the correct adapter to make it
work with your Mac. These Macs don't produce VGA-standard video
scan rates (which are 60 Hz vertical and 31.5 kHz horizontal), and they
don't use the same video synchronization signal, but a multiscan,
multisynch monitor can adapt itself to the Mac's scan rates and video
synchronization method. Call the monitor's manufacturer and ask if
the monitor can support Mac video scan rates (which are 66 Hz vertical
and 35 kHz horizontal). If it can, then you only need to find the correct adapter for it.

■ If you have a Mac LC, Quadra, IIvx, IIvi, Centris, or Performa model, it
can put out VGA-standard video. You can use any VGA-standard monitor, as long as you have the right adapter to connect it to your Mac.
The connector's pin configuration determines the video scan rates and
type of synchronization signal the Mac puts out. Ask the monitor's
manufacturer or your Mac dealer for the right connector.

Chapter 21

Printers

In this chapter, we'll look at some common problems related to specific models of Apple printers. The chapter is divided into two sections, one for LaserWriters and the other for StyleWriters and ImageWriters. When a problem is specific to a certain LaserWriter, StyleWriter, or ImageWriter model, the model is mentioned in the problem heading.

LaserWriter problems

Your LaserWriter prints a startup page each time you turn it on, and you don't want it to.

Problem: Every PostScript-compatible LaserWriter automatically prints a startup page.

Solution: Use the LaserWriter Utility (version 7.0 or later) to disable or enable the startup page.

Pages print blank or very lightly.

Problem: Either the toner cartridge is empty or it's not distributing toner, or the print density dial is set too low.

Solutions:

■ Check the print density dial on the back of the LaserWriter and make sure it's not turned all the way down. Try turning it up and printing again.

279

- If you've just replaced the toner cartridge and nothing is printing at all, make sure the sealing tape has been removed from cartridge.

- If the cartridge isn't new, try removing it, holding it lengthwise between your hands, and then rocking it toward and away from you a few times to redistribute the toner. Even if the cartridge is getting empty, this should allow you to print a few more pages.

The LaserWriter's print is too dark.

Problem: The print density setting is probably too high.

Solutions:

- Turn down the density dial on the back of the printer and try printing again.

- Look inside the LaserWriter and see if it needs cleaning. Look for excess toner spilled inside the mechanism. Usually, though, a dirty mechanism causes random darkness or splotches, not uniform darkness.

- Try replacing the toner cartridge. A failing cartridge can sometimes cause print that's too dark.

There are random white spots on pages.

Problem: The toner isn't being distributed evenly, or the printer may need cleaning.

Solutions:

- Try removing the cartridge, holding it lengthwise between your hands, and rocking it toward and away from you a few times.

- Replace the toner cartridge.

- If the above steps don't work, take the printer in for cleaning or consult a printer troubleshooting book (like *The Dead Mac Scrolls*) for instructions on how to clean it yourself.

There are black spots at random on a page, or toner seems unevenly distributed.

Problem: The toner cartridge is probably running out.

Solutions:

- Try removing the cartridge and rocking it a few times to redistribute the toner inside it. If this doesn't work, replace the toner cartridge with a new one.

- If replacing the cartridge doesn't solve the problem, the printer drum is probably dirty. Take it in for cleaning, or consult a printer trouble-shooting book (like *The Dead Mac Scrolls)* for instructions on how to clean it yourself.

There are black smudges on the back of each printed page.

Problem: The printer needs cleaning.

Solution: Take the printer in for service, or consult a printer troubleshooting book (like *The Dead Mac Scrolls)* for instructions on how to clean it yourself.

You upgraded a LaserWriter II to a IIg or IIf, and now it doesn't recognize the external hard disk where your fonts are stored.

Problem: The LaserWriter IIg and IIf have different SCSI termination schemes than the LaserWriter II, and so the upgraded printer isn't recognizing the hard disk.

Solution: Use the black terminator from a Mac IIfx to terminate the hard disk. You can get one from your Apple dealer.

Your LaserWriter suddenly won't download the fonts you've specified in your document, even though the fonts are available on your hard disk.

Problem: The system software or LaserWriter driver is corrupted.

Solution: Check for multiple System Folders on your hard disk and eliminate them, then replace the system software in the System Folder that remains.

You can't select the grayscale option in the Print dialog box (or you get an error message when you try) when you're printing on a StyleWriter or non-PostScript LaserWriter from a Mac Plus, SE, Portable, Classic, or PowerBook 100.

Problem: The Mac Plus, SE, Portable, Classic, and PowerBook 100 don't have color QuickDraw in ROM, and you need this to print in grayscale on a non-PostScript printer. You can only print in black and white from these Macs.

Solutions:

■ Print the document from a different Mac.

■ Connect the StyleWriter or non-PostScript LaserWriter to a Mac that does have color QuickDraw, use GrayShare to share the printer over a network, and then print on it from your own Mac. Because the printer is connected to a Mac that does support grayscale, you'll be able to use this option.

You want to use the GrayShare driver to share an ImageWriter, StyleWriter, or non-PostScript LaserWriter, but you can't select one of these printers.

Problem: The GrayShare driver only supports the StyleWriter II, LaserWriter Select 300, Apple Color Printer, and newer QuickDraw-based printers. Other printers can't be shared with it.

StyleWriter and ImageWriter problems

The printer's select light doesn't come on, even though the power is on.

Problem: The printer's cover isn't completely closed.

Solution: Check the printer cover to make sure it's completely closed.

The print density is uneven.

Problem: You need a new ribbon or ink cartridge.

Solutions:

■ Replace the ribbon or ink cartridge.

■ If this doesn't solve the problem, there may be something wrong with your platen or print head. Take the printer in for service.

The print is too light.

Problem: Either the ribbon or the ink cartridge needs to be replaced, the paper thickness lever is set wrong, you're using the wrong paper, or the ribbon isn't advancing properly.

Solutions:

- Check the setting of the paper thickness lever. This lever changes the distance between the print head and the paper; if the print head is too far away, the print will be too light. Move the lever up or toward the back of the printer to move the print head closer to the paper.

- If you're using a StyleWriter, purge the ink cartridge. See the printer manual for instructions.

- If you're using a StyleWriter, make sure you're using bond paper in 16 to 24 pound weights. Other weights or types of paper don't retain the ink as well.

- If this isn't the problem, replace the ribbon or ink cartridge.

- If the above solutions don't work, take the printer in for service.

Characters are blotchy or have gaps in them.

Problem: The ribbon or ink cartridge is wearing out, the paper thickness lever is set wrong, you're using the wrong paper weight (on a StyleWriter), or the print head is dirty.

Solutions:

- Check the paper thickness lever to make sure the print head isn't too far away from the paper. Moving the lever back or up moves the print head closer to the paper.

- If you're using a StyleWriter, make sure you're using bond paper in 16 to 24 pound weights. Other weights or types of paper won't retain the ink as well, and you might get blotchy results.

- Replace the printer ribbon or ink cartridge. If the ImageWriter's print head is dirty, a new ribbon will probably clean it. (The ink contains a lubricant that can free up sticky wires in the print head.)

- If the above solutions don't work, take the printer in for service or consult *The Dead Mac Scrolls*. If the printer is a few years old, the print head may simply be worn out.

You've just replaced the ink cartridge in a StyleWriter I and now it doesn't print anything at all.

Problem: New ink cartridges often have a little air in them, and you need to purge the air before ink will come out.

Solution: If you have a StyleWriter I (the StyleWriter II doesn't have this problem), turn the printer off, press the *Form Feed* and *On* buttons at the same time, then turn the power switch on. This forces ink through the print head and purges the air bubble.

Fonts seem jagged or low-resolution when you print from a StyleWriter, even though you have TrueType fonts or ATM and PostScript fonts installed.

Problem: The StyleWriter defaults to using bitmapped fonts if they're available in the System Folder or Fonts folder. For example, if you have a bitmapped version of Times installed in your Mac, the StyleWriter uses that version before it uses the TrueType or PostScript version.

Solution: Remove the bitmapped versions of fonts from your System Folder or Fonts folder. The StyleWriter is then forced to use TrueType (or PostScript fonts, if you have ATM installed), and you get much better quality.

The print is tiny and there are big gaps between words.

Problem: You're using the Draft quality setting in the Print dialog box.

Solution: Select a different quality setting in the Print dialog box before you print the document.

Some characters are missing when you print from a StyleWriter.

Problem: A screen-saving program may be disabling print processing.

Solution: Check your Mac to see if you have a screen saving utility installed, then turn it off and print the document again. If it prints okay, the screen saver is interfering with the print processing. Make sure you turn off the screen saver when you print long documents.

On an ImageWriter, there's extra space or not enough space between the first and second lines of text on a page, or the first line becomes offset somewhere between the left and right margin.

Problem: The printer's platen isn't set correctly. When the platen is between click stops, it can fall into place either while printing one line, or between the first and second lines of the document.

Solution: Make sure the platen is set on a click stop by rolling it back and forth before you print a page.

There's too much or too little space between lines on a printout.

Problem: If this happens with every document in every program, the printer's DIP switch settings are probably off.

Solutions:

- First, check the line spacing setting in the document to make sure it's what you want.

- If the line spacing is set properly, look in your printer's manual to see how its DIP switches should be set. One setting controls the amount of space after each carriage return.

There's too much space or not enough space between pages on a continuous-feed printout.

Problem: Either the page size or margins are set wrong in the document, or the printer's DIP switch settings are wrong.

Solutions:

- Make sure the document's page size and top and bottom margins are what you want them to be. Use the *Page Setup* command to check the paper size option.

- If the paper size and margins settings are okay, check the printer manual for the proper DIP switch settings. One setting controls paper sizes, and your printer may be set to standard sizes for a different country.

The paper advances too far before printing the first line.

Problem: The top margin is too large or the top-of-form setting is off.

Solutions:

- Check the top margin setting in the document to make sure it's not too large.

- If the margin setting is okay, reset the top of form. Turn the printer off, advance the paper until its top edge is just under the print head, and then turn the printer on again. If your printer has a *Top Of Form* button, align the paper's top edge under the print head and then press the *Top Of Form* button.

You're printing single sheets on an ImageWriter, ImageWriter II, or ImageWriter LQ, and the top margin shrinks on the second page of a document and on each page after that.

Problem: You probably have the *Continuous Feed* option set in the Print dialog box. When printing on continuous paper, ImageWriters reverse the paper slightly before printing new pages.

Solution: Check the Print dialog box and make sure the *Manual Feed* option is set.

You're using continuous-feed paper in an ImageWriter and it becomes mis-aligned after a few pages are printed.

Problem: You have the printer's platen set to friction feed instead of pin feed.

Solution: Move the feed selection lever backward to the pin feed position and then load the paper so the holes in its margins are over the pins at the edges of the platen.

When you print large boxes from a graphics program on a StyleWriter or StyleWriter II, the box ends up shorter than it was drawn in the application.

Problem: StyleWriter printers overlap each printed line to blend lines or characters more completely for better resolution. Unfortunately, this overlapping has a cumulative effect with graphic objects that occupy most of a page, so the objects end up shorter than they were originally drawn.

Solution: When exact sizes matter, use a PostScript printer.

Mailing label stock jams in an ImageWriter II.

Problem: Either the platen release lever isn't locked all the way down or, more likely, the label stock you're using is old or curved from being in the printer too long.

Solutions:

- Carefully remove the label page from the printer. If any labels have come loose, make sure you clear them completely out of the paper path. If any label gum has gotten on the platen, clean it off with type-writer platen cleaning fluid from an office supply store.

- Examine your label stock and make sure the labels on it aren't loose (this happens when label stock gets old). If the labels are loose, buy new label stock.

- Carefully feed a new, straight sheet of labels into the printer and then print immediately. Don't leave label stock in the printer for any longer than necessary, because it soon curves, and curved paper easily jams in an ImageWriter II.

- If you can't clear the paper path completely or the above steps don't solve the problem, take the printer in for service.

The paper jams in an ImageWriter II.

Problem: Either the platen release lever isn't locked all the way down, the paper path is obstructed, the paper is crooked or curved, or the paper guide is broken.

Solutions:

- Remove the paper and check the paper path for pieces of paper or labels. Even a small scrap can cause a jam.

- Make sure the platen release lever is pressed all the way down.

- If you're using continuous-feed paper, make sure the first sheet of paper isn't curved (from being in the printer for a long time). If it is, tear it off and start with a new, straight page.

■ Feed the paper carefully into the printer, using the roller to advance the paper until its front edge is under the print head. (Don't use the *Form Feed* button.)

■ If the above steps don't solve the problem, the paper guide may be broken. Take the printer in for repairs.

Colors overlap at the top and bottom of text characters when you use a color ribbon on the ImageWriter II.

Problem: The ribbon is improperly adjusted.

Solution: Turn the ribbon cam adjustment ring and try reprinting until the colors don't overlap. Check the ImageWriter II manual for instructions.

The StyleWriter makes a clicking noise when it picks up paper.

Problem: This is a normal sound created by the printer's paper pickup mechanism, and there's nothing you can do about it.

Chapter 22

Microsoft Word

In this chapter, we'll look at common problems you may run into when using Microsoft Word. The chapter is divided into four sections to help you zero in on problems:

- Working with files

- Entering and editing information

- Formatting and printing

- Miscellaneous

Most of these problems deal with user error—they explain things that many people are confused about, and they're not specific to a particular version of Word. This chapter assumes that you're using either Word 4 or Word 5.

As to bugs, most of the common ones in Word 4 occurred in early versions of that product, so you can avoid a lot of them by using a later version. Word 5 has proven to be relatively bugless.

To find out which version of Word you're using, select the Word icon on the desktop and then choose *Get Info* from the File menu in the Finder. If you're using Word 4, there should be a letter after the version number in the info dialog box. If this letter is *a* or *b*, you should upgrade. If you're a registered Word 4 user, you can get a free maintenance upgrade by calling Microsoft.

If you're running System 7, you should probably upgrade to Word 5. Word 4 isn't fully System 7 compatible, although you can get a maintenance release of Word 4 that makes it partially System 7-compatible and fixes some bugs that occur when you run under System 7.

Working with files

Word's performance seems slower than usual.

Problem: There are several possible reasons for this:

- When you use the Fast Save option, Word keeps track of all the edits you make and tacks them onto the last saved version of the file instead of rewriting the file from scratch. This makes file-saving faster, but it also makes for larger, slower files.

- You're running in color instead of black and white.

- You have several large documents open.

- You have something large on the Clipboard.

Solutions:

- If you've been working on the document for a long time, use *Save As* to save the document instead of *Save*—this rewrites the entire file to disk, eliminates all the added-on editing changes, and slims down the file. Then reopen the document.

- If you're running your monitor in color mode, open the Monitors control panel and switch to Black and White. It takes the Mac a little longer to do anything in color.

- Try closing other documents you're not using.

 If you're using Word 5.0 or later, the program automatically does a normal save of the file every so often to keep the file in fighting trim, even if you have the Fast Save option set, so bloated files shouldn't be a problem.

- If you recently copied and pasted a large graphic or text selection and you no longer need this information on the Clipboard, select a single character and copy it twice to reduce the amount of memory being used by the Clipboard.

Your Mac has crashed and you want to recover data from a Word Temp file, but you can't find the file or it doesn't contain anything.

Problem: When you open a document and work on it, Word creates a Word Temp file and keeps track of the changes you make to the document. If you save your work normally and quit Word properly, the Temp file is automatically deleted. If Word or your Mac crashes, however, the Temp file remains on your disk. Theoretically, you can open the Word Temp file to retrieve your work, but in practice you may not know where to look for this file, the file may not contain anything when you do open it, or it may not contain all the work you lost.

Solution: If you're using System 7 and your Mac crashes, the system software creates a folder called Rescued Items inside your Trash, and you'll find it there when you restart the Mac. The Word Temp file is inside this folder. If you're using System 6, the Word Temp file is located right inside the System Folder. To open the file:

1. If you're using System 7, drag the Word Temp file out of the Rescued Items folder and onto the desktop.

2. Open Word, then choose the *Open* command from the File menu.

3. Choose the *All Files* option from the List Files of Type pop-up menu, then navigate to the desktop (or to the System Folder under System 6). You should see the Word Temp file on the list.

4. Double-click the Word Temp file to open it.

Once you open the file, don't expect it to look like your document. Instead, you'll see a plain-formatted file that may contain just a few strings of text, or whole paragraphs, or even some garbage characters. What Word has saved depends on how long you've had the document open, whether or not you have the Fast Save option checked in the Save As dialog box, and how recently you saved the document to disk before the crash occurred. If you just opened the file and edited a few characters before the crash, for example, the Word

Even though the Word Temp file is a readable file, it won't show up in a list of files when you have the *Readable Files* option selected on the List Files of Type pop-up menu.

Temp file won't contain anything, while if you've worked on the file for hours, saving regularly, the Word Temp file will contain a lot of text.

The Word Temp file can help you recover some edits you made to a document, but the best protection against power outages and system crashes is to save your document to disk very frequently. Then, when the system crashes, you can open the document itself and you should have lost only a little work.

Files seem larger than normal.

Problem: There are two possible causes of larger-than-normal files.

 Word 5 periodically consolidates changes and rewrites a file when you use its *Save* command to eliminate the file-bloating problem. You can also disable the *Fast Save* option in Word 5.0 or later by using *Preferences* command. Choose *Preferences* from the Tools menu, click the Open and Save icon, and then click *Allow Fast Saves* to remove the X from the checkbox.

- Graphics make files much larger. If your document contains one or more graphics, the character count in the document window is significantly smaller than the file size listed in the Finder.

- You may be using the *Fast Save* option, which speeds up file saving by writing only changes to the last saved version of the file, rather than rewriting the file completely.

Solution: There's not much you can do about graphics making a file larger, but if you have the *Fast Save* option checked in the Save As dialog box, use the *Save As* command to save the entire file. Unlike the *Save* command, *Save As* rewrites the whole file instead of just adding changes to an older version.

Entering and editing information

When you scroll the document, some lines seem to be missing, or double-spaced lines become single-spaced.

Problem: This is usually a temporary problem with screen refreshing.

Solution: Scroll to another part of document, then scroll back. This should clear up the problem. If it happens again, scroll away from the problem area and then back to clear it up, save and close your document, and quit Word. Then restart and go back to work. This procedure will clear up any potential memory corruption problems.

One or more lines in your document don't wrap at the right margin—they wrap well before the right margin.

Problem: The line has probably been broken manually with a line break character.

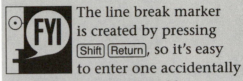 The line break marker is created by pressing Shift Return, so it's easy to enter one accidentally when you're typing quickly.

Solution: Choose *Show ¶* from the View menu to display hidden formatting characters, and look at the end of the line for a character like this: ↵

This is the line-break marker. It shows where lines are broken without beginning a new paragraph. Select it and delete it to eliminate the line break.

Word beeps when you try to backspace to remove a paragraph marker.

Problem: You can't remove a paragraph marker by simply backspacing when the marker separates two paragraphs with different formats.

Solution: If you really want to remove the marker, select the marker itself and delete it. The paragraph above the marker takes on the format of the paragraph that was below the marker before you deleted it.

You've moved the insertion point from an early page of a long document to a page near the end of the document, and now you want to go back to where you were before without scrolling and searching for the old location.

Problem: When you're working with a multipage document, it's sometimes hard to remember exactly where you were when you move the insertion point to a different location to check some text or make a change. When comparing text at two ends of a document, you can wind up doing a lot of scrolling and scanning to move between two locations.

Solution: Press 0 on the numeric keypad or ⌘ Option Z to choose the *Go Back* command. Word remembers the last four locations of the insertion point, so pressing 0 or ⌘ Option Z once moves back to the previous location, pressing the command again moves you back to the location before that, and so on.

You paste in a graphic and it screws up the line or word spacing in your document.

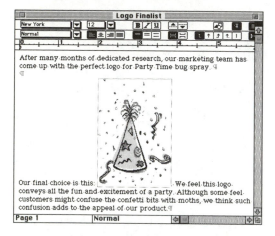

Problem: Normal pasting puts graphics in line in a document. A graphic is treated like a text character, and other lines or characters move out of the way to accommodate it.

Solutions:

■ Create a two-column table one row high, and then paste the graphic into one of the two cells. You can then paste text into the adjacent cell, display the table without a border, and it looks as if the graphic and text are in two separate columns.

■ Create a frame and paste the graphic into the frame. You can then position the frame anywhere, and text automatically rearranges itself around the frame.

 There are two *Frame* commands in Word, one on the Insert menu and one on the Format menu. Use the one on the Insert menu to create a frame or to turn a selection of text or a selected in-line graphic into a frame. Use the *Frame* command on the Format menu to change the size or position of a frame.

You want to select just one column of text from a multi-column table, but Word keeps selecting all the text on each document line.

Problem: When you hold down the mouse button and drag the pointer up or down, Word assumes that you want to select everything on a line.

Region	City	Sales
East	New York	149,000
East	Boston	133,000
Midwest	Chicago	147,000

Solution: Press (Option) and then drag the pointer across only the column of text you want to select. Word selects only that column.

Formatting and printing

Word always uses 12-point New York in new documents, but you want a different look.

Problem: Word has a default font and style that applies to all new, untitled documents. Word always uses 12-point New York unless it's not available, and it defaults to the Normal style. Fortunately, you can change the font and style easily.

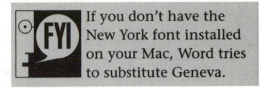

If you don't have the New York font installed on your Mac, Word tries to substitute Geneva.

Solutions:

- To change only the default font, choose the *Preferences* command from the Tools menu, check the *Default Font* option, and choose a different font or size from the pop-up menus.

- To change text styles, paragraph indents, line spacing, indents, or other character or paragraph formats, choose the *Styles* command from the Format menu and either change the Normal style or select the style you prefer and make it the default style.

You paste in text that is formatted the way you want it, but its format changes to match the paragraph into which you paste it.

Problem: Pasted text always takes on the format of the paragraph into which it is pasted in a Word document.

Solution: Reformat the text.

You're trying to align several rows of text or numbers in a column, but they don't quite line up.

Region	City	Sales
East	New York	149,000
East	Boston	133,000
Midwest	Chicago	147,000

Problem: You're probably trying to align the text by pressing [Spacebar]. This always worked on a typewriter because each character was exactly the same width. But because characters on the Mac are different widths, it's difficult or impossible to precisely align rows of text by pressing the [Spacebar].

Solution: Press [Tab] or use paragraph indents to line up several rows of text precisely.

There are two Header styles (or two other styles with the same name) on the list in the Style dialog box.

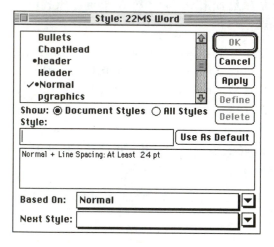

Problem: You're working with a document in which a second Header style has been imported from another document, or a second Header style has been created and named. Each new Word document includes a standard Header style, but you can create another one if you like.

Solution: Select each Header style in turn and look at its definition in the box below. If they're the same, delete one of the styles. If they're not the same, give one of the styles a different name.

The standard styles Word includes in every new document are identified with bullets on the list in the Style dialog box. When you delete a style, any text formatted with that style is assigned the Normal style. To copy a particular style from one document to another in Word, select the paragraph containing that style, copy it, and paste it into the other document. The style is pasted with the selection. To copy *all* the styles from one document to another, choose the *Style* command in the document into which you want the new styles copied, then choose the *Open* command from the File menu and open the document whose styles you want to import. Instead of opening the document, Word opens the document's style sheet and copies the styles there into the document you already have open.

You modify the Normal style in the Style dialog box, and other styles in your document change as well.

Problem: To make it easier for you to create new styles, Word lets you base each new style on a previously existing style. For example, all the standard styles (Header, Footer, and so on) included with new documents are based on the Normal style (they use the same font), and any new style you create will automatically be based on the style of the paragraph where the insertion point is currently located. However, since some styles are based on others, changing a style upon which others are based also changes those files as well.

Solution: To keep each new style completely separate, delete the style name from the Based On pop-up menu before you define the new style.

A graphic becomes distorted when you drag its handle to resize it.

Problem: Graphics stored in MacPaint and TIFF file formats sometimes don't resize smoothly.

Solution: Hold down the ⌘ key and double-click the graphic to return it to its normal size. Unfortunately, there's no good way to smoothly resize a MacPaint or TIFF image if it's becoming distorted. Instead, copy the image to a paint or drawing program, save it in either PICT or EPS format, and then insert that image in your document. Images in these formats resize more smoothly.

You've placed a border around a document heading, but the border's box is a lot wider than the text it contains.

Table of Contents

Problem: Borders are as wide as the current paragraph margins.

Solution: Select any or all text inside the border and then drag the left and right indent markers in the ruler to make the paragraph itself narrower.

You've selected a hairline border, but it doesn't show up when you print the document.

Problem: The *Hairline* border option only works on PostScript-compatible printers. If you're using a StyleWriter or ImageWriter, it won't print.

Solution: Choose the *Single* line option for a border, or print the document on a PostScript-compatible printer.

You've created a title at the top of a document and added a border around it, but now the border extends when you press Return**, and you don't want it to.**

Table of Contents¶
¶

Problem: Word always continues the formatting of the previous paragraph into the next paragraph, so if the insertion point is at the end of a heading that has a border around it, pressing Return creates a new paragraph and extends the border.

Solution: Select the new paragraph marker and then use the *Border* command on the Format menu to change the border for that paragraph back to None. The border moves back up to the end of the previous paragraph.

Page breaks are different in a printed document than they are on your screen.

Problem: If page breaks are different on a printout, it probably means that Word repaginated your document just before printing, changing the positions of page breaks. Word repaginates documents either automatically or manually, depending on whether you've checked *Background Repagination* in the Preferences dialog box. Even with *Background Repagination* set, however, Word doesn't always repaginate documents immediately, so you don't always see true automatic page breaks on your screen. When you print, Word always repaginates just before sending the document to the printer.

Solution: To see the current placement of page breaks, choose *Repaginate Now* from the Tools menu just before you print. Better yet, choose *Print Preview* from the File menu to see exactly where the page breaks fall.

You've created a new section in the middle of a page and you're expecting a page break, but the section mark doesn't generate a page break when you print the document.

Problem: Word's default with sections is no new page break. You have to format the section to cause a page break.

Solution: Choose the *Section* command from the Format menu, then choose the *New Page* command from the Start pop-up menu in the upper right corner.

 If you want page numbers to restart at 1 after a section, check the *Restart at 1* box in the Page Numbers area of the Section dialog box.

When you print a document, the pages come out in reverse order, so the first page is always on the bottom of the output tray.

Problem: Word normally prints documents from front to back, so the first page is the first one out of the printer. If your printer delivers pages face down, the document is in the proper order, but if it delivers pages face up, the order is backwards and you have to rearrange the pages.

Solution: Check the *Back to Front* option in the Print dialog box before printing the document. Word then prints the last page first.

Miscellaneous

Word rounds amounts and creates an inappropriate result when you use the *Calculate* command.

Problem: Word calculates numbers to the level of precision indicated by the most precise value in the numbers being calculated. For example, it calculates 2525/3 as 841, while it calculates 2525.00/3 as 841.67.

Solution: Make sure that at least one of the numbers being calculated has enough decimal places to produce a calculation at the level of precision you need.

You've spell-checked your document, but when you compile a table of contents or index from hidden text, there are spelling errors that Word didn't catch.

Problem: Word doesn't check hidden text if it's not displayed in a document.

Solution: Use the *View* options in the Preferences dialog box to display hidden text, then run the spelling check again. With the hidden text in view, Word can check it.

The Grammar Checker checks spelling in a document even though you've already used the spelling checker.

Problem: One of the style characteristics the Grammar Checker looks for is word spellings, but you can tell it to ignore these if you like.

Solution: Choose the *Preferences* command from the Tools menu, click the Grammar icon (you'll have to scroll the list at the left side of the dialog box to see it), and then click the checkmark next to the *Open vs. Closed Spelling* option to remove it.

You used the *Hyphenation* command to add automatic hyphens to a document. You now think the document looks dumb, but it's too late to use the *Undo* command to remove them.

Problem: Word's *Undo* command only undoes the very last thing you did, so you have to use it right away to cancel operations.

Solution: You can use the *Replace* command to search for automatic hyphens and then replace them with nothing. Just choose *Replace,* choose *Optional Hyphen* from the Special menu below the *Find What* box to enter the code for this marker in the *Find What* box, leave the *Replace With* box blank, and click *Replace All*.

 You can eliminate lots of mistakes using the Format and Special pop-up menus in the Replace dialog box. Before you panic and start removing unwanted items from a document manually, check out the Replace dialog box's menus to see if Word can search for the item you want to remove.

Chapter 23
Microsoft Excel

In this chapter, we'll look at common problems you may run into when using Microsoft Excel. The chapter is divided into seven sections:

- Working with files

- Entering and changing data

- Calculating

- Formatting and printing

- Macros

- Charting

- Miscellaneous

Some of the problems covered here are version-specific. In that case, the problem heading says so. As it happens, a lot of Excel's incompatibilities and bugs can be solved by using the right version of the program.

- If you're using Excel 2.2, make sure you're using version 2.2a or later. There were lots of bugs in version 2.2 related to locating files in folders and to crashing on the Mac IIsi and newer machines (or under System 7).

- If you're using Excel 3.0, make sure you're using version 3.0a or later. Otherwise, you'll have trouble printing from the Finder or selecting certain printing options when printing to a Personal LaserWriter LS.

To find out which version of Excel you're using, select the Excel icon on the desktop and then choose *Get Info* from the File menu in the Finder. If you're a registered Excel 3 user, you can get a free maintenance upgrade by calling Microsoft. Excel 2.2 users should upgrade to Excel 4.

Working with files

You've used a newer version of Excel to open, change, and save an Excel file from an older version, but the original file you opened hasn't changed.

Problem: When you open an Excel document from an older version of the program, Excel converts it to the format for the current version, considers it a new file, and saves the new file to the same folder from which you launched Excel. The original file (in the old Excel version's format) remains unchanged on the disk.

Solution: Delete the old version of the file or use the *Save As* command to save the new, converted file to the same folder as the old version of the file, thereby replacing it.

You're running At Ease on a Macintosh Performa, you've set it up to save files to a floppy disk, and you get an error message when you try to save an Excel file to a folder on the floppy.

Problem: Excel can't save files to a folder on a floppy disk if you've set the options to require a floppy or to add a button to At Ease.

Solution: Open the At Ease Setup control panel, click the *Set Up Documents* button, and make sure that neither of the options (*Add A Button To At Ease* or *Require A Floppy Disk*) is checked.

You want to automatically open a macro sheet or a chart when you open a worksheet file.

Problem: Macros and charts are stored in separate files in Excel.

Solution: Drag the macro sheet or chart file inside the Preferences folder in your System Folder, or (under System 6) inside the System Folder itself.

Entering and changing data

You enter a long number into a cell, but when you press ⌐Return⌐, the number is converted to scientific notation.

Problem: When a number contains too many digits to be displayed in a cell at the current column width, Excel converts it to scientific notation. The positive or negative number in the notation indicates the number of zeroes to the left (positive) or right (negative) of the decimal point. For example, the number above represents 132,456,000,000.

B2		132456000000	
	A	**B**	**C**
1		January	February
2	Cost of Goods	1.3246E+11	
3			

Solutions:

If you don't want to view the number in scientific notation:

■ Widen the column so it can display the full number.

When you use the ROUND function, remember that it will change the stored number. A number rounded off to two decimal places is converted to the two-decimal number, while a number formatted to two decimal places is still stored as the larger original value.

■ Use the *Number* command on the Format menu to select a fixed-decimal format for the number to limit the number of decimal places.

■ Use the ROUND function in a formula to round the number off so it can be displayed in fewer digits.

You can't enter data into a cell.

Problem: Excel's worksheet protection feature is turned on.

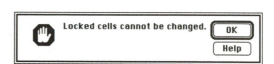

Locked cells cannot be changed.
OK
Help

Solution: Choose the *Unprotect Document* command from the Options menu and then enter the password required to unlock the document. If you don't know the password, ask the worksheet's owner.

You've selected a range of cells into which to enter data, but as soon as you press an arrow key to move from one cell to the next, the range is deselected.

Problem: You can only use $\boxed{\text{Tab}}$, $\boxed{\text{Shift}}$ $\boxed{\text{Tab}}$, $\boxed{\text{Return}}$, and $\boxed{\text{Shift}}$ $\boxed{\text{Return}}$ to move within a selected range. If you use an arrow key, Excel automatically deselects the range.

Solution: Don't use arrow keys to move within a selected range.

You've moved formulas containing relative references from one location to another, but the references in them didn't adjust to their new locations.

Problem: Relative cell references only adjust automatically when you copy a formula, not when you move it using the *Cut* and *Paste* commands or the drag-and-drop feature in Excel 4.

Solution: Use *Copy* instead of the *Cut* to move formulas, and their relative references will adjust.

Calculating

You enter a simple formula with values and operators, but the result isn't what you expected.

Problem: Excel performs calculations in a certain order: it always performs operations inside parentheses first, followed by multiplication and division, and then addition and subtraction. Unless you've used parentheses to specify the order of calculations within a formula, you may not get the result you want. For example, *3+5*2* equals 13, while *(3+5)*2* equals 16.

Solution: Always use parentheses to specify the order of calculations when you enter complex formulas.

Excel displays negative numbers in financial formula results and you don't want it to.

Problem: Some financial formulas (loan payment calculations, for example) produce negative results, because the result represents negative cash flow. In many cases, however, you don't want the result displayed as a negative.

Loan Amount	$10,000
Loan Term	36
Mo. Int. Rate	0.83%
Mo. Payment	($322.67)

Solution: Use the ABS function to calculate the absolute value of the number. Select the cell, click just to the right of the equal sign at the beginning of the formula bar, type *ABS(*, then click at the very end of the formula and type *)*. Once you enter this formula you'll be calculating the absolute value of the expression, which returns the positive version of any negative number.

A financial formula produces a loan payment amount that seems way too high.

Problem: Typically, the problem is that the values specified for the loan's term and interest rate don't agree. You've probably specified a loan term in months and have specified the annual interest rate. Under this scenario, the annual rate amount is being applied to each month's payment, and the payment is far higher than it should be.

Loan Amount	$10,000
Loan Term	36
Interest Rate	12.00%
Mo. Payment	($1,220.64)

Solution: When entering values in financial formulas, make sure the loan period and interest values are expressed for the same time period. If you're calculating a monthly payment, the loan period must be specified in months and the interest rate must be a monthly rate.

Excel displays an error value instead of a number in a cell as the result of a formula.

Problem: The formula can't be resolved because of some mathematical or referential error. Excel uses seven different error values to help you determine what the problem is.

#DIV/0! The formula is trying to divide by zero, usually because it refers to an empty cell. This can happen when you've copied a formula into another cell—although the original formula works fine, the copy contains a relative reference that refers to an empty cell.

#NAME? The formula contains a name reference or constant, but either the name reference is invalid or the constant isn't entered in the correct format. For example, you may have used a range name in a formula, but the range name has been deleted, or you spelled it wrong when defining the formula. In a text formula, you may have entered the text string without quotation marks around it, so Excel tries to evaluate the text as a range name instead.

#VALUE! The formula is supposed to calculate numbers, but one of the cells or ranges referred to contains text. For example, if the formula is =A35+A43 and cell A43 contains text, you get the #VALUE! error as a result.

 To quickly locate all the cells or ranges referred to in a formula, double-click the cell containing the formula; Excel selects the cells or ranges referred to in that formula. If a referenced cell has a note attached to it, however, that cell won't be selected when you use this technique.

#REF! One of the cells or ranges referred to in a formula has been deleted from the worksheet. For example, if your formula refers to cell D7 and you later delete row 7 from the worksheet, you see this message as the formula's result.

#N/A! This error only occurs when a formula contains cells that themselves contain the value *#N/A* or *#n/a*. If the cells are blank, the formula assumes that the cells contain the value zero.

 You use #N/A in a cell when you want a formula that refers to that cell to show that the information isn't available yet. This reminds you that some cells referred to don't yet contain data.

#NUM! Usually means that the formula contains or has produced an invalid numeric result. You see this message if the formula produces a result that's too large to be displayed with the current cell format, or if you use a mathematically invalid expression such as taking the square root of a negative number.

#NULL! This message appears when the formula tells Excel to locate information in a cell that doesn't exist—for example, if a formula tells Excel to sum cells that are common to two different ranges, but the two ranges actually have no cells in common.

Formatting and printing

Your worksheet doesn't display zeroes in cells that contain zero values, or it does and you don't want it to.

Problem: Either the display option is set wrong in the Display Options dialog box, or the cells have a custom format that hides their contents.

Solutions:

- Choose *Display* from the Options menu and check or uncheck the *Zero Values* checkbox (depending on whether you want values showing or not showing), then click the *OK* button.

- If a cell still doesn't display information, choose *Number* from the Format menu and choose a standard format code from the list that appears, then click the *OK* button. The cell may have had a custom format that instructed Excel to hide its contents.

Dates or times are shown as apparently meaningless numbers.

Date	32835
Time	0.47

Problem: The cell containing the date or time has a number format instead of a date or time format. Internally, Excel stores dates as the number of days since January 2, 1904, and it stores times as a decimal fraction of 1, where 12:00 midnight equals 0 and 12:00 noon equals .5.

Solution: Select the cell and apply a date or time format to it.

You have a long label in column A, and rather than widening the column you want to break the label up so it's distributed in the cells directly beneath it.

A2		Figures adjusted to include finance charges.

	Worksheet1	

	A	B	C	D	E
1			January	February	March
2	Figures adjusted t	Salaries	$132,500	$132,500	$140,500
3		Material	$56,234	$57,139	$57,300
4		Leases	$18,000	$18,000	$18,000

Problem: When a label is wider than a column, widening the column isn't always the best solution because it uses up precious horizontal space on the screen or paper. In the example here, it would be better to distribute the words in this label into cells A3 and A4 rather than widening Column A to show the whole label in one cell.

Solution: Select the cell containing the label along with several cells directly beneath it, then choose *Justify* from the Format menu. Excel breaks up the label and distributes it across the cells in the range you selected.

You want row or column titles to print on every page, but they only print on the first page.

Problem: Normally, row and column titles only appear on the page on which they appear in your worksheet, but this can make it difficult to identify rows and columns in subsequent pages.

Solution: Choose *Set Print Titles* from the Options menu, check the *Titles for Columns* box, then select the column or columns whose titles you want to appear on each page. Then check the *Titles for Rows* box and select the row or rows whose titles you want to appear on each page. Click *OK* to define these titles. When you print the document, these rows and columns will print on each page.

A worksheet's header or footer overlaps data when you preview or print.

Problem: The top or bottom page margin is too small. Excel automatically places headers or footers half an inch from the top or bottom of a page, and the default top and

Sales Figures For First Quarter of 1994, based on projection in previous quarter.		Worksheet 1 2:50 PM		
		January	February	March
Figures adjusted	Salaries	$132,500	$132,500	$140,500
to include finance	Material	$56,234	$57,139	$57,300
charges.	Leases	$18,000	$18,000	$18,000

bottom margins are 1 inch each. However, you may have made these margins smaller to squeeze more worksheet rows on a page, or your header or footer may contain more than one line of text.

Solutions:

There are two ways to resize worksheet margins:

- Choose *Print Preview* from the File menu and then drag the handle at the end of the line dividing the header or footer from the data in the document.

- Choose *Page Setup* from the File menu and type larger numbers in the Top and Bottom margin boxes.

Macros

A macro name doesn't appear on the list in the Run Macro dialog box.

Problem: The macro sheet containing that macro isn't open.

Solution: Locate and open the macro sheet. The names of macros on it are automatically added to the list in the Run Macro dialog box. When you close any macro sheet, the names of macros on that sheet are automatically removed from the list in the Run Macro dialog box.

You want to use a macro sheet to run macros, but you don't want the sheet's window cluttering up your screen.

Problem: A macro sheet must be open before you can use the macros in it.

Solution: Activate the macro sheet window and choose *Hide* from the Window menu. The window is hidden, but the macro sheet is still open so you can run its macros.

You've defined a macro, but nothing happens when you run it.

Problem: Either the macro wasn't defined as a command or function macro when you named it, or something actually is happening and you're just not aware of it.

Solutions:

■ Activate the macro sheet, select the first cell of the macro, then choose *Define Name* from the Formula menu. Select the macro name in the list at the left and check out the buttons below to make sure that either the *Function* or *Command* button is selected. If neither of these is selected, Excel will name the cell you selected, but it won't consider it the start of a macro.

■ If the macro name is properly defined, the macro may be performing an action that isn't apparent, either because it's taking place in a different part of the worksheet or because it's being performed on an empty cell. (Results are only visible if the cell contains data.) To check the macro's operation as it is executed, resize and rearrange both the macro sheet and the worksheet where you're running the macro so you can see them both at once. Then set the macro sheet to display values instead of formulas by unchecking the *Formulas* box in the Display Options dialog box (choose *Display* from the Options menu). Finally, run the macro and watch the values change in the macro sheet to see how they affect your worksheet.

A Macro error has occurred.

Problem: There are lots of reasons for macro errors, but in general this message means the macro contains an invalid formula.

Solutions:

■ Click the *Go To* button to activate the macro sheet and select the cell in which the error occurred. Examine the formula there to be certain it makes sense (be sure to enclose text in double quote marks, for example).

If your macro contains subroutines, run the subroutines by themselves to make sure they're okay before you debug a macro that contains them.

■ If this inspection doesn't reveal any problems, run the macro again to display the error message and then click the *Step* button. Clicking this button executes the macro one cell at a time and displays the formula in the Single Step dialog box. In that dialog box, click the *Evaluate* button to have Excel calculate each part of the formula and display its results. Watch the results to make sure they're what you want. If they're not, you need to examine and rewrite the formula.

Problem: Every macro must end with a RETURN() or HALT() function. If you don't include this function at the end of the macro, the macro may still run, but you get this message.

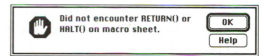

Solution: Always end macros with a RETURN() or HALT() function.

When you use the Macro recorder, Excel records the macro in the top cell of the first empty column in the macro sheet, but you want the macro recorded someplace else.

Problem: Excel's macro recorder always chooses the top of the first empty column in which to record macros.

Solution: Select the cell in which you want the macro recording to begin and then choose *Set Recorder* from the Macro menu. Excel begins recording the macro in the cell you chose.

You're recording a macro, but there's no more room left in the recorder range you selected in which to record the macro steps.

Problem: When you select a certain range of cells (rather than just one cell) in a macro sheet and then set them as the recorder range, Excel displays the above message if you record a macro whose steps require more space than the range you selected. Recording stops automatically when you see this message.

Solution: Activate the macro sheet, select and delete the steps you recorded in the macro so far, and then select a single cell in an empty column (or below any existing macro in that column) and choose *Record* from the Macro menu. Excel then uses the entire column to record macro steps, so it won't run out of room.

Charting

You selected a range of cells and have made a chart, but Excel has plotted the data backwards: rows have become data series and columns have become points in each series, or vice versa.

Problem: Excel always assumes that your charts contain more data points than different series, so it makes the larger part of a selection (rows or columns) into data points, and the smaller part into the series themselves. In a bar chart like the one here, for example, the selection included five rows (the five expense categories) and three columns (the three months), so Excel has made the rows into data points and the columns into series. But this probably isn't what you want.

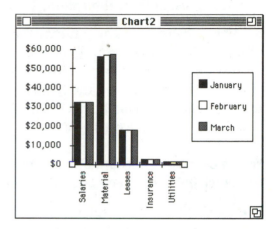

Solutions:

■ If you use the ChartWizard to create a chart, click the *Rows* or *Columns* button in the Step 4 of 5 dialog box to indicate which of these elements you want used for the data series. If you already used the ChartWizard and didn't get what you wanted, try it again and click the opposite button than the one you clicked before in this dialog box.

■ If you made the chart by selecting data and opening a new chart window, you can't change the chart that you've already created. Instead, you'll need to create a new one. Select the worksheet data that you want charted and choose *Copy* from the Edit menu. Then open a new, blank chart window and choose *Paste Special* from the Edit menu. Click the *Rows* or *Columns* button to select whether you want the values (data points) taken from rows or columns. Click the *OK* button and your chart appears.

You want to plot different rows or columns in the same chart, but the rows or columns aren't adjacent to each other.

Problem: You can only select a contiguous range of cells to plot in a chart, but there are lots of times when you want to plot, say, columns that contain quarter totals, but not the columns containing monthly data between them.

Solution: Hide the rows or columns that separate the two areas you want to plot (use the *Row Height* or *Column Width* command on the Format menu to set row heights or column widths to zero). Next, select the rows or columns, choose *Select Special* from the Formula menu, click the *Visible Cells Only* button, and click *OK*. Finally, open a new chart window. Excel now plots only data from the visible cells.

You've changed some formatting options for a chart (the scale or bar colors, for example), but Excel changes them again when you switch chart types.

Problem: Excel always displays new chart types in the default formats, so if you change a chart's format and then select a different chart type, the formats will probably be reset to that chart type's defaults.

Solution: Always select a chart type before messing around with the chart's formats.

Some of the bars or lines on a chart are so close to the X axis that you can't discern changes in them from one data point to the next.

Problem: The chart probably includes values in such a broad range that changes in values at the smaller end of the range don't show up very well. For example, the chart at right actually contains five data series (or bars), but only three of them show up. The other two are so short that they blend into the X axis.

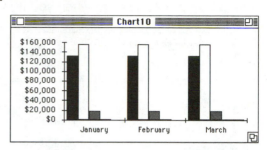

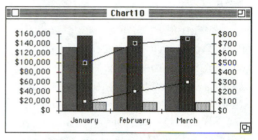

Solution: Add a chart overlay and a second Y axis to the chart. This creates a combination chart and shows the smaller values plotted against the right-hand Y axis. Here's what to do:

- Activate the chart window and choose *Add Overlay* from the Chart menu. Excel splits the chart, taking half of the original chart's data series and plotting them as a line instead of a bar, or vice versa. However, since the chart only has one Y axis scale (based on the larger numbers), the lines (or bars) probably still don't show up very well.

Excel always divides your data series in half when it decides which ones to overlay. If you select an odd number of series (five columns, for example), Excel overlays the smaller half (two columns, in this case). Series are selected for overlays by their position in the selection: if you select five columns, for example, Excel overlays the two right-hand columns. If you select four rows, Excel overlays the two bottom rows.

- Choose *Axes* from the Chart menu, click the *Value (Y) Axis* checkbox in the Overlay area, and then click *OK*. A right-hand Y axis is added to the chart, and the smaller values are plotted against it, as in the lower chart above.

Miscellaneous

You get an error message when you try to name a cell or a range.

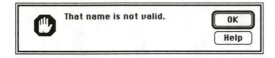

 You can add a list of defined ranges or cell names to your worksheet so you can easily see which range is which. Select a cell at the top left corner of an empty area of your spreadsheet where there are at least two columns and several rows blank, then choose *Paste Name* from the Edit menu and click the *Paste List* button. Excel pastes a list of names and their ranges into your worksheet.

Problem: Excel won't accept range names that begin with numbers or symbols, that contain any space characters, or that look like cell references (A1, for example).

Solution: Use letters to begin range names, and don't use letter and number combinations that look like cell references. If you want a name to have more than one word, use the underline character instead of a space to separate words.

You use the *Find* command to search for a number you know is in the worksheet, but Excel can't find it.

Problem: Excel may be searching the wrong worksheet elements (as defined in the Find dialog box), or you may have entered the wrong search string.

Solution: Choose *Find* from the Formula menu and check out the *Look In* buttons to make sure that Excel is searching in formulas, values, or notes, as you want it to. If you have the right button selected, make sure the string you've entered in the Find What box *exactly* matches the string you want to find. For example, if you're looking for 8,000.00, Excel won't find it if you've entered *8000* in the Find What box. Excel is very literal this way.

You've imported data into an Excel worksheet from another program, but what should be entries in individual columns are bunched together in column A.

Problem: In order for Excel to recognize and separate data into individual columns, the data in each column must be separated by tab or comma characters, and data in each row must be separated by return characters. If the data isn't separated this way, Excel puts everything in one cell.

Solution: Use the *Parse* command to separate the data in each cell and have Excel distribute it into different columns. Select the cells you want to parse (they must be in the same column), then choose *Parse* from the Data menu. In the dialog box that appears, insert bracket characters ([ ]) around each piece of data you want

 Before you parse data, make sure there are enough empty columns to the right of the selected column to contain the parsed information (insert some columns if necessary). Otherwise, Excel overwrites any existing data in its path.

separated into a different cell. (Click the *Guess* button if you want Excel to insert brackets where it thinks they should go, instead of inserting them yourself.) When you're done, click the *OK* button. Excel separates the data and moves it to adjacent cells to the right.

Chapter 24
Aldus PageMaker

Aldus PageMaker has been updated more slowly than many other programs. Although version 5.0 has just been released at this writing, the last major revision (4.0) was three years ago. Therefore, the problems and solutions in this chapter focus on versions 4 and 4.2 of PageMaker. If you're still using version 3.0, I strongly suggest that you upgrade.

This chapter is divided into five sections:

- Working with documents

- Placing and editing text

- Formatting and layouts

- Working with graphics

- Printing

At the end of some sections, there are a few problems and solutions that are specific to certain versions of PageMaker or certain Macintosh models. Watch the problem headings for these.

Working with documents

It takes a long time for PageMaker to redraw the screen when you switch pages or make major changes.

Problem: PageMaker takes longer than word processing programs to redraw the screen because it has to calculate precise placements of every element on the page. However, there are a couple of ways to speed things up.

Solutions:

■ Don't set any of your layouts to display in color. Choose the *Black and White* option in your Monitors control panel.

■ Use the *Preferences* command on the Edit menu to set a larger font size for Greeked text when you're working on a layout. PageMaker displays Greeked text much more quickly, and you can always change the value back to a smaller font size when you want to actually read text on the layout.

■ Display one page on the screen at a time. If your layout has facing pages, don't display them (uncheck the *Facing Pages* option in the Page Setup dialog box). It takes longer to draw two pages than one.

■ Change the selection on the Page menu to view the document at a reduced size.

Your PageMaker disk files seem much larger than they should be.

Problem: Your document may contain a lot of graphics, or this problem may be due to the way documents have been saved. PageMaker has two ways of saving documents. A minisave stores the current state of the document along with all the recent deletions you've made whenever you use the *Save* command, or whenever you turn to a different page, change the page setup, add or delete pages, copy something, or print the document. A full save simply saves the current state of the document without all the extra stuff. If you always use the *Save* command instead of the *Save As* command, the file will grow much larger than it should be.

Solutions:

■ If your document contains lots of graphics, consider linking them to the document instead of storing them in the same file. Select each graphic, choose *Links* from the File menu, and then uncheck the *Store Copy in Publication* box.

- Use *Save As* once in awhile to purge all the stored deletions and other change information from the file, so only the current state of the file is saved.

You want to display the entire pasteboard surrounding a document, but choosing the *25% size* command from the Page menu doesn't quite do it.

Problem: You may store extra blocks of text, lines, boxes, or graphics on the pasteboard temporarily, but then it's hard to see the whole pasteboard at once, and scrolling the screen takes a long time.

Solution: Hold down the [Shift] key while choosing *Fit in window* from the Page menu. This selects the "Fit in world" magnification level, which shows the entire pasteboard surrounding your document.

You're tired of changing the default values for page setup, type specifications, or line or fill patterns each time you open a new document.

Problem: PageMaker has default formatting values for each new document, but you can change them.

Solutions:

- To create a custom set of formatting values and even store default text, graphics, or master pages, create a document and save it as a template.

- To change the defaults that are set when you open any new document, choose menu commands for the settings you want without having a document open on the screen. When you make menu selections without a document open, these become the defaults for all new documents.

You're tired of having to click two or three buttons to get out of deeply nested dialog boxes.

Problem: Many PageMaker commands produce dialog boxes which themselves produce other dialog boxes when you select further options. It's a pain to have to click two or more buttons to return to your document layout.

Solution: Hold down the ⌷Option⌷ key while clicking *OK* or *Cancel* in the current dialog box. PageMaker automatically closes all other dialog boxes and returns you to the layout.

You're running At Ease on a Macintosh Performa. You've set it up to save files to a floppy disk, and you get an error message when you try to save a PageMaker file to a folder on the floppy.

Problem: PageMaker can't save files to a folder on a floppy disk if you've set the options to require a floppy disk or to add a button to At Ease. This problem occurs with several different Macintosh programs.

Solution: See page 304 in Chapter 23.

You're using PageMaker 4.0 under System 6 and you've imported a PICT2 file into a document, but the graphic isn't displayed completely.

Problem: PageMaker has a problem displaying PICT2 format files under System 6, although they will print out properly. Some applications are saved in PICT2 format rather than the older PICT format when you choose the PICT format from their Save As dialog boxes.

Solutions:

- Make sure your graphics program saves the image in PICT (not PICT2) format. If you're not sure which format it uses, save the image in TIFF format.

- To solve the problem completely, upgrade to System 7.

PageMaker 4.0 and 4.01 won't run on a Macintosh Quadra when the cache is on.

Problem: Some of the import filters supplied with PageMaker 4.0 and 4.01 are incompatible with the Quadra's cache.

Solutions:

There are two ways around this Problem: remove the filters that are causing the problem, or upgrade to PageMaker 4.02 or later.

- If you upgrade, you'll have to manually delete the old Story Importer filter from the Aldus folder. This filter was renamed in later versions of PageMaker, so it's not removed from the Aldus folder when you install the new version of the program.

■ If you decide not to upgrade, look in the Aldus Filters folder inside the Aldus folder in your System Folder for any of the following filters:

Smart ASCII Import   Story Importer
Smart ASCII Export   RTF Import
Word 4.0 Import

If any of these filters is present, drag it outside the System Folder and restart the Mac. PageMaker should now run.

Placing and editing text

You've selected a story to place with the *Place* command and have clicked the *OK* button to place it, but now you've changed your mind.

Problem: Once you click *OK* to place a story, you can't undo this action from the Edit menu.

Solution: Instead of clicking in the document to place the story, click the Pointer tool in the toolbox. This cancels the place operation.

You placed a story in a layout, but the text in the first line is squished against the right side of a column, or it doesn't flow completely to the margin on one side of the column.

Problem: Paragraph indents from the original document are preserved when you place stories in layouts. In the example here, the story that was placed had a first-line indent greater than the width of the column.

has been well
received in over-
seas markets,

Solution: Reset the paragraph indents. Select the Text tool and click in the affected paragraph (or select the whole story, if necessary), choose *Indents/tabs* from the Type menu, click the *Reset* button, and then click *OK*.

Formatting and layouts

You want to be able to vary the space between columns on a multicolumn layout, but only the column widths change when you drag a column boundary.

Problem: You can vary column widths in PageMaker, but you can't vary the spacing between columns.

Once you've set a variable-column layout, the only way to vary the space between columns is to reset it with the *Column guides* command on the Options menu. Once you do this, however, PageMaker resets all the layout's columns to equal widths, and you have to drag column boundaries to create variable-width columns again. The moral is to set the space between columns with the *Column guides* command before creating variable-width columns.

When you isolate one text block, the blocks on either side of it remain linked, and any changes in the preceding block ripple through to the following block, skipping over the isolated block.

Solution: Set the spacing between columns to the smallest amount you want between any two columns, and then create extra, blank columns to serve as spacers. Since you can reset any column's width independently by dragging its borders, you can make a blank column exactly wide enough to give you the extra space you need between one "real" column and the next.

You want to resize a text block that's part of a story, but you don't want the resizing to change the positions of text in other blocks that are part of the same story.

Problem: When text blocks are linked in one story, any changes you make to the formatting or contents of one ripple through to other blocks, changing text positions there too. But sometimes you want to reformat just one block without affecting others.

Solution: Select the block with the Pointer tool, cut it to the Clipboard, and then paste it back into the layout. The block is no longer part of the story.

Leading is inconsistent between one line of text and another in the same paragraph.

Problem: PageMaker defaults to auto line leading unless you tell it otherwise. In this case, auto-leading is probably set and you've changed the font size of one character or word in the line, so PageMaker has increased the leading for that line.

Our new product, the BlastMaster®, has really taken off in Europe. It seems our friends across the ocean just can't get enough of American-style leaf blowing.

Solution: Select the whole paragraph or story and choose a fixed leading size from the Type menu. With a fixed size set, the leading doesn't change when you resize characters. The drawback is that you may run out of space between lines if you make characters in one line too large.

You want to paste several horizontal lines or other items exactly the same distance apart, but it's hard to do this using the ruler.

Problem: Parallel lines can make your eyes play tricks, and it can take a lot of time to manually align several objects so they're exactly the same distance apart. (The example here shows what can go wrong.)

Solution: Draw the first object, select it, and copy it. Then hold down the (Option) key and paste the object. Drag the copy to where you want it (the distance from the first object), and then (Option)-paste again. The third object is exactly the same distance from the second as the second is from the first. Repeat this process as many times as you like to create evenly spaced lines for forms or other projects.

You want to design a full-bleed layout for printing on a LaserWriter, but the LaserWriter won't print within ½" of the page edges.

Problem: LaserWriters have a nonprintable area at the edges of each page, but there's a partial solution to this problem.

Solution: Print the layout on a larger paper size and then trim the nonprintable area from it. For example, design a full-bleed layout that runs to the top of an 8½ x 11 page, then print it on 8½ x 14 paper and trim 1½" from the top and bottom. This doesn't help with bleeds at the sides of the layout, however, unless the layout bleeds to a 7-½" width and you trim ½" off each side.

You've made changes to the ruler guides on a master page, but the changes didn't appear on one or more regular pages of your document.

Problem: Guides on regular pages are only linked to master page guides as long as you don't move or change any of the guides on a regular page. Once you move a regular page guide, the page becomes unlinked from the master page, and changes to guides on a master page are no longer reflected on it.

Solution: To relink a regular page with a master page's guides, display the regular page and choose *Copy Master Guides* from the Page menu.

Working with graphics

You've wrapped text around a graphic, but you want to change the wrap boundary from a rectangle to an irregular shape.

Text normally reformats after each boundary change you make, but by holding down the Spacebar as you drag handles, you can suspend text reformatting until you release the Spacebar. To add handles to the text wrap boundary, just click anywhere along the boundary's dotted line where a handle doesn't already appear. PageMaker automatically adds one. Each new handle makes the screen redraw more slowly, however, so don't get carried away.

Problem: The Text Wrap dialog box only allows you to specify rectangular boundaries around graphic objects.

Solution: Choose *Text wrap* from the Element menu, specify the wrap and text flow options, and click *OK*. Then click the graphic to display the text wrap boundary as a dotted line. You see reshaping handles along the boundary, and you can drag any handle to reshape the boundary so it more closely matches the shape of the graphic.

A graphic becomes distorted when you drag its handle to resize it.

Problem: Bitmapped graphics can become distorted when you resize or reshape them to sizes or shapes that aren't exact multiples of the original. PageMaker can't break the original image's pixels into fractions of pixels, so it adds or eliminates pixels to compensate, which often results in unwanted moiré patterns.

 To return a distorted shape to its original size, hold down the [Shift] key while clicking one of the image's resizing handles. After a couple of seconds, the image is returned to its original size.

Solution: Hold down the [⌘] key when you resize an image. This constrains resizing or reshaping to exact multiples of the original.

You want to create or fill an object with a different gray percentage than is available on the Fill menu.

Problem: There are several holes in the selection of gray shades on the Fill menu. If you want a shade that isn't listed, you'll have to create it.

Solution: Choose *Define colors* from the Element menu, click the *New* button, and then set the color values to zero in the Cyan, Yellow, and Magenta boxes. Then set the Black value to the gray shade percentage you want. Finally, type a name for the new shade and click the *OK* button twice (in the current and preceding dialog box). This "color" is added to PageMaker's color palette, and you can select it there any time you want to create an object with that shade.

Printing

You want to print a document in the background on your LaserWriter using PrintMonitor, but the standard Print dialog box doesn't support this feature.

Problem: The Aldus printer driver gives you lots of extra options for printing your layouts, but it doesn't support PrintMonitor, so you have to tie up your Mac each time you print something from PageMaker.

Solution: Hold down the [Option] key when you choose the *Print* command. Page-Maker opens the standard LaserWriter driver instead. The dialog box contains

This trick only works for the LaserWriter driver. If you're using a StyleWriter or ImageWriter, you're out of luck. some of the PageMaker-specific options you'd find in PageMaker's Print dialog box, but not all of them. However, you'll be able to use PrintMonitor to print the document in the background.

Some of your layout's headlines or display type don't print when you use the *Proof Print* option in the Aldus Print dialog box.

Problem: PageMaker substitutes a graphics placeholder for real graphics when you make proof prints, so if the headline or display type was imported as a PICT file, it won't show up in a proof.

Solution: Print the layout as a normal document.

You changed the Print dialog box settings and printed a document, but the next time you open it, the dialog box settings are back to what they were before.

Problem: PageMaker doesn't save custom Print dialog box settings unless you save the document when they are in effect.

Solution: Save your document before closing it to preserve custom print dialog box settings.

Your print job crashes the printer or Linotronic, or it prints really slowly.

Problem: This usually means that you have too many complex bitmaps, overlaid objects, patterns, fonts, styles, or other elements on a page, and the printer gets overloaded trying to sort them all out.

Solutions:

■ Make sure the file size is as small as possible by using *Save As* to save the file before printing.

■ Try printing with the standard LaserWriter driver, if you're not using it already.

■ Remove some of the more complex elements from each page.

■ Break the document into smaller components and print them separately.

Your document comes back from a service bureau with the wrong fonts or formatting.

Problem: The service bureau isn't using the same fonts you used to create the document, or it's using a different printer driver.

Solutions:

Before you send a floppy disk copy of your layout and any linked files to a service bureau, open the document from the floppy to make sure all the links are still in place and that all the linked files are also on the floppy. Otherwise, the service bureau will have to figure out which file goes where, and they may not have all the files they need.

- ■ Include copies of all the font files you used in your document when you send your document for printing. You can't assume the service bureau has exactly the same fonts you used to design the document, even if you and the service bureau have fonts with the same names. Same-name fonts from different manufacturers can have different thicknesses and character spacing that will throw off the look of your layout.

- ■ If you're certain the service bureau is using the same fonts, make sure you used the same printer driver as the service bureau when you chose the Page Setup options for your document. Different printers have different page size, print area, and print quality characteristics.

Chapter 25

QuarkXPress

QuarkXPress is an extremely powerful program, and it has become the most popular page composition system for professionals. In this chapter, we'll look at some basic conceptual and operating problems you may encounter with QuarkXPress if you're a new or occasional user of the program. The chapter is divided into five sections:

- Working with documents
- Working with text
- Working with graphics
- Working with boxes
- Printing

Working with documents

You selected a page size that matches your output paper size in the New dialog box, but the document prints too close to the margins.

Problem: Even though it contains buttons that let you select standard paper sizes as a layout's size, the Page Size area in the *New* command's dialog box refers to the size of finished QuarkXPress pages, not to the paper size. You set the paper size in the *Page Setup* command's dialog box.

Solution: Enter the dimensions of the finished layout in the *Width* and *Height* boxes of the Page Size area in the New dialog box, not the dimensions of the paper you're printing on. If the layout size happens to match a standard page size, click one of the buttons instead, and the dimensions of that standard page are automatically entered in the *Width* and *Height* boxes.

You specified two or more columns in the New dialog box, but although the new page has column guides on it, there are no text columns.

Problem: The Column Guides options in the *New* command's dialog box tell QuarkXPress to display column guides, not to create text columns. The guides are like blue lines on layout paper—they help you align objects within columns on the page, but you still have to create and place the columns themselves.

Solution: Use the Text tool to draw text boxes that match the column guides, if you want columns that size.

You've changed a default tool setting, but QuarkXPress reverts to the old setting when you open the next document.

 Any settings you choose in the *New* command's dialog box become the defaults, and will appear the next time you use this command. Be sure to check all the settings in the New dialog box each time you create a document to make sure you'll get what you want.

Problem: The effect of changing a default setting depends on whether you have a document open at the time. When a document is open, the setting applies only to that document. When no documents are open, the setting applies to all new documents.

Solution: To change a default for all new QuarkXPress documents, change it when no documents are open.

Working with text

You selected a text box and now want to import a story into it, but the _Get Text_ command is dimmed on the File menu.

Problem: You selected the text box with the Item tool.

Solution: Use the Content tool to select the text box. The _Get Text_ command is now available.

You imported a story, but the indents, style sheets, and other format attributes didn't transfer consistently.

Problem: QuarkXPress has problems importing formatting and style sheets from any program other than Microsoft Word, and in order to import style sheets from a Word document, the Microsoft Word filter must be inside the QuarkXPress folder when you launch QuarkXPress.

 If one particular style sheet didn't transfer from a Word document but the others did, it's because a style sheet with that name already exists in the QuarkXPress document.

Solutions:

- Make sure the Microsoft Word filter is installed in your QuarkXPress folder before you launch the program.

- If you're importing a story from a word processor other than Word, save the word processing file in Microsoft Word format, open and adjust its formatting in Word if necessary, then save the Word file and import that into your layout.

You selected some text in one box and you want to paste it into another box, but nothing happens when you use the *Paste* command.

Problem: You must paste with the same tool you used to select and copy information in QuarkXPress. You use the Item tool to select boxes, and the Content tool to select text inside boxes.

Solution: Make sure the Content tool is selected when you paste text.

You want to create more space between the first line of text and the top of a box, but changing the leading doesn't do it.

We feel this logo conveys all the fun and excitement of a party. Although some feel customers might confuse the

Problem: Leading affects the space between lines in a paragraph, but it doesn't alter the space between the first line in a box and the top of the box itself.

Solution: Select the box with the Content or Item tool, choose *Modify* from the Item menu, and enter a value in the First Baseline box.

Working with graphics

You imported a picture into a picture box, but it doesn't appear.

Problem: Either the picture isn't positioned in a visible part of the box, or the import didn't work.

 If you imported an EPS file that didn't include a PICT or TIFF version of the image, the imported picture appears as a gray box with the EPS file name on it.

Solutions:

■ If the box still has an X in it, the import didn't work. Try using the *Get Picture* command again.

■ If the box is blank, with no X in it, the picture is there but it's outside the visible part of the box. Choose the Content tool and drag the blank part of the picture box down and to the right. The picture should come into view.

You try to paste a graphic into a box, but the Mac just beeps or nothing happens.

Problem: You're probably trying to paste the graphic into a text box, and QuarkXPress won't allow you to do this.

 You can't import a picture into a text box, either. When you have a text box selected, the *Get Picture* command on the File menu becomes *Get Text*.

Solution: Create a picture box using the Rectangle, Rounded Rectangle, or Oval picture box tool (the top three shapes with the Xs through them on the palette), then paste the graphic into the box.

You want to resize the graphic inside a picture box as you resize the box itself.

Problem: When you select and drag a handle on a picture box, only the size of the box changes, not the size of the graphic inside it.

Solution: Hold down the (Shift) key as you resize the box, and the graphic inside it is resized as well.

 If you resize a graphic and you don't like the result, here's how to restore it to its original size: double-click on the picture box with the Item tool to display the Picture Box Specifications dialog box, then type *100*% in the Scale Across and Scale Down boxes.

You want to resize the graphic inside a picture box without resizing the box itself.

Problem: When you (Shift)-drag a picture box handle, both the box and the picture in it are resized.

Solution: Select the picture box with the Content tool, hold down (⌘⌘)(Option)(Shift), and then press (<) or (>) to resize the picture. Each time you press the (<) or (>) key, you shrink or enlarge the picture by 5 percent.

You want to rotate a graphic without rotating the picture box that contains it.

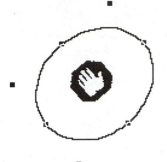

Problem: When you select a picture box with the Rotate tool, you rotate both the picture box and the graphic inside it.

Solution: Display the Measurement palette if it's not showing by choosing *Show Measurements* from the View menu. Select the picture box with the Content tool, and then type the angle of rotation into the picture angle field at the far right side of the Measurement palette.

 You can also specify the picture angle by double-clicking on the picture box with the Item tool to display the Picture Box Specifications dialog box, and then typing the angle's value in the Picture Angle box. If you rotate a picture and don't like the result, you can return it to its previous position by entering the same angle with a minus sign in front of it. For example, if you rotated a picture 37 degrees, you can undo that action by rotating it -37 degrees.

You're using QuarkXPress under System 6. You've imported a PICT2 file into a document, but the graphic isn't displayed completely.

Problem: QuarkXPress has a problem displaying PICT2 format files under System 6, although they print fine when you print a document. Some applications are saved in PICT2 format rather than in the older PICT format when you choose the PICT format from their Save As dialog boxes.

Solutions:

■ Make sure your graphics program saves the image in PICT (not PICT2) format. If you're not sure which format it uses, save the image in TIFF format.

■ To solve the problem completely, upgrade to System 7.

Working with boxes

New pages are automatically added to your document when text you type or import overflows the text box on the current page, and you don't want this to happen.

Problem: If you check the *Automatic Text Box* option in the New dialog box when you create a new document, QuarkXPress automatically inserts more pages if the text box on the current page isn't large enough to hold all your text.

Solution: Choose *Document* from the Preferences submenu off the Edit menu, and then choose *Off* from the Auto Page Insertion menu.

You've selected a box and pressed Del to delete it, but nothing happens.

Problem: You've selected the box with the Content tool, so QuarkXPress is trying to delete contents inside the box, rather than the box itself. If the box is empty, nothing happens.

If you're unable to select multiple items on the same page or spread by Shift-clicking, it's also because you're selecting with the Content tool rather than the Item tool.

Solution: Select the box with the Item tool and then press Del. The box is deleted.

You've selected a linked text box and have tried to copy or duplicate it, but QuarkXPress won't let you.

Problem: You can't duplicate or copy text boxes that are linked to other text boxes, because QuarkXPress wouldn't be able to keep the links straight if it had to link text from one box to more than one copy of the next box.

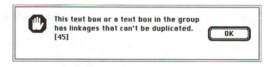

This text box or a text box in the group has linkages that can't be duplicated. [45]

OK

Solutions:

- To copy text inside the box, select the Content tool and then select and copy the text.

- To copy the box itself, select the box with the Unlinking tool. The link arrow appears between the box and the previous linked box. Click on the arrowhead in the box you want to unlink to break the link. Then select the box with the Item tool and copy or duplicate it. To relink the box after you've made a copy or duplicate, select the Linking tool, click on the previous linked box, then click on the box you just unlinked to link it again.

You rearranged the pages in your document, and now the links between text boxes don't make any sense.

Problem: QuarkXPress doesn't automatically adjust text box links when you move pages around, so if you move a later page ahead of an earlier one, text bounces forward a page and then back again in linked text boxes on those pages.

Solution: Use the Unlinking tool to unlink the text boxes on the pages you'll be moving, then use the Linking tool to relink them once the pages are in the order you want.

You want to unlink a box from the middle of a story without breaking the links to boxes after it.

Problem: When you use the Unlinking tool to break a link to a text box, it also breaks all the links to boxes that come after it.

Solution: Hold down ⌜Shift⌟ as you click on the box with the Unlinking tool. The link to that box is broken, but links to others after it remain.

You can't remember the order in which text boxes are linked.

Problem: Links between text boxes don't show up once you've created them, so it can be difficult to remember which is the next or previous text box in a layout that has many pages containing different stories.

Solutions:

■ To find all the boxes that contain linked text from the same story, click inside a text box with the Content tool, then choose *Select All* from the Edit menu. All the text in the story is selected, and you can scroll through the document to see which boxes contain selected text.

■ To move quickly from one linked text box to the next, move the insertion point to the end of the current text box and press ⌜→⌟. QuarkXPress automatically moves to the beginning of the next linked text box. If that box is on another page, QuarkXPress scrolls to that page. To move to the previous linked text box, move the insertion point to the beginning of the current box and press ⬅.

You set an item for text runaround, but it disappears when you drag it onto a box containing the text you want to run around it.

Problem: The item you set for text runaround is in a layer behind the text you want to run around it.

Solution: If the item's selection handles are still showing (as in the example here), choose *Bring to Front* from the Item menu. If the item's selection handles aren't visible, use the Item tool to select the text box and then choose *Send to Back* from the Item menu.

> **Spring Festivities**
>
> The annual Groundhog Day party was a big success, as usual. Bob Feemish spent most of the time passing out smiley buttons, and everyone felt that Sharon Smithers' furry centerpieces added just the right touch of groundhog sensitivity to the occasion.

 If you create a new box on top of the existing text box and set the new box for text runaround, text automatically wraps around it because the new box is already in a layer on top of the old one.

Printing

The margins aren't what you expect when you print a document on your laser printer, even though you checked them before printing.

Problem: You may have the wrong printer type set in the Page Setup dialog box.

Solution: Check the Printer menu in the Page Setup dialog box. The printer shown there should be the same as the one you have selected in the Chooser. If the printer you've selected in the Chooser isn't shown on the Printer menu in the Page Setup dialog box, choose *LaserWriter* there. This choice should work with most PostScript printers.

Chapter 26
FileMaker Pro

FileMaker Pro is powerful program that's relatively simple to use. As a result, lots of people learn only the barest basics about FileMaker Pro and are then cast into bewilderment when some of the program's more complex or powerful features rear their heads. In this chapter, we'll look at some common problems you may have when using FileMaker Pro. This chapter assumes you're using FileMaker Pro rather than earlier versions, as this version of the program has been out for nearly three years now.

The chapter is divided into six sections:

- Working with files

- Viewing, entering, and changing information

- Finding and sorting

- Formatting and layouts

- Reports and printing

- Miscellaneous

Working with files

A message says the file is damaged.

Problem: Files can become damaged in various ways, but FileMaker Pro usually warns you about such damage so you can repair it.

Solutions:

■ If you get such a message while working with a file, close the file immediately and open it again. You'll probably see a message that says the file needs minor repairs. Click the button to repair the file. If you get the message again after repairing the file, close it and use the *Recover* command on the File menu to rebuild the file.

■ If the message says the file can't be opened, use the *Recover* command on the File menu to rebuild it.

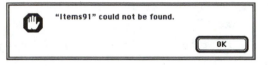

Problem: You've selected a field that triggers a lookup of information from another file (called the lookup file), and either the lookup file has been deleted or renamed, or you don't have the access privileges to open it.

Solutions:

■ If you're using the file as a guest user, ask the file's host to open the lookup file. Only a file's host can open lookup files.

■ If you're the file's host or its only user, search your disk for the lookup file and open it if you find it. If you can't find the file, you're out of luck.

You want to close a file, but a message says others are using it.

Problem: If you were the first one to open the file, you're the file's host, and if others have opened the file after you, you can't close it until the other users close it from their Macs.

Solution: Click the *Ask* button in the alert box. This sends a message to the file's guest users asking them to close it. Once all the guest users have closed the file, you can close it yourself.

Viewing, entering, and changing information

You see parts of two records on the screen at once.

Problem: You have the *View As List* command checked on the Select menu. In this mode, you can scroll through records as if they're in a list, so it's possible to display parts of two or more records on the screen at once by clicking or dragging in the vertical scroll bar.

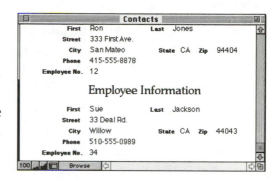

Solution: Either scroll the screen or resize the window so only one record is displayed, or choose *View As List* from the Select menu. When this command is not checked, FileMaker Pro displays only one record at a time, and the vertical scroll bar scrolls within one record, not from one record to the next.

Information takes a long time to appear in certain fields.

Problem: The file you're using is stored across a network, and/or the layout you're working with contains summary fields that must be calculated before the total amount appears.

To quickly determine which of the file's layouts contain summary fields, choose *Overview* from the Access Privileges submenu off the File menu, then select each layout name in the Layouts list in the dialog box. As you select each layout name, the Fields list shows which fields are on each layout.

Solution: If you don't need to see the summary information, try switching to a layout that doesn't contain any summary fields. Otherwise, you'll just have to be patient.

A field contains a question mark instead of data.

Problem: If the field is a calculation field, either the for- mula stored in it can't be calculated properly, it's being forced to divide by zero or perform some other illogical operation, or the calculation produces a numeric result and there simply isn't enough room to display the entire result. If the field is a numeric field, the value in it is too long to be displayed properly given the current field format settings.

Solutions:

- If the field is a numeric (and not a calculation) field, switch to Layout mode and make the field wider until the entire number in it can be displayed. If you don't want to change the field's size, use the *Number Format* command on the Format menu to change its format so the value can be displayed in fewer numbers.

- If the field is a calculation field, choose *Define Fields* from the Select menu, click on the name of the calculation field, and then click the *Options* button to display the field's formula. Check the formula to see that it makes sense.

- If the formula looks okay, try viewing other records in the file. It may be that the calculation formula can't be performed in the record you're viewing because one or more of the fields referred to in the formula is blank or contains the wrong kind of information. For example, if it's a mathematical formula and one of the fields referred to contains text, the text will be evaluated as zero by the formula.

 You can't always tell a field's name by viewing a layout in Browse mode, because text names in Browse can be different from the actual field name. To find out a field's real name, switch to Layout mode and look inside the field's data space—the actual field name is shown there.

- If the calculation produces a number, check the number format (double-click in the field in Layout mode to display the Number Format dialog box), and see how many decimal places the result is formatted for. FileMaker Pro can calculate to 22 digits of precision, and if the field isn't wide enough to display all the digits, you see a question mark. In this case, either change the number format to display fewer digits or widen the field in Layout mode.

Data is chopped off in a field.

Problem: The field isn't wide or tall enough to display all the data in it on the layout you're viewing.

State Cali

Solution: Choose *Layout* from the Select menu to switch to Layout mode, then select the field and drag its border to make it larger. Then choose *Browse* from the Select menu to switch back to Browse mode and make sure the field is large enough.

Remember, each FileMaker Pro layout can contain a different selection of fields, and fields can be different sizes on different layouts

You've opened a file as a guest user. A field is covered up by a gray box and you can't select it.

Problem: You haven't been given access privileges to view or change that field. If the file has been set up with passwords and access privileges, different passwords grant their users different types of access privileges. In some cases, a password restricts which fields or even which layouts you can see or change.

Employee Information

First	Ron		Last	Jones		
Street	333 First Ave.					
City	San Mateo		State	CA	Zip	94404
Phone	415-555-8878					
Employee No.	12	Salary Rate				

Solution: Ask the file's host to grant you access to the field.

A field isn't covered up, but you can't enter data into it.

Problem: The field is a calculation or summary field, and you can't enter data into these fields because they calculate their own data. There's no workaround for this problem.

In FileMaker Pro version 2.0 and later, you can select data inside a calculation or summary field in order to copy it. In earlier versions of the program, you can't even select such a field in Browse mode.

You've defined entry options to produce a list of entries for a field, but the list doesn't appear when you tab into the field in Browse mode.

Problem: Even though you define a list of entry options when you define a field, the list of options won't appear unless you format the field to display them.

Solution: Choose *Layout* from the Select menu, select the field in question. Then choose the *Field Format* command from the Format menu, click the *Using Field's Value List* button, and choose a display option from the pop-up menu next to the button.

Finding and sorting

You can't enter Find criteria into a field.

Problem: Either you're not in Find mode or you're trying to enter the criteria into a summary field. FileMaker Pro won't search for information in a summary field.

Solution: Choose *Find* from the Select menu to display the Find mode screen if it's not showing. Make sure you're not trying to enter the criteria into a summary field.

Problem: Either you haven't entered any criteria for FileMaker Pro to search for, or you've entered criteria that FileMaker Pro isn't capable of searching for. FileMaker Pro won't search for symbols such as *, &, and $.

Solutions:

- Click the *Modify Find* button to return to the Find screen, and make sure you've entered at least one criterion for FileMaker Pro to search for.

- If you're trying to search for symbols, use a font like Zapf Dingbats or Symbol to enter the symbols in records and in a Find request. Use only the symbols generated with standard alphabetical or number keys. These keys have the same ASCII codes as standard letters and numbers, and because FileMaker Pro selects characters by their ASCII codes, the program is able to find them.

A sorted file is unsorted when you use the *Find* command.

Problem: Whenever you search for records with the *Find* command, FileMaker Pro always returns a file to its unsorted state when it displays the found records.

Solution: If you use Find mode a lot to select groups of records and you have a particular sort order you want restored after you find records, create a script that stores the sort command and then play the script after you find records each time.

Formatting and layouts

FileMaker Pro always adds a new field to the bottom of the current layout, and you don't want it to.

Problem: Whenever you define a new field, FileMaker automatically adds it to the bottom of the current layout unless you tell it not to. Often you don't want new fields added automatically, because you may not be displaying a layout where you want that new field to

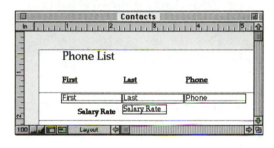

appear. For example, the new Salary Rate field here has been added to a telephone list layout.

Solution: Choose *Preferences* from the File menu and uncheck the *Add Newly Defined Fields To Current Layout* box.

It's difficult to line up objects precisely on a layout.

Problem: When you view a layout in actual size and you're working with lots of objects, it can be hard to line them up precisely.

 If you created objects without the grid on, choosing *Align to Grid* won't help you line them up afterwards. In fact, if you're trying to align objects manually, make sure the *Align To Grid* command is not checked on the Arrange menu.

 To make it easier to line things up manually, click the zoom-in control in the lower left corner of the layout to magnify everything.

Solutions:

■ If you'll be adding a lot of objects to a layout and you want them to line up as you create them, choose *Align to Grid* from the Layout menu. Each object snaps to the grid as you create it, and it's easy to drag them into line.

■ If you've already added a lot of items to a layout and you then want to align them, select all of the objects, choose *Alignment* from the Arrange menu, and choose the alignment option you want there.

It's hard to select an object on a layout because other objects are too close.

Problem: When objects are very close together, it can be difficult to select one of them—you often end up selecting the wrong object because it's so close to the one you really want.

Solutions:

■ Once you've selected the wrong object, choose the *Lock* command from the Layout menu. This locks that object and sends it to the back layer of the document, making it easier to select the one you really want. To unlock an object later, select it and choose *Unlock* from the Arrange menu.

■ As an alternative, click the zoom-in control in the lower left corner of the Layout screen. This magnifies everything on the layout (including the space between objects), making it easier to select a particular object.

Reports and printing

You want a report to perform calculations on data in a summary field, but that field's name isn't available when you try to define the formula.

Problem: When you define a summary field, you have limited selection of calculations you can perform, and you can't specify another summary field as the field whose data is to be calculated. There are many times, however, when you'll want to take the data from a summary field and perform other calculations on it.

Solution: Create a calculation field and then use the SUMMARY function to extract summarized information from a summary field. The SUMMARY function pulls information from the field named in its argument, and you can then use other functions to calculate that information in a variety of ways. The SUMMARY function requires not only the name of the summary field whose data you want to calculate, but also the name of the break field, or the field on which the file is sorted to obtain the proper summaries.

For example, suppose a file contains a summary field called Total Sales, which sums all the data from a field called Sales to produce total sales of all stores. Now suppose there's a Region field that identifies the region to which each store belongs, so that when the file is sorted on the Region field, the Total Sales field produces summaries that total the sales of all stores within each region. To find out the average of the total sales for each region, you would define a new calculation field containing the formula:

=AVERAGE(SUMMARY(TOTAL SALES,REGION))

Once you've defined a field with this formula, the file has to be sorted on the Region field in order to produce correct results.

Summary data doesn't print in a sub-summary part.

ITEMS Database - 7/5/93 - Page 1		
No. **Item Name**	**Class Code**	**Value**
432 1/4 sheet cake baked & decorated	Edibles	$30.00
433 A handmade puppet	Kids Stuff	$50.00
434 A 5-gallon camelia plant	Home & Garden	$20.00
435 An Esprit sweatshirt, size 11	Clothing	$30.00
436 $25 worth of butcher shop meats &	Edibles	$25.00
437 A gingerbread house	Holiday	$25.00
	Total Value	$180.00

Problem: The file probably isn't sorted on the proper field in order for the summary information to be calculated. When you create a sub-summary part, you specify the field on which the file must be sorted to produce the summary in that part. In the example here, a sub-summary totals item values when the file is sorted by Class Code, but because the file isn't sorted by Class Code, the sub-summary part doesn't appear. A grand summary totaling all the item values does appear, because it doesn't require a particular sort order.

Solution: Choose *Layout* from the Select menu and then look at the sub-summary part label on the layout to see which field the part is supposed to be sorted on. Sort the file on that field before printing.

Margins are too large or too small when you print a layout.

Problem: FileMaker Pro has no document margin commands like word processing or spreadsheet programs. Instead, you must move objects in Layout mode to set the amount of space between them and the edges of your page. Normally, however, it's hard to tell how much space there is between items on a layout and the edges of a page.

Solution: Choose *Layout* from the Select menu and choose *Rulers* from the Layout menu to display rulers at the top and left sides of the layout. Then choose *Non-Printable Area* from the Show submenu off the Layout menu. FileMaker Pro displays a dotted line showing the nonprinting edges of the document. You can now drag objects and, using the rulers, determine exactly how much space is between them and the edges of the page.

Data creeps up or down when you print on a labels layout, so it doesn't print within each label.

Problem: Either the data is too close to the edges of the layout or FileMaker Pro is deleting lines from labels when certain fields in a record don't contain any data.

Solutions:

- First, make sure each label contains the same number of lines of data. Typically a label has one line for the name, one or two lines for the street address, and one line for the city, state, and zip code. Check all the labels on a page and make sure each label has the same number of lines.

- If the labels all have the same number of lines, then the label stock is slipping slightly as it moves through the printer, and data is too close to one of the layout's edges. As a result, data creeps over the line between one label and the next when the label stock slips. To correct this problem, switch to Layout mode and move the fields and other objects farther away from the layout's edges. Try to allow ⅛" of blank space between data or other layout objects and the edges of the layout. This allows for slippage when the label stock moves through the printer. If you can't move objects closer together, try making objects smaller or using smaller fonts or font sizes for text. If you don't want to make objects smaller, make a new layout using a larger label size.

- If the labels don't have the same number of lines, then you have FileMaker Pro set to delete a blank line and close up the layout part when a field contains no data. For example, if the layout contains two fields for a person's address (one for the street address and a second for the building number or mail stop, for example) and a particular record contains no data in the second address field, FileMaker Pro eliminates the blank space and makes that label shorter. This causes the label below it to move up one line, which throws off the alignment of label data on the label stock. To remedy this problem, switch to Layout mode, select all the fields on the layout, choose *Slide Objects* from the Arrange menu, and uncheck the box that says *Also Reduce the Size of the Enclosing Part*. This way, FileMaker Pro leaves a line blank (instead of eliminating it) when a field contains no data.

An object or data doesn't appear in the body of a layout when you print it.

Item No.	Size	Price
OC102	24"	$12.50
	48"	$15.00

Problem: The object or field boundary is probably touching or slightly overlapping another part boundary. If an object touches or overlaps a summary or header part above the body, for example, that object or field is considered as part of the header or summary part, not the body. In the example here, a photo is supposed to appear to the right of the price information, but because the picture field is touching the boundary of the part above it, the photo isn't showing in the body.

Solution: Switch to layout mode, use the zoom-in control in the lower left corner of the window to magnify the layout, and then make sure the object or field in question isn't overlapping the part boundary above the body.

Miscellaneous

You've imported records, but they replace existing data instead of adding to it.

Problem: You had the wrong option set when you imported the records. FileMaker Pro gives you the choice of replacing all the records in the current found set or adding new records to the file, but you must set the option you want before importing.

Solution: Once you've imported records and they've replaced other records, the records that were replaced are gone for good unless you have a backup copy of the file. To avoid replacing records in the future, click the *Add New Records* button in the Field Order dialog box that appears when you select the fields of data to be imported from a file.

The *Import Movie* command is dimmed on the Import/Export submenu.

Problem: You don't have the QuickTime extension installed. You can't import or play movies unless your Mac is running QuickTime.

Solution: Install the QuickTime extension in your System Folder and then restart your Mac.

Chapter 27

Microsoft Works

Microsoft Works, now in its third revision, has long been the most popular integrated program for the Macintosh. Version 3 of Works has been out for about a year now, but many people continue to use version 2 because some of the "improvements" in version 3 are actually steps backward. For example, Works 3 is noticeably slower than Works 2. On the other hand, the drawing program and database in particular are much improved in Works 3.

If you've decided to stick with Works version 2, make sure you're using one of the later releases. Versions 2.00a and 2.00b in particular had some serious bugs related to opening and saving files. If you're a registered Works 2 owner, you should be able to get a later, less buggy version of Works 2 from Microsoft for free.

This chapter is divided into seven sections:

- Working with files

- The word processor

- Spreadsheets and charting

- The database

- The drawing program

- The communications program

- Integration and macros

Working with files

Works slows down as you use it.

Problem: Works stores most of its program code and all of any open documents in memory. Along with this, it stores changes you've made to support the *Undo* command. As you work with one or more documents and make lots of changes, the Undo buffer gets bigger and, depending on how much memory you have and how large your documents are, Works can slow down noticeably.

Solutions:

- Save and close all your open documents and restart the program. This clears the Undo buffer and should speed things up.

- If the problem occurs frequently, try increasing Works' current memory size with the *Get Info* command in the Finder (see page 35), eliminating any extensions or inits you don't absolutely need, and reducing the size of the RAM Cache in the Memory control panel. (If you're using System 6, try turning the RAM Cache off completely.)

You've opened a Works 2 document with Works 3 and Works presents a save alert message when you try to close it, even though you've already saved the document with the *Save* command.

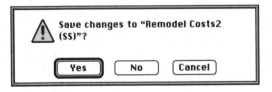

Problem: This is a bug in Works 3 that occurs with files that have been converted from the Works 2 format.

Solution: Select all the information in the converted file, then create a new Works 3 file and copy all the information from the old file into it. Since the new file has been created in Works 3 (rather than converted), you won't see the alert message unless there really are changes that haven't been saved when you try to close the file.

The word processor

You want to make a character superscript or subscript, set an odd-size font, or change the color of text, but there are no options for these actions on the Style menu.

Problem: These options are available in the Format Character dialog box.

Solution: Choose *Format Character* from the Style menu and click the checkboxes there to choose superscript, subscript, or other character styles, or use the pop-up menu to select a text color.

 When the insertion point is on text that is formatted with options not shown directly on the Style menu, a check mark appears next to the *Format Character* command.

You've used the *Increase Size* or *Decrease Size* command to set an odd-sized font size, but the font size jumps to the next even size instead.

Problem: *Increase Size* and *Decrease Size* set the next higher or lower font size, according to what's available. If you're using fixed-size fonts instead of TrueType fonts (or PostScript fonts with Adobe Type Manager), Works chooses the next fixed size. For example, if you're using fixed-size Geneva fonts and you have 12, 14, and 18-point sizes installed, using the *Increase Size* and *Decrease Size* commands only selects these sizes, not the ones in between.

Solution: Install TrueType fonts on your Macintosh, or install PostScript fonts and Adobe Type Manager.

You want to store and reuse standard paragraph formats.

Problem: Works doesn't have paragraph style sheets, so you can't name and save custom paragraph styles.

Solution: A partial solution is to use the *Copy Ruler Settings* and *Paste Ruler Settings* commands on the Document menu. This allows you to copy a paragraph format and apply it to other paragraphs.

 Paragraphs with copied formats aren't linked the way paragraphs formatted with style sheets are. If you change the format of the original paragraph, the paragraphs containing the copied format don't automatically change.

You used the *Insert Current Time* command, but the time shown isn't the same as the current time on your Mac's system clock.

Problem: The *Insert Current Time* and *Insert Current Date* commands place a marker in the document. The marker reads the current date or time as the last recorded modification time for that document. Therefore, if you've had a document open without saving it for, say, 15 minutes, and you use the *Insert Current Time* command, the time inserted is 15 minutes behind the actual current time.

Solution: Save the document. The time or date marker is automatically updated to the current time. (Of course, the time shown is immediately out of date, because time marches on.)

Footnotes appear at the end of each page, and you want them to appear at the end of the document instead.

Problem: You have the footnote preferences option set wrong.

Solution: Choose *Preferences* from the Edit menu, click the Word Processor icon if it's not selected, and then click the *End of Document* button in the Footnotes area.

Spreadsheets and charting

A spreadsheet always opens at the top of the document (the part showing cell A1), but you want it to open and display a different part of the document.

Problem: Works defaults to displaying the beginning of any spreadsheet document.

Solution: Drag the horizontal split bar to divide the spreadsheet window into two separate panes, scroll the lower pane to the part of the spreadsheet you want to show when the document opens, then save and close the document. The pane positions and scrolling positions will be preserved when you open the document the next time.

The *Freeze Titles Horizontal* and *Freeze Titles Vertical* commands are dimmed on the Format menu.

Problem: These commands aren't available unless you've divided the spreadsheet window into two or more panes.

Solution: Drag the vertical split bar from the lower left corner of the window to the right to activate the *Freeze Titles Horizontal* command, and drag the horizontal split bar from the upper right corner of the window down into the document to activate the *Freeze Titles Vertical* command.

Format	Options	Chart
Format Cells...		
Column Width...		
Protect Cell		
Set Page Break		
Remove Page Break		
Freeze Titles Horizontal		
Freeze Titles Vertical		
Format Character...		

You want to print just one page or portion of a spreadsheet.

Problem: You can select specific page numbers to print in the Print dialog box, but it's often difficult to tell which page is which.

Solutions:

■ The simplest way to print just one section of a spreadsheet (whether it's more or less than one full page) is to select the cells you want to print and then choose *Print* from the File menu. You see a message saying that only the selected cells will be printed, and you can click the *OK* button to print them.

■ If you want to print whole pages by specifying page numbers in the Print dialog box, remember that Works displays horizontal and vertical page breaks as dashed lines, and that it prints from left to right across the spreadsheet first, and then down. In a spreadsheet that's two pages wide and two pages long and that has the default column widths, for example, pages are divided like this:

■ Page 1—columns A through F and down to row 50

■ Page 2—columns G through L and down to row 50

■ Page 3—columns A through F and from row 51 to row 100

■ Page 4—columns G through L and from row 51 to row 100

If you're not sure which data prints on which page, use the *Print Preview* command to display the pages on the screen before you commit them to paper.

You've drawn a chart and you want to change the Value and Category labels on the X and Y axes.

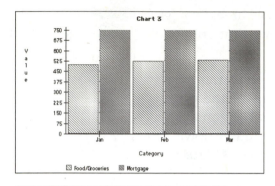

Problem: Works automatically includes these labels on any bar or line chart. Although you can change the chart legend and axis labels with the *Define Chart* command, the Value and Category labels can't be changed this way.

Solution: Select the chart and choose *Touch Up* from the Chart menu, then select the axis label you want to change. To delete the label, just press (Delete). To change the label, choose the Text tool from the tool palette, select the text inside the label, and type in the label you want.

 You can use *Touch Up* to select and change any chart element, including the patterns in bars or pie slices, or the font or size of any chart title or labels.

You've drawn a chart and want to print it, but the *Print* command is dimmed on the File menu.

 Actually, the easiest way to print a chart is to select it and copy it into a new Draw document, and then print the Draw document. With the chart in the Draw document, you have many more options for adjusting the chart's formatting.

Problem: You can only print charts when you're in spreadsheet mode.

Solution: To print the chart from within the spreadsheet, drag the chart to a separate page of the spreadsheet, click the Spreadsheet tool at the top of the tool palette (it's the one on the far left in the top row), and then choose *Print* from the File menu and print that one page.

The database

You want to perform a multilevel sort, but the *Sort* command only lets you sort on one field at a time.

Problem: Works can only sort on one database field at a time.

Solution: Perform a sort for each sort level you want, sorting on the least important field first. For example, to sort by the Account field and by date within each Account category, sort on the Date field first, and then on the Account field.

You're in design view, but you can't select, move, or resize a field.

Problem: You're probably in draw mode, not in design view, and Works won't let you select a field when you're in draw mode. It's easy to switch from design view to graphics mode without noticing, because the only indication of the change is that the Graphics tool is selected in the tool palette and the palette itself grows longer, as in the example at right.

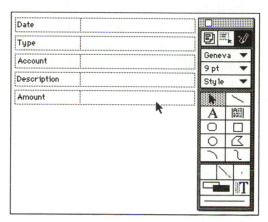

Solution: Click the Design View tool in the tool palette (to the left of the pencil at the top) to switch to design view, then select the field.

You're using PrintMonitor to print labels, and data starts printing outside label boundaries after you print several pages of labels.

Problem: Apple's system software can only print 128 documents in one spool file, and each individual label you print is considered a document. After 128 pages are printed, applications are supposed to automatically create a new spool folder, spool the next 128 documents into it, and delete the old spool file. Works has trouble doing this. In effect, it "burps" after the 128th document and causes the data to shift about half a label when it switches from one spool file to another.

Solution: Use Works' database filters to select portions of your database containing fewer than 128 records, and then print the labels in these smaller groups.

 If you want to display category subtotals, make sure the file is sorted on the appropriate field before you copy the totals from the report. For example, if you want subtotals by categories in an Account field, make sure the file is sorted on the Account field first, and that you've selected the Account field in the report and have chosen *Subtotal when Contents Change* from the Totals menu.

You want to quickly view the totals in a report without printing or previewing the report.

Problem: Totals you've specified for a report aren't shown on the screen in report view.

Solution: Display the report and choose *Copy Totals* from the Edit menu, then choose *Show Clipboard* from the View menu to display the Clipboard's contents. The totals from the report are shown there.

The drawing program

Works always selects the Pointer tool after you draw an object, and you don't want it to.

Problem: When you use any drawing tool except the pointer, Works normally selects the Pointer tool immediately afterwards. However, there's a way to lock tools so they remain selected after you use them.

 A selected tool is highlighted in gray on the tool palette, while a locked tool is highlighted in black.

Solution: Double-click a tool to lock it, or hold down the Shift key while you click the tool. The tool is then locked and remains selected until you select a different one.

You want to edit part of an object, but you can only select the whole object.

Problem: Works doesn't include a paint program you could use to edit objects one pixel at a time. However, you can break up a shape into component segments, and you may also be able to ungroup a series of objects that has previously been combined. If not, you can often draw on top of part of an object to change its appearance.

Solutions:

Be careful with the *Break Up* and *Join* commands. Once you drag an object's component line segments apart, it's difficult to reassemble the object with the *Join* command. Segments must be put back exactly where they were originally in order for *Join* to work properly.

- Select the object and choose *Ungroup* from the Arrange menu. If the object is composed of several individual objects that were previously grouped, it is broken up into its component parts again. (The *Ungroup* command isn't available if the selected object isn't composed of several grouped objects.)

- If the object isn't grouped, select it and choose *Break Up* from the Draw menu. The selection handles disappear, and you should then be able to select any single arc or line segment that makes up the object and edit it.

- As an alternative, you can modify part of an object in limited ways by drawing on top of portions of the object with lines or shapes of different colors or patterns. For example, to erase part of a rectangle, select the Rectangle tool, select a white fill pattern with a no-fill line pattern, and then draw a white rectangle on top of the part you want to erase. It is covered up with white, which looks the same as if you erased it.

You've turned the grid on to align objects, but the objects don't align precisely when you drag them.

Problem: The grid only works to align objects if you turn it on *before* you draw the objects. If you don't, the object edges usually fall at locations between grid points, and dragging them so they snap to the grid doesn't align object edges.

To create and align several identical objects like those shown above, draw the first one and choose *Duplicate* from the Edit menu. The duplicate is drawn below and slightly offset from the original, but once you turn the grid on and drag the object, the duplicate snaps to the same vertical or horizontal line as the original.

Solutions:

- If you know you want to align objects, draw them after you choose *Snap to Grid* from the Arrange menu.

- To align an object after you've drawn it, select and copy the object, choose *Snap to Grid,* and then paste the object into the document. Since the grid is on when you paste the object, its edges snap to the grid. As an alternative, leave the grid off and use the arrow keys on the keyboard (or click the arrow icons in the tool bar above the document) to nudge selected objects in any direction, one pixel at a time.

You want to set tabs or indents for text inside a draw document, but Works won't let you.

Problem: Works doesn't support tabs or indents in text in draw documents or in the draw layer of other document types. There's no workaround for this problem.

The communications program

Nothing happens when you type in a communications document.

Problem: You can only enter or paste text into a communications document when you're connected to a remote computer.

Solution: Establish a connection to a remote computer, then type or paste text into the communications document window.

You received some text in the communications document window and saved the document, but the text isn't there the next time you open the document.

Problem: Text displayed in a communications document window is stored in a buffer called the overflow area that is automatically emptied when you close a document, even if you save the document. Saving a communications document only saves the communications settings you've chosen.

Solution: Copy the data out of the overflow area and paste it into a word processor document to save it, or set up a captured text file so that incoming text is automatically saved to a text file on your disk as you work with the communications document.

You've set up a captured text file, but after you close the communications document and open the captured text file with the word processor, the file doesn't contain all of the text you received.

Problem: Works only saves text that you receive after you open a captured text file. Any text that is displayed on the screen at the time you open the file isn't captured.

Solution: Set up Works to automatically open a captured text file as soon as you make a connection to a remote computer. Choose *Preferences* from the Edit menu, click on the Communications icon if it isn't selected, and check the box that says *Always Capture Text*. Then, when you open a connection each time, Works displays a dialog box asking you to name a new captured text file, and it is open from the time you're first connected to the other computer. This way, all the text you receive is captured.

Integration and macros

Nothing happens when you paste a graphic into the database list view.

Problem: You must be in the database's data or design view or in a header window in report view to paste in a graphic.

Solution: Switch to data or design view, or open the header window in report view and then paste in the graphic. Works automatically switches to the draw layer so you can resize or otherwise manipulate the graphic.

Nothing happens when you press a macro key sequence.

Problem: Most likely, the macro file that stores that macro isn't open. Works doesn't automatically open a macro file when you start it up: you must remember to open it manually.

Solution: Choose *Macros On* from the Macro submenu off the Window menu, then choose *Open Macro File* and open the file containing the macro you want to run. Then try pressing the macro keys again.

A macro runs, but it doesn't do what you expected.

Problem: Either you have the wrong document or document type open, you have the wrong macro file open, or you're in the wrong document mode (so the macro key sequences or mouse movements are performing other commands or operations). Macros perform literally the keystrokes and mouse movements you made when you recorded them. Unless you're in the same document or document type, a key sequence might choose a different command than the one you had in mind. (For example, ⌘ I chooses the *Insert* command in the spreadsheet, but it selects the Italic character style in the word processor.)

Solutions:

- Make sure you have the correct document type open.

- If you have the correct document type open, make sure you're in the right document mode (form view instead of design view in the database, for example.)

- If the macro stores mouse movements, they may be specific to a particular document, and you're trying to play them in another document. Macros play back mouse movements by position only, so if you use the mouse to choose a command in one document type or mode, and you're in a different document type or mode when you play it back, the movement may well choose a different command from a different menu that happens to be in the same position.

- If you've created several different macro files, make sure you have the correct macro file open. The same macro keys can execute entirely different macros, depending on which macro file you have open.

Chapter 28

ClarisWorks

ClarisWorks includes six different applications, so we have a lot of ground to cover in this chapter. The chapter is divided into eight sections:

- Working with documents
- The word processor
- Spreadsheets and charts
- The database
- The drawing program
- The painting program
- The communications program
- Working with frames

Space constraints limit the number of issues we can cover in each section, but many of the conceptual problems you may have with parts of this program are the same ones you'll find in other programs of the same type. Therefore, if you're having a problem in the ClarisWorks database and it's not listed here, for example, check the chapter on FileMaker Pro—many aspects of these two programs are similar. Check the chapter on Excel for problems related to displaying or calculating numbers in the ClarisWorks spreadsheet. And check the chapters on Microsoft Works (under *The drawing program*) and FileMaker Pro (under *Formatting*) for more solutions to drawing problems.

367

Working with documents

You want to open a non-ClarisWorks document, but you can't find the document's name in the list when you use the *Open* command.

Problem: ClarisWorks defaults to displaying only ClarisWorks documents in the list when you use the *Open* command, but it can display other types of documents if you choose another option from the Document Type pop-up menu.

Solution: Use the Document Type pop-up menu to choose the type of ClarisWorks document you want to create when you open and convert the existing file on your disk. For example, if you're opening a Microsoft Word file, choose *Word Processing* from the Document Type menu. Once you do this, you should be able to see other types of documents.

You've created and saved a stationery file, but its name doesn't appear on the Stationery menu in the New Document dialog box.

Problem: Stationery documents only appear on the Stationery Menu if you've saved them to the ClarisWorks Stationery folder inside the Claris folder in your System Folder.

Solution: Move the document to the ClarisWorks Stationery folder. Its name then appears on the Stationery menu.

You want to use the Shortcuts palette in ClarisWorks 2.0, but you're having trouble remembering which shortcut icon does what.

Problem: With dozens of different shortcuts among the different document types, it's not always easy to remember which shortcut icon does what. However, you can easily display shortcuts as names or get a description of any shortcut icon.

Solutions:

■ Choose *Preferences* from the Edit menu, click the Palettes icon, click the *Show Names* box at the bottom of the dialog box, and press Return.

Shortcuts are then displayed as names rather than as icons. (You click a name instead of an icon to execute the shortcut.)

 You can also use the Palette preferences to automatically display the Shortcuts palette when each document is opened. ClarisWorks doesn't normally display the palette unless you choose *Show Shortcuts* from the Shortcuts submenu.

■ If you prefer the icon palette and only want to get a description of a particular icon, choose *Edit Shortcuts* from the Shortcuts submenu off the File menu, and then click any icon for which you want a description. The shortcut's description appears in the Description box below.

You want to choose a command, but you can't find the command or the menu that contains it.

Problem: Menus and the commands on them change depending on what mode you're working in. In any ClarisWorks document (except communications) you can be working in the native document mode, in graphics mode, or inside a paint, text, or spreadsheet frame. The menus you see depend on which mode you're in.

Solution: To return to a native document mode, click in the document itself (not in a frame or on a graphic object). If you have the tool panel displayed, you can tell which mode you're in because that mode's tool (the graphics Pointer, Text tool, Paint tool, or Spreadsheet tool) is selected.

Paragraphs have strange indents when you print to a StyleWriter.

Problem: There's a bug in ClarisWorks versions 1.0 and 1.0v2 that causes problems with paragraph indents when you print to a StyleWriter.

Solution: Print the document to a different printer, or contact Claris for an upgrade to ClarisWorks version 1.0v3 or later.

The word processor

You want to hide the blank margin space around the sides of the document window.

Problem: ClarisWorks normally displays document margins in word processor documents, so you get a WYSIWYG page preview at all times. However, showing the margins wastes a lot of space inside the document window when you want to focus on editing text.

Solution: Choose *Document* from the Format menu and uncheck the *Show Margins* box, then press Return. The margins disappear and text runs from one edge of the document window to the other.

A time inserted with the *Insert Time* command doesn't match the time on your Mac's system clock.

Problem: See page 358 in Chapter 27 for an explanation of this problem.

Columns

○ Equal width
◉ Variable width

Number of   3

Column width   1 ▼   2.04 in

Space between   0.17 in

[Cancel]   [OK]

You want to vary the space between columns in a multicolumn document, but the Columns dialog box only lets you change the values for column widths, not the space between columns.

Problem: You can use the *Columns* command to define the number of columns or to set up variable column widths, but you must use the mouse to change the space between columns.

Solution: Hold down the Option key as you point to one of the dividing lines between two columns, and then drag the dividing line to change the space between columns.

 You can also change column widths by holding down Option and dragging with the pointer between two column dividing lines, rather than dragging one of the

You want to paste a graphic into a document, but doing this screws up a paragraph's line spacing.

Problem: If you paste a graphic while you're working in the word processor layer of a document, the graphic is treated as a text character, and the line spacing automatically adjusts to accommodate the graphic's height.

Solution: Create a paint frame in the document and paste the graphic into it. Since the graphic is in a frame separate from the document's text, you're able to move or resize the frame without affecting the formatting of text.

> Our second quarter financial results can only be characterized as pathetic. Expenses were up, sales were off, and somebody went around the office pasting little stickers like this on all the telephones and filing cabinets. We are not amused.

FYI Once you've created the frame, you can switch to the document's graphics layer by clicking the Pointer tool in the tool panel, and then selecting and resizing the frame, or make text wrap around it by choosing *Text Wrap* from the Options menu.

Spreadsheets and charts

Your spreadsheet is only 40 columns wide and you need more room.

Problem: All new ClarisWorks spreadsheets have a default size of 40 columns by 500 rows, but you can adjust the size if you need more room.

Solution: Choose *Document* from the Format menu and enter the number of columns and rows you want in the Size area. A spreadsheet's maximum size is 256 columns and 16,384 rows.

A label is too wide to fit inside a cell, but you don't want to widen the column to display it.

Problem: Sometimes you need to use a long label in a cell, but widening the column enough to show the whole label isn't a good option because it means you won't have enough room to print other columns on the same page.

	A	B	C	D	E
1		January	February	March	April
2	Rent	750	750	750	750
3	Food	250	250	250	250
4	Medical Insur	100	100	100	100
5	Car Payment	225	225	225	225

Row heights and column widths in ClarisWorks are expressed in points— 72 points equal an inch.

Solution: Format the cell to wrap the text. Select the cell (A4 in the example above), then choose the *Wrap* command from the Alignment submenu off the Format menu. The text wraps down to a second line inside the cell. You won't be able to see the second line without making the row taller, however. To make the row taller, choose the *Row Height* command and enter a larger value for the row height.

Some cells are locked.

OK

Problem: You've tried to move, paste, sort, or enter data in a cell, but ClarisWorks displays a message saying that some cells are locked.

Solution: Select the cell you want to unlock and then choose *Unprotect Cells* from the Options menu.

After sorting, the labels in a spreadsheet column no longer match the values in adjacent columns.

	A	B	C	D	E
1		January	February	March	April
2	Car Payment	750	750	750	750
3	Food	250	250	250	250
4	Medical Insu	100	100	100	100
5	Rent	225	225	225	225

Problem: In some spreadsheets you sort entire spreadsheet rows, but ClarisWorks allows you to sort individual groups of cells. As a result, you can rearrange cells in one column without affecting the cells in other columns. (Compare the example above with the one on page 371.)

Solution: Always check out the Range box in the Sort dialog box to see which groups of cells you're about to sort, and make sure you're sorting the cells you want. If you perform a sort and it's not what you want, choose *Undo Sort* immediately from the Edit menu to put things back the way they were.

You can't see the page breaks in a spreadsheet.

Problem: ClarisWorks only displays its standard page breaks in a spreadsheet document when you're using page view. If you insert manual page breaks, on the other hand, they are indicated with dashed lines whether you're in page view or not.

Solution: Choose *Page View* from the View menu. You see the page margins and the breaks between pages.

Data from rows is used for each chart series, and you wanted data from columns used for each series.

Problem: ClarisWorks and most other spreadsheets assume that the largest number of data points should be used as series (the x-axis labels above), while the smaller number should make up the values within each series (the bars above).

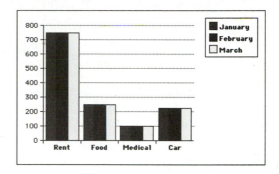

Solution: Choose *Modify Chart* from the Options menu, click the *General* button at the left side of the dialog box, and then click the *Series in Columns* button.

You want to change the color or pattern of a bar or pie slice in a chart.

Problem: ClarisWorks' chart modification options don't offer any way to change a chart's colors or patterns.

Solution: Copy the chart to a draw document, choose *Ungroup Picture* from the Arrange menu to break the chart up into its component bars or pie slices, and then select the bar or slice you want and choose a different pattern or color for it from the tool palette.

 When you paste a chart into a draw document and choose the *Ungroup Picture* command, ClarisWorks doesn't break up smaller components like the patterns and text inside a chart's legend. To break up these elements further, select the object and then choose *Ungroup* from the Arrange menu.

The database

You see parts of two or more records on the screen at once.

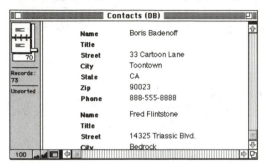

Problem: ClarisWorks' default display mode is to show records in a scrollable list, as shown above.

Solution: Choose *List View* from the Layout menu to remove the checkmark from this command. You then see only one record at a time.

You're trying to find information, but the Find/Replace window doesn't allow you to search for information in specific fields.

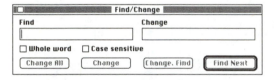

Problem: The *Find/Replace* command on the Edit menu is a global feature that works in most ClarisWorks document types. It lets you search for text anywhere in the document. In the database, however, you use the Find mode to search for data in specific database fields.

Solution: Choose *Find* from the Layout menu to use the database's Find mode.

You added a header or footer to a layout, but now it appears in every layout, rather than just on the one where you added it.

Problem: The *Insert Header* and *Insert Footer* commands on the Format menu work with any ClarisWorks document. In the database, these add a header or footer to every layout in your database document, not to a particular layout.

Solution: To add a header or footer to a particular layout, choose the layout name from the Layout menu (to display that layout), Choose *Layout* from the Layout menu (to switch to Layout mode), and then choose the *Insert Part* command from the Layout menu to add a header or footer part to that particular layout.

You want to insert a second copy of a field on a layout, but the Insert Field dialog box doesn't show the field name, and nothing happens when you try to copy the field in Layout mode.

Problem: You can't have more than one copy of a field on any layout in the ClarisWorks database.

Solutions:

- If you're trying to add another calculation formula to a layout (placing the same total formula in both a sub-summary and grand summary part, for example), simply define a new calculation field with the same formula and a slightly different name. For example, you could name one field GRTOTAL and the other SBTOTAL.

- If you need to use multiple copies of the same field (using the FirstName field twice in a form letter, for example), switch to FileMaker Pro, which has no problem with multiple copies of the same field in a layout.

The drawing program

It's hard to keep lines straight when you drag an endpoint to resize them.

Problem: You have to keep the mouse on the same plane as the line itself in order to maintain a straight line when you drag one of its endpoints. Otherwise, the line becomes jagged.

Solution: Hold down ⟨Shift⟩ as you drag the line's endpoint. This keeps the pointer on the same path as the original line.

You want to draw an arc that has a different angle than 90 degrees.

Problem: The default setting for arcs is a start angle of 90 degrees and a total angle of 90 degrees, so you're limited as to the position of every arc you draw.

Solution: Draw the arc, then leave it selected and choose *Modify Arc* from the Options menu. Then you can change the arc's start angle and total angle (called the Arc Angle in the dialog box) by entering new values for them.

Shapes you draw cover up objects beneath them.

Problem: The default fill color for shapes is white, and the default pattern is opaque. Since the Mac's screen is white, it looks as if you're drawing a transparent shape, but you're not.

Solution: Select the object and then choose the transparent fill pattern from the fill pattern palette. If you don't want to change a shape's pattern, select it and choose *Move to Back* from the Arrange menu to put it in a layer behind anything else it was covering up.

You've changed a fill pattern or line attribute, but after you draw the current object it changes back to what it was before.

Problem: If you have an object selected when you change a fill or line attribute, you change it only for that object.

Solution: To change the setting so it's the same for all new objects, choose the setting when no objects are selected.

The painting program

A new paint document is too small, or you get out-of-memory messages as you use a paint document.

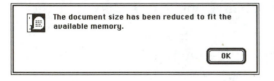

Problem: There's not enough memory to make the document larger or to allow you to continue working with it. Paint documents use a lot of memory, and the document size depends on how much memory is available at the time. If you have no other documents open, the document size is one full page.

Solutions:

- If you see a message like the one above, open the document anyway, choose the *Document* command from the Format menu, and try enlarging the document by changing its size in the Document dialog box.

- If you get an out-of-memory message, close the paint document or other documents and then try opening a new paint document again.

Paint documents can only be one page no matter how much memory you have. If you want to create a multipage document, use the drawing program.

- If you still can't make the document large enough, choose *Resolution and Depth* from the Format menu and select a lower resolution or a smaller number of colors or gray shades. As you choose the options in the Resolution and Depth dialog box, you'll see how much memory the document is using—you use less memory with lower resolution or depth settings.

- If you don't want to live with a lower resolution or depth, quit ClarisWorks and change its current memory size with the *Get Info* command to allow it more memory space (see page 35).

You used the paint bucket to fill an object, but your whole screen got filled instead.

Problem: The paint bucket fills any enclosed object. If the object isn't completely enclosed, it fills your whole screen (except for other objects that are completely enclosed).

Solution: Choose *Undo Paint* from the Edit menu to cancel the fill operation. Then close up the object you want to fill and try using the paint bucket again. If you have trouble closing up an object because you can't spot the gap in its border, click the zoom-in control to magnify the object.

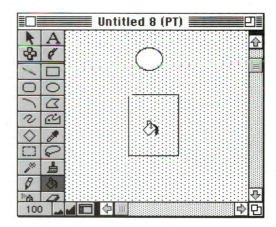

You moved an image so part of it extends past the edge of the paint document, and now you can't get that part back.

Problem: Anything that hangs off the edge of a paint document is no longer in memory once the image is deselected.

Solutions:

■ If you haven't selected anything else yet (the selection marquee is blinking around the edges of the image that are still visible on your document), drag the image back toward the middle of the document. The missing part reappears.

■ If you deselected the image but you haven't done anything else yet, choose *Undo Deselect* from the Edit menu. The entire image is selected again, and you can drag it back onto the document.

You darkened an image with the *Darker* command on the Transform menu and now want to lighten it again, but when you choose the *Lighter* command the image doesn't return to its original state.

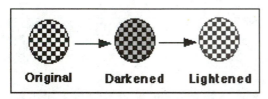

Original   Darkened   Lightened

Problem: The *Darker* command darkens an image permanently. You can lighten the darkened image with the *Lighter* command, but this doesn't return the image to its original state.

 To try out effects like this, duplicate the original image and try the effect on the duplicate. That way, you still have the original if you don't like the effect and can't change it back.

Solution: If you haven't done anything else since darkening the image, choose *Undo Darker* immediately from the Edit menu. Otherwise, you're out of luck.

The communications program

You're trying to create and store a log-on macro, but you can't choose the *Macro Wait* **command from the Shortcuts submenu.**

Problem: The *Macro Wait* command tells ClarisWorks to wait for a particular log-on prompt from the remote computer. This command is only available when you're actually connected to a remote computer.

Solution: Record the first part of the log-on macro by making a connection to the remote computer. Once you see the log-on prompt, select it and copy it in the work area, choose *Macro Wait,* and then paste the prompt into the Wait For box in the Macro Wait dialog box. Once you've done this, press Return and finish recording the macro.

Working with frames

**You want to add a frame to a database document,
but the tool panel doesn't show any frame or graphic tools.**

Problem: The tool panel in the database only shows frame and graphic tools when you're in Layout mode, because this is the only place where you can add frames or graphics.

Solution: Switch to Layout mode and then add the frame.

**You're working in a frame, but it's not large enough and
there are no scroll bars you can use to view another part of it.**

Problem: Frames don't have scroll bars you use to navigate in them. In a text or spreadsheet frame, you can actually move the insertion point or cell selection to a part of the frame you can't see, and there's no simple way to scroll to and view that area of the frame

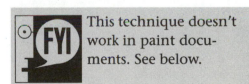 This technique doesn't work in paint documents. See below.

Solution: Click once in the document to switch to draw environment. The frame should be selected as a graphic object. If it isn't, click on it once to

select it. Then drag one of the frame's selection handles to make it larger. Finally, click inside the frame to move into its data environment and continue working.

You want to work with data in a frame that's in a paint document, but the frame's menus don't appear when you click on it. Instead, the pointer turns into a pencil.

	A	B
1		January
2	Food	250
3	Rent	750
4	Utilities	75
5	Insurance	100
6	Medical	50

Problem: Once you create a frame and click away from it in a paint document, the frame is converted to a bitmapped image, and there's no way to modify data in it any further.

Solution: Create a new frame and modify the data in it before you click away from the frame.

That is the startup disk; its contents can't be replaced. 169

That name is not valid. 318

The <program name> document <name> could not be opened, because it is in the Trash. To use this item, first drag it out of the Trash. 161

The alias <name> could not be opened, because the original item could not be found. 161

The application <name> has unexpectedly quit, because an error of type 1 occurred. 189

The Clipboard could not be read. 187

The control panel <name> cannot be used now, because not enough memory is available. 183

The desktop file couldn't be created on the disk <name>. 177

The disk <name> can't be used, because an error of type -192 occurred. 154

The disk <name> can't be used, because an error of type -192 occurred. 192

The disk <name> could not be erased, because it is the startup disk, which contains the active system software. 178

The disk <name> could not be put away, because it contains items that are in use. 153

The disk <name> could not be put away, because it is being shared. 239

The disk <name> needs minor repairs. Do you want to repair it? 148

The disk is so full that the folder changes couldn't be recorded. 153

The document <name> could not be opened, because the application that created it could not be found. 158

The document size has been reduced to fit the available memory. 376

The drive failed its test. 145

The driver could not be installed. 145

The file <name> couldn't be read and was skipped (the file is busy). 238

The file <name> couldn't be written and was skipped (unknown error). 171

The file <name> couldn't be written and was skipped (unknown error). 238

The file server is closing down in <number> minutes. 240

The file/folder could not be renamed. 173

The folder <name> could not be opened, because you do not have enough access privileges. 236

The folder/disk <name> couldn't be opened (file server is no longer connected). 239

The folder/disk <name> couldn't be opened (the file/folder is missing). 160

The Installer did not find any Installer documents and cannot run without one. 132

The printer has been initialized with an incompatible version of the Laser Prep software. To reinitialize and continue printing, click OK or click Cancel to stop printing. 209

The selected items are from different disks. Please move, copy, or duplicate them separately. 171

The selected items can't all be opened/printed at once. 160

The startup application on <disk name> cannot be set (not a startup volume). 178

The Trash cannot be moved off the desktop. 172

The volume <name> could not be made the startup volume (can't switch systems when using MultiFinder). 132

The volume <name> could not be made the startup volume (can't switch systems when using MultiFinder).163

The volume <name> could not be made the startup volume (Finder is older version). 162

The volume <name> could not be made the startup volume (System is older version). 132

There are no initialized Macintosh volumes on this drive. 144

There are not valid criteria in this request. Type a valid request before clicking Find. 348

There is not enough memory to keep the window <name> open. 161

There is not enough room on the disk <name> to copy <file name> (an additional <number> MB must be thrown away first. 165

There isn't enough Finder memory to complete this command. 176

There isn't enough Finder memory to eject the startup disk. 152

There isn't enough Finder memory to work with the disk <name>. 152

There may be items in <folder name> that are not visible; try to remove it anyway? 175

There's a problem with the disk <name>. Installation cannot continue. The disk <name> may not be a usable startup disk. (Error # -54) 135

These items need to be stored in special places inside the System Folder in order to be available to the Macintosh. Put them where they belong? 165

This disk is damaged. Do you want to initialize it? 148

This disk is locked, so you cannot make changes here. Do you want to create the alias on the desktop? 178

This file is used by the system software. It cannot be opened. 159

This is not a Macintosh disk: Do you want to initialize it? 146

This text box or a text box in the group has linkages that can't be duplicated. [45] 339

This version of Font/DA Mover is out of date. To install a font, drag it to the System file. To put a desk accessory in the Apple menu, drag it to the Apple Menu Items folder. 214.

Too many desk accessories on <disk name> to install <file name>. 134

Unable to find a suitable drive connected to the SCSI port. 142

Unable to identify this drive. 143

Unable to mount volume. 143

Unknown user or log on is disabled. Please retype the name or contact the server's administrator. 234

You are about to start file sharing without having given yourself a password, and this is not advised. 231

You are not connected to any file servers. 238

You cannot copy <file name> onto the disk <name>, because the disk is locked. 167

You cannot duplicate in the folder <name>, because there isn't enough memory available. Closing windows or quitting application programs can make more memory available. 166

You cannot duplicate in the folder <name>, because you do not have the privilege to make changes. 237

You cannot move <file name> to the folder <name>, because it cannot be found. 166

You cannot move <file name> to the folder <name>, because the disk is full. 166

You cannot move <folder name> from the disk <name>, because the disk is locked. 175

You cannot move <folder name> to the folder <folder name> because it cannot be moved into itself. 170

You cannot open more than one Finder at a time. 163

You cannot replace the <program name> document <name>, because a file cannot be replaced by a folder. 170

You cannot replace the folder <name>, because it contains items that are in use. 168

You cannot switch launch to an older version of the Finder. 162

You do not have the access privileges to see all items in <folder name>; copy the visible ones? 237

You don't have enough access privileges to see all the items if they are put into <folder name>. Put them there anyway? 237

Your owner name needs to be entered before file sharing can be enabled. 231

Index

387